FROM DEEP TO SURFACE STRUCTURE
AN INTRODUCTION TO TRANSFORMATIONAL SYNTAX

Marina K. Burt
Ph.D. candidate, M.I.T. and Harvard University

Harper & Row, Publishers
New York, Evanston, San Francisco, London

FROM DEEP TO SURFACE STRUCTURE: An Introduction to Transformational Syntax

Copyright © 1971 by Marina K. Burt

Library of Congress Catalog Card Number: 78-132656

SBN 06-041069-8

To My Father, Gerrit Klaver

CONTENTS

Foreword

One of the most acute problems that a beginning student in syntax encounters is how to gain some facility in following a syntactic argument. The present book grew out of an attempt to help students over this first hurdle. Its exercises, which have been tested extensively in classes in various universities, have been successful in assisting a good number of aspiring linguists to acquire the skills necessary to comprehend a reasonably complex argument in syntax.

Comprehending such arguments is, of course, only part of the battle. The next task is to gain insight into what makes a good argument in syntax so that one may then construct such arguments himself. A good means for achieving this is to examine carefully good arguments which have worked in the past. A selection of such arguments is given in the book, so that students may be exposed to them from the very beginning of their career. If these are presented in such a way as to stimulate the students' minds rather than to burden their memory, a great deal can be learned. Needless to say, learning to appreciate and to construct good arguments is a never-ending task, for the invention of good arguments of a type previously unknown is the major step whereby advances in any scientific discipline are achieved. But even the longest journey must begin with one step. To help students take this step and to instruct them in a few of the steps that immediately follow is the modest aim of this volume.

To help students achieve these objectives has been the author's main aim and she has been very successful in attaining it. We are sure that her book will be a useful tool for all those who are seriously interested in learning about the most complex intellectual feat accessible to all humans, the use of their native tongue.

NOAM CHOMSKY
MORRIS HALLE
JOHN ROBERT ROSS

Preface

The main text of this book is concerned with establishing the relative ordering of about thirty transformational rules of grammar which have been regularly included in the introductory course of transformational grammar presented at M. I. T.'s Department of Linguistics (by Professors Morris Halle and John R. Ross), for the last three years (1967-1970). Although new rules have been motivated and discussed since this time, the rules presented in this book are exemplary of the basic insights achieved by advocates of the transformational approach to English syntax, and thus seem essential for any student interested in learning some fundamentals of transformational grammar. We would inform the reader, however, that this book is intended to be a workbook which should be used as a supplement to, not a substitute for, a course in introductory transformational syntax.

The order in which these rules are presented is determined primarily by their simplicity in terms of the range of their applicability (to simple or complex sentences) and the ease with which their relative ordering can be illustrated. The purpose of the book is to establish the ordering of the transformational rules as they are listed on page 253.

The book consists of four main sections. Part I deals with rules pertaining to the analysis of the auxiliary as presented in Chomsky's Syntactic Structures,* and with rules which illustrate the basic structures of independent simplex sentences (that is, sentences which do not contain embedded sentences in them). Part II deals with relative clauses and related structures. Part III deals with the grammar of some complement structures. Part IV is concerned with more complicated structures and presents some motivations for the transformational cycle in English syntax.

MARINA K. BURT

---

*Noam Chomsky, Syntactic Structures (The Hague: Mouton, 1957), pp. 38-42.

Preliminaries

Language is something everyone knows. Its knowledge is not dependent upon IQ, socioeconomic status, color, or education. Everyone can understand new sentences heard every day, and invents and produces new ones naturally. The sentence I am now making up can be easily understood by anyone, and yet no one has seen or spoken exactly this sentence before. Why is this so? What kind of knowledge do native speakers of every known language possess that allows them to understand and produce novel sentences every day of their lives?

Although attempts are being made to answer these questions, unfortunately, their solutions will depend on much more research. Little can be said now, since so very little is known. However, we can make some rather simple observations about the facts of English which every native speaker of English knows. Let us consider, for example, a group of adjectives which denote emotion. Generally, these adjectives, when they have objects, are followed by the preposition <u>toward</u>. We have:

> friendly toward
> hostile toward
> benevolent toward
> affectionate toward

but not:

> *friendly at[1]
> *affectionate at

There is an exception to this generality, however. <u>Mad</u> is also an adjective denoting emotion, but we do not have:

> *mad toward

Instead, we have:

> mad at

This kind of exception must be learned by every speaker of English.

Let's take another illustration. In general, there is no change in the basic shape of adjectives in forming comparatives and superlatives. For most common adjectives the general rule is that <u>er</u> is added to the adjective to form comparatives, and <u>est</u> is added to form superlatives. Thus we have:

> big, bigger, biggest
> nice, nicer, nicest
> tall, taller, tallest

Again, however, there are exceptions to the general rule, for we do not have:

> good, *gooder, *goodest
> bad, *badder, *baddest

Instead, everyone must memorize the irregular forms:

[1]An asterisk preceding a sentence or phrase means it is not acceptable. See pp. 245-246, for an explanation of all symbols and abbreviations used in this book.

1

good, better, best
bad, worse, worst

Let us consider one more example—plural formation. The general rule to form plurals is to add some form of _s_. Thus we have:

boy, boys
house, houses
pleasure, pleasures

But this rule, too, is not without its exceptions. We do not have:

man, *mans
child, *childs
sheep, *sheeps

Rather, we must memorize these irregular forms:

man, men
child, children
sheep, sheep

On the word level, then, we see that there are exceptions to general rules which everyone must learn.

Can we find parallel cases for whole sentences? That is, are there any general rules for the formation of English sentences, and can we find any exceptions to these? Traditional grammar has always said that all English sentences, as a general rule, must consist of at least a subject and a verb. Thus we have, along with all the sentences already written here:

1) Who did this?
2) Everyone knows it is impossible to maintain such a theory.

The following sentence is an exception to this rule, for it is not at all clear what its subject and verb are, or if they exist at all:

3) like father, like son.

Here the sentence and its meaning are simply learned together as a whole, since they are exceptions to the general rule.

In the case of adjectives, it would be quite conceivable to learn the comparative and superlative form for each separately, as there are only a finite number of adjectives. Since there is obviously a rule at work, however, we first learn the rule, and later the exceptions to it.

Can we say the same about sentences? If we had no rules to describe the basic regularities of English sentences, could we still memorize all of them? We could not, because it is impossible to list all the sentences of English. Since we cannot give the sentence which is the longest possible one (i.e., we can always add _and such and such..._, or another _very_ to _very, very funny_, etc.), we would never come to the end of our list. More important, there is an infinite number of sentences, no two of which are exactly alike. To expect a child to memorize all the sentences he will ever produce is absurd. Grammarians, therefore, attempt to discover the underlying regularities of sentence formation by trying to find rules which correctly describe sentences. For example, what is the rule which allows

1) Who did this?

but not

1a) *did who this?

Or, why do we accept

2) Everyone knows it is impossible to maintain such a theory

but not

2a) *Theory a such maintain to impossible is it knows everyone?

The theory of transformational syntax attempts to explain why certain groups of words are accepted as good English, and why some are not, by attributing to every speaker not only the knowledge of a number of rules, but also the knowledge of how these rules interrelate. It is the violation of these rules which leads to unacceptable constructions like 1a) and 2a).

The sort of rules we are concerned with are called transformational rules. Stated simply, these rules change a sentence into a related one. We will view a sentence as a string of words with an associated structure. The sentence:

4) The boy will hit the ball

is a grammatical string of words. Traditional grammar is concerned with the parts of speech of the words in a string and with how sequences of parts of speech constitute larger phrases. Thus, in our example, since _boy_ and _ball_ are nouns (N), _hit_ a verb (V), _will_ an auxiliary (Aux), and _the_ a determiner (Det), the first step in providing a diagrammatic representation of (A) might be:

$$Det - N - Aux - V - Det - N^2$$

The boy will hit the ball.

Furthermore, according to the traditionalists, the sequences _the boy_ and _the ball_ form larger groups or phrases.

$$[Det - N] - Aux - V - [Det - N]$$

Phrases of the same type have roughly the same privileges of occurrence. That is, they often may be interchanged with each other. In our example, we may exchange the NP's _the boy_ and _the ball_. This gives us:

[Det N] Aux V [Det N]
The ball will hit the boy.

The meaning, of course, is changed, but the sentence is quite normal.[3]

---

[2]The dashes indicate boundaries between two elements. They have the same meaning as pluses did in earlier literature, e.g., Chomsky, _Syntactic Structures_, 1957.

[3]We could not, however, exchange the node V with a NP node, as is clear from: "hit will the boy the ball.

We can diagram the information we have so far as follows:

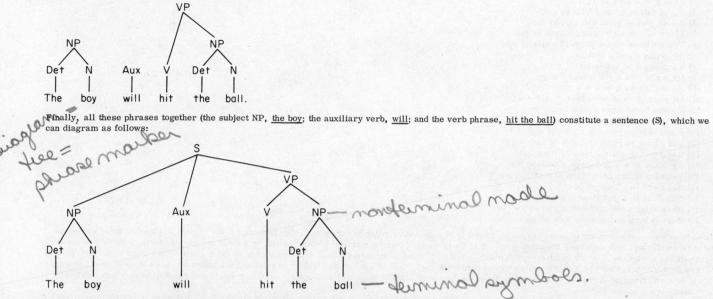

The group of words <u>hit the ball</u> also makes up a phrase, called a <u>verb phrase</u> (VP). In our example the VP consists of the verb (V) and its direct object (NP). Diagrammatically, we now have:

Finally, all these phrases together (the subject NP, <u>the boy</u>; the auxiliary verb, <u>will</u>; and the verb phrase, <u>hit the ball</u>) constitute a sentence (S), which we can diagram as follows:

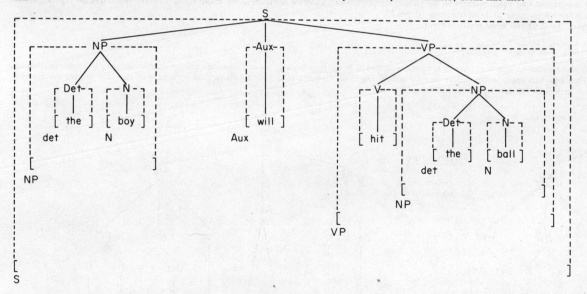

This entire diagram is called a <u>phrase marker</u>, or <u>tree</u>, and the labels S, NP, Det, N, Aux, VP, and V, which appear above or <u>dominate</u> other nodes of the tree, are referred to as <u>nonterminal</u> nodes. The words <u>the</u>, <u>boy</u>, <u>will</u>, <u>hit</u>, and <u>ball</u>, which are not connected by any lines to lower nodes, are called <u>terminal</u> symbols. A linear equivalent of this phrase marker, determined directly from the phrase marker, looks like this:

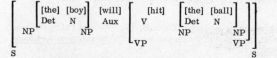

Thus, directly from the phrase marker above, we have determined its exact linear equivalent, which can be abbreviated as follows:

$$\begin{bmatrix} \begin{bmatrix} [\text{the}] & [\text{boy}] \\ \text{Det} & \text{N} \end{bmatrix}_{NP} & \begin{bmatrix} [\text{will}] \\ \text{Aux} \end{bmatrix} & \begin{bmatrix} [\text{hit}] \\ \text{V} & \begin{bmatrix} [\text{the}] & [\text{ball}] \\ \text{Det} & \text{N} \end{bmatrix}_{NP} \end{bmatrix}_{VP} \end{bmatrix}_{S}$$

3

The entire string, bounded by the outermost brackets, is a sentence (S). (The outermost brackets are so labeled.) The next three large constituent breaks are between the subject noun phrase, which contains the determiner <u>the</u> and the noun <u>boy</u>, and the auxiliary, which contains the auxiliary verb (also called the <u>modal</u>) <u>will</u>, and finally the verb phrase, which contains the verb <u>hit</u> and the object noun phrase <u>the ball</u>. The object noun phrase, just like the subject noun phrase, consists of a determiner <u>the</u> and a noun <u>ball</u>. We could just as easily determine the phrase marker from the linear form by reversing the process. We will consider only the phrase markers (as opposed to the linear representations) of the following examples because it is upon phrase markers that transformational rules (or T-rules) operate. These rules map one phrase marker onto another phrase marker, that is, they change the structure of a tree in some way to produce another, <u>derived</u> tree.

One important reason why we have rules which change one phrase marker into another is that certain sentences and phrases are felt to be related to each other in a clear way. For example:

1) I will give a girl a book.
2) I will give a book to a girl.
3) A girl will be given a book by me.
4) A book will be given to a girl by me.
5) There will be a girl given a book by me.
6) There will be a book given to a girl by me.
7) my giving a girl a book
8) my giving a book to a girl
9) for me to give a girl a book
10) for me to give a book to a girl
11) for a girl to be given a book by me
12) a girl's being given a book by me
13) for a book to be given a girl by me
14) a book's being given to a girl by me
15) that a book be given to a girl by me
16) that a girl be given a book by me
17) for there to be a girl given a book by me
18) for there to be a book given to a girl by me
19) that there be a book given to a girl by me
20) that there be a girl given a book by me
21) there being a book given to a girl by me
22) there being a girl given a book by me

These twenty-two sentences and phrases are all perceived to be somewhat similar to each other. Our intuitions about English tell us that these sentences and phrases all mean approximately the same thing. It is the purpose of transformational syntax to state, in a clear and precise form, exactly how these sentences are alike—how they are related to each other by means of specific syntactic rules. Our formulation of these rules leaves much to be desired, but there is no doubt that rules which relate sentences and phrases to each other in a consistent fashion do exist and are known by every speaker of the language. This is how we recognize the above twenty-two examples as "somehow alike": In each of us there are certain grammatical rules at work which relate all these sentences to each other.

Transformational grammarians assume that certain sentences are <u>basic</u> (they are called <u>deep structure</u> strings)[4] and that other sentences are <u>derived</u> from these basic sentences by means of applying certain T-rules to the deep structure strings. <u>Derived sentences</u> are called surface structure strings. Exactly how a derived sentence is related to a basic sentence is determined entirely by which rule was applied to the structure of the basic sentence. Since, as we have mentioned, transformational rules operate on the phrase markers which underlie sentences, the relationship between basic and derived sentences is stated in terms of the rules which apply to these phrase markers.

Consider, for example, the first and third sentences on p. 4.

1) I will give a girl a book. (active)
3) A girl will be given a book by me. (passive)

We will assume, with no justification at this time that 1) is basic, and that 3) is <u>derived</u> from it (as are all of the others on this page) by a transformational rule, called <u>Passive</u>. This rule will apply to the phrase marker underlying 1) (in diagram (a)), and will change the structure of this tree to give the derived phrase marker (b), which underlies 3), in roughly the following manner:[5]

(a)   (b)

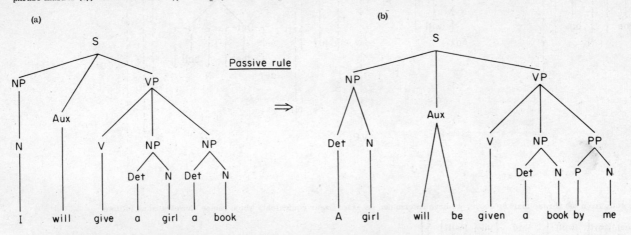

[4]Earlier works referred to these as "kernel" sentences. See Z. Harris, <u>Methods in Structural Linguistics</u> (Chicago, University of Chicago Press, 1952) and "Co-occurrence and Transformation in Linguistic Structure," <u>Language</u> 33:283-340, reprinted in Fodor and Katz, <u>The Structure of Language</u> (Englewood Cliffs, N.J., Prentice-Hall, 1964), pp. 479-518; and Chomsky, <u>Syntactic Structures</u>.

[5] $\Rightarrow$ means "is transformed into." PP = <u>prepositional phrase</u>, and P = <u>preposition</u>. See also explanation of symbols and abbreviations on pp. 245-246.

The Passive rule will be stated and discussed in detail below (pp. 37-46). It is by means of such a rule that we relate this pair of active and passive sentences to each other, i.e., by means of a rule which changes one basic (or underlying) phrase marker (a) into another, derived phrase marker, (b).

Consider sentences 1) and 2) (p. 4). These, too, are felt to be related.

1) I will give a girl a book.
2) I will give a book to a girl.

These two sentences are related to each other by means of another transformational rule applied to 1) (which is stated and discussed on pp. 38-41). That is, the phrase marker (a), which underlies 1), is changed, by application of a rule called Dative, into the phrase marker (c), which underlies sentence 2). This change in structure is approximately as follows:

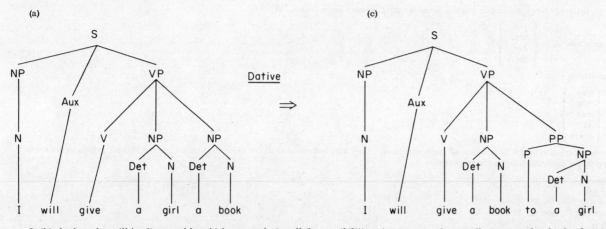

In this book, rules will be discussed by which we can derive all the possibilities given on page 4, as well as many other kinds of sentences, from the deep structure (a). From the above examples, we see that the transformational rules can capture the notion related sentence by relating in a clear and precise way the phrase markers which underlie these sentences.

Now to our question: how can these rules help us determine why some sentences are ungrammatical, while others are not? If we are correct in saying that some kinds of rules which change one kind of sentence into another are known in some way by every speaker of English, we can explain why certain constructions are never produced by any speaker. In other words, we can explain the distribution of words and phrases in English.

Earlier (p. 1), we mentioned the distribution of the prepositions toward and at, with respect to the adjectives they follow:

affectionate toward

but not

*affectionate at

and we have:

mad at

but not

*mad toward

As we said, these are facts which must be learned by every speaker of English. We cannot make up general rules to account for this distribution.

But let us turn to a more complex group of words, whose distribution we will also attempt to describe. These are the reflexive pronouns: myself, yourself, himself, herself, itself, ourselves, yourselves, themselves, and the normal pronouns I, you, he, she, it, we, me and they. As a sample of the occurrence of these pronouns, consider the following table:

	I	II	III
1.	*I wash me	you wash me	he washes me
2.	I wash you	*you wash you	he washes you
3.	I wash him	you wash him	*he washes him[6]
4.	I wash her	you wash her	he washes her
5.	I wash it	you wash it	he washes it
6.	I wash us	you wash us	he washes us
7.	I wash them	you wash them	he washes them
1a.	I wash myself	*you wash myself	*he washes myself
2a.	*I wash yourself	you wash yourself	*he washes yourself
3a.	*I wash himself	*you wash himself	he washes himself
4a.	*I wash herself	*you wash herself	*he washes herself
5a.	*I wash itself	*you wash itself	*he washes itself
6a.	*I wash ourselves	*you wash ourselves	*he washes ourselves
7a.	*I wash themselves	*you wash themselves	*he washes themselves

---

[6]This form is not acceptable if the he and him are intended to refer to the same person. If him and he refer to different people, the sentence is acceptable. Note that with the starred examples in columns I and II, this ambiguity cannot arise. For example, I wash me (col. I) can only mean that I and me are the same person. Hence this sentence is unacceptable. The same is true of you wash you (col. II). Both you's can only refer to the same you. Hence, this form is also unacceptable.

In all three columns, we see a perfect complement in the distribution of normal pronound and reflexive pronouns in second (object) position.

Nonreflexive pronouns, in comparison, can occur almost anywhere. They all appear in subject position:

(a)
$$\left\{\begin{array}{l} \text{I} \\ \text{you} \\ \text{he} \\ \text{she} \\ \text{it} \\ \text{we} \\ \text{they} \end{array}\right\} \quad \text{will go}$$

or they may appear in indirect object position in slightly modified (or inflected) form (see fn. 8):

(b)
$$\text{I will write a note to} \left\{\begin{array}{l} \text{you} \\ \text{him} \\ \text{her} \\ \text{them} \end{array}\right\}$$

or in direct object position:

(c)
$$\text{I wash} \left\{\begin{array}{l} \text{you} \\ \text{him} \\ \text{her} \\ \text{it} \\ \text{them} \end{array}\right\}$$

However, there is one restriction on the appearance of these pronouns. They <u>may not occur in direct object position when the subject refers to the same person.</u> That is, we do not have the following sentences:

(d) *I wash <u>me</u>
    *you wash <u>you</u>
    *he washes <u>him</u> (see fn. 5)
    *she washes <u>her</u> (") (see fn. 5)
    *it washes <u>it</u>   (")
    *we wash <u>us (we)</u>
    *they wash <u>them</u>

Nor may these pronouns occur in indirect object position when the subject of the sentence is the same as the indirect object. The following examples are ungrammatical:

(e) *<u>I</u> will write a note <u>to me</u>
    *<u>you</u> will write a note <u>to you</u>

We see from the distribution of the reflexive pronouns that they do not occur in subject position:

(f) *myself will go
    *yourself will go
    *himself will go
    *herself will go
    *itself will go
    *ourselves will go
    *themselves will go

Secondly, a reflexive pronoun may not occur in direct object position, <u>unless</u> the subject is identical to it; i.e., we do not have forms like:

(g) *you wash myself
    *I wash yourself
    *I wash himself
    *I wash herself
    *I wash itself
    *I wash themselves

but only

    I wash myself
    you wash yourself
    we wash ourselves
    they wash themselves
        etc.

In addition, a <u>reflexive pronoun never occurs in indirect object position unless</u> the subject of the sentence is identical to it. That is, we do not have:

(h) *I will write a note <u>to yourself</u>
    *I will write a note <u>to himself</u>
    *I will write a note <u>to herself</u>
    *I will write a note <u>to themselves</u>

but only

    I will write a note to myself
        etc.

We can now describe the distribution of regular and reflexive pronouns with the help of the following two sets of rules: The first set of rules will account for the facts about the gaps in the distribution of regular pronouns:

I. <u>you</u>, <u>him</u>, <u>her</u>, <u>it</u>, <u>us</u>, <u>them</u> may appear as direct or indirect object if the subject is <u>I</u>.[7] (This excludes *<u>I wash me</u>, and *<u>I wrote a note to me</u>.)

II. <u>me</u>, <u>him</u>, <u>her</u>, <u>it</u>, <u>us</u>, <u>them</u> may appear as direct or indirect object if the subject is <u>you</u>. (This excludes *<u>you wash you</u>, and *<u>you wrote a note to you</u>.)

III. <u>me</u>, <u>you</u>, <u>her</u>, <u>it</u>, <u>us</u>, <u>them</u> may appear as direct or indirect object if the subject is <u>he</u>. (This excludes *<u>he washed him</u>, and *<u>he wrote a note to him</u>, where he is meant to refer to the same person as <u>him</u>.)

IV. <u>me</u>, <u>you</u>, <u>him</u>, <u>her</u>, <u>us</u>, <u>them</u> may appear as direct or indirect object if the subject is <u>it</u>. (This excludes *<u>it washed it</u>, and *<u>it did something to it</u>, where both <u>its</u> refer to the same thing.)

V. <u>me</u>, <u>you</u>, <u>him</u>, <u>her</u>, <u>it</u>, <u>them</u> may appear as direct or indirect object if the subject is <u>we</u>.[8] (This excludes *<u>we washed us</u>, and *<u>we wrote a note to us</u>.)

VI. <u>me</u>, <u>you</u>, <u>him</u>, <u>her</u>, <u>it</u> may appear as direct or indirect object if the subject is <u>they</u>. (This excludes *<u>they washed them</u>, and *<u>they wrote a note to them</u>, where <u>they</u> refers to the same ones <u>them</u> refers to.)

That is, any nonreflexive pronoun may appear in direct or indirect object position so long as it is not identical with the subject of the sentence. (Of course, all nonreflexives may appear in subject position.)

The distribution of the reflexive pronouns can be described by the following set of rules:

I. No reflexives may appear in subject position.
II. <u>myself</u> may appear as direct or indirect object only when the subject is <u>I</u>.
III. <u>himself</u> may appear as direct or indirect object only when the subject is <u>he</u>.
IV. <u>herself</u> may appear as direct or indirect object only when the subject is <u>she</u>.
V. <u>itself</u> may appear as direct or indirect object only when the subject is <u>it</u>.
VI. <u>yourself</u> may appear as direct or indirect object only when the subject is <u>you</u>.
VII. <u>themselves</u> may appear as direct or indirect object only when the subject is <u>they</u>.
VIII. <u>yourselves</u> may appear as direct or indirect object only when the subject is <u>you</u>.
IX. <u>ourselves</u> may appear as direct or indirect object only when the subject is <u>we</u>.

By comparing the two sets of rules above, we see that there is a gap in the distribution of both kinds of pronouns. There are some environments where the regular pronouns cannot occur. And exactly where regular pronouns cannot occur, the reflexive pronouns do occur. There is a larger gap in the distribution of reflexives, i.e., they occur much less often than do the regular pronouns. But again, just where the reflexives cannot occur, the regular pronouns do. All these facts are correctly described by the fifteen rules given on this page.

However, there is yet another way to analyze these facts. Since the regular pronouns appear almost everywhere, suppose we allow these to occur freely. That is, in deep structure, we will allow them to appear everywhere—in subject position (as in (a), p. 6), in indirect object position (as in (b), p. 6), or in direct object position (as in (c), p. 6). This will give us all the possibilities of (a)-(e), p. 6, <u>including</u> all the unacceptable sentences of (d) and (e):

*I wash $\left\{ \begin{array}{c} \text{me} \\ \text{I} \end{array} \right\}$.

*I will write a note to $\left\{ \begin{array}{c} \text{me} \\ \text{I} \end{array} \right\}$.[9]

Now we will say that any time we generate a sentence in which there are two identical noun phrases, there will be a rule which causes the second noun phrase in that sentence to assume its reflexive form. That is, in deep structure we will generate (i.e., allow to occur) all the sentences of (d) and (e). But because in each of those sentences there are two identical noun phrases, our rule (called <u>Reflexive</u>), will automatically cause the second of the identical noun phrases to assume its reflexive form. So, for example:

(d) *<u>I</u> wash <u>I</u> $\implies$ I wash <u>myself</u>.
becomes, via
<u>Reflexive</u>

and

(e) *<u>I</u> will write a note to <u>I</u> $\implies$ I will write a note to <u>myself</u>.
becomes, via
<u>Reflexive</u>

All of the unacceptable sentences in (d) and (e) will thus be obligatorily transformed by our rule, <u>Reflexive</u>, and this will give us the correct reflexive pronoun in each case.

With this single rule, we can now account also for the ungrammatical sentences of (f, g, h), p. 6. First, our rules will never generate the examples in (f) because the reflexive form may only be assumed by the <u>second</u> of two identical NP's within a sentence. Therefore forms like:

*myself will go
*yourself will go

cannot ever arise. Likewise, our rule will also explain why the examples in (g) are impossible. Since we only <u>derive</u> reflexive forms when there are two identical NP's in a sentence, it is impossible to generate:

*I wash yourself

because this would have to be derived from the deep structure string:

I wash <u>you</u>.

---

[7]Actually, this is somewhat oversimplified, for *<u>I washed us</u> is somewhat strange. If the pronouns are reversed, the string is definitely impossible (*we washed me). However, we can disregard this additional complication for present purposes.

[8]See fn. 6.

[9]After prepositions and verbs, pronouns show up in the objective form $\left\{ \begin{array}{c} \text{me} \\ \text{him} \\ \text{her} \\ \text{us} \\ \text{them} \end{array} \right\}$ by processes which need not concern us.

Since I and you are not identical in deep structure, the Reflexive rule could not apply to give *I wash yourself. Instead, the string I wash you simply remains I wash you in surface structure. It is only by violating the rule of Reflexive that we can derive this string, so our rule correctly reflects the English speaker's knowledge that something is wrong with the string. Exactly the same is true for the examples in (h), p. 6. Our rules cannot produce the surface structure:

> *I will write a note to yourself

because this would have to have been derived from:

> I will write a note to you

by another violation of the rule of Reflexive. Since I and you are not identical, the Reflexive rule cannot apply to this deep structure; and we will end up in surface structure with the same string we had in deep structure, namely I will write a note to you. Thus, by postulating one transformational rule, we can explain the distribution of regular and reflexive pronouns shown in the table on p. 5 and discussed on p. 6.

The theory of transformational syntax, by distinguishing between deep structure and surface structure, avoids all the necessary statements about distribution such as the 15 given on p. 7. All these facts can be accounted for by postulating one rule, Reflexive, which operates on certain deep structure strings and converts them to the proper surface structures. There are many other cases in syntax where exactly this kind of rule is helpful. Consider, for instance, imperative sentences such as the following:

1) Go home!
2) Come here!
3) Shut up!

These sentences appear to have no subject. But we know in all these cases that you is understood as the subject. For instance, 1) cannot be a command

> for Bill to go home, or
> for mother to go home, or
> for them to go home, or
> for us to go home,

but only for you to go home. The same holds true for 2) and 3).

In the preceding examples of reflexive sentences, we accounted for the surface structure forms of these sentences by positing a different deep structure. The rule of Reflexive then converted these deep structures to give us the surface forms. With the imperative sentences, too, we might say that a subject you is actually present in the deep structure, and that there is a rule which deletes it. There is evidence for the existence of such a rule—the Reflexive rule. In imperative sentences, we get reflexives, but only one:

4) wash yourself (or yourselves)
5) *wash myself
6) *wash himself
7) *wash herself
8) *wash itself
9) *wash themselves

This ties in perfectly with our Reflexive rule. That is, we know this rule converts the second of two identical noun phrases into its reflexive form. Since the only reflexive pronoun occurring in imperative sentences is yourself, the subject NP (i.e., the first NP) must have been you at some time. These two facts together—1) that imperative sentences are understood to have you as their subject, and 2) that the only reflexive pronoun occurring in imperatives is yourself—suggest that there is a rule which deletes you under some conditions, after the Reflexive rule has applied. We call this rule Imperative, and it is stated roughly as follows (for a fuller discussion of this rule, see pp. 12-13.)

Imperative
you - Aux - VP ⟹
O - O - VP

Now, with reference to what was just said, let us consider sentences like the following:

10) Bill craned his neck.
11) Mary craned her neck.
12) We craned our necks.
13) They craned their necks
14) You craned your neck.
15) I craned my neck.

However, we do not have:

16) *I craned Bill's neck.
17) *We craned your neck.
18) *They craned our necks.
19) *You craned his neck.
20) *Mary craned my neck.
21) *I craned Mary's neck.

What we see in 10)-15) is that the possessive pronoun must be a copy of the subject NP of the sentence in these constructions, for otherwise we get unacceptable sentences like 16)-21).

The facts above indicate the need for postulating a Subject Copying rule in the grammar of English. It is stated as follows:

Subject Copying[10]

NP	Aux	crane	neck	
NP	Aux	crane	$\begin{bmatrix} NP's \\ + PRO \end{bmatrix}$ neck	⟹

---

[10]Actually, this rule must be extended to apply not just to sentences containing the VP crane neck, but to a wide variety of other VP's, like keep (one's) cool, hold (one's) breath, watch (one's) step, give (someone) a piece of (one's) mind, etc.

The feature [+ PRO] means that the possessive modifier of <u>neck</u> will be a pronoun (<u>John craned his neck</u>), not a full NP (*<u>John craned John's neck</u>).
With these two independently motivated rules of <u>Imperative</u> and <u>Subject Copying</u>, we can explain the fact that we have the sentence:

    22) Crane your neck.

but not:

    23) *Crane my neck.
    24) *Crane his neck.
    25) *Crane her neck.
    26) *Crane our necks.
    27) *Crane their necks.

Let us require the <u>Subject Copying</u> rule to apply <u>before</u> the <u>Imperative</u> rule. That is, the <u>Subject Copying</u> rule applies to the string:

    you crane -- neck

$\Longrightarrow$ <u>Subject Copying</u>

giving:

    <u>you</u> crane <u>your</u> neck

Then the rule deleting the subject noun phrase, <u>you</u>, will apply to the output string of the <u>Subject Copying</u> rule. That is, the <u>Imperative</u> rule applies to the derived string, after <u>Subject Copying</u> has applied

    you crane your neck

$\Longrightarrow$ <u>Imperative</u>

giving:

    crane your neck

It is this kind of explanation which transformational grammar seeks to give for sentences which are acceptable and for those which are not. We will postulate certain rules of grammar as being at least part of the knowledge every native speaker must have about his language.

The rule <u>Imperative</u> is necessary to describe the data in 1)-9) on p. 8, and the rule <u>Subject Copying</u> is necessary to describe the facts in 10)-21) on p. 8. With these two independently motivated rules, we <u>explain</u> the occurrences of the sentences 22)-27) above, <u>simply by ordering the process of Subject Copying</u> before the rule deleting the subject noun phrase, <u>you</u> (Imperative). Explaining the variety of new facts by using only those rules which are a necessary part of the grammar anyway brings us a little closer to what may be going on in the heads of native speakers concerning their knowledge of English. The above examples are rather simple, but the rules which will be illustrated and discussed below will involve more complex constructions.

In the following examples, the same general format will be used as above. Each derivation will begin with an illustration of the underlying or deep structure of a sentence (a structure to which no transformational rules have yet been applied). This will be given in the form of a tree diagram with labeled nodes of the sort we have discussed.

In the beginning of a derivation, the terminal string of each underlying tree will be divided into a number of parts. There will be a number for each part, and there will be as many numbers as there are parts. The way we determine how the tree is to be divided is completely dependent upon the grammatical rule to be applied. Each grammatical rule has two parts—a <u>structural description</u> (S. D.) and a <u>structural change</u> (S. C.). When we wish to apply a rule to a tree, this tree must be divided so that the parts correspond exactly to the parts given in the S. D. of the rule. This is called the <u>proper analysis</u> of a tree, with respect to the rule in question. For example, we consider the underlying structure for the sentence <u>John hates himself</u> to be:

(a)

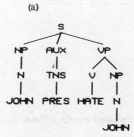

Since the rule of <u>Reflexive</u> is obligatory (see p.12), we must apply it to this structure, provided we can find a "proper analysis" with respect to the rule of <u>Reflexive</u>. <u>Reflexive</u> is stated as follows:[11]

        X - NP - Y - NP - Z

S. D.: 1   2   3   4   5

$\Longrightarrow$ oblig

S. C.: 1   2   3 $\begin{bmatrix} 4 \\ + \text{refl} \end{bmatrix}$ 5

Condition: 2 = 4

A proper analysis of (a) with respect to <u>Reflexive</u> must divide the terminal string of (a) into the same number of parts as there are in the S. D. of <u>Reflexive</u>—five. The first part can be any string at all, the second must be an NP, the third can be any string, the fourth must also be an NP, and the fifth can again be any string. Furthermore, if the division into five parts is to be a proper analysis, the NP in the second part must be identical to the NP in the fourth part. (This is what the condition 2 = 4 means.) A division of (a) in this manner can be performed. It is shown in (b). (The symbol O designates <u>nothing</u>, i.e., the first and fifth parts are not filled, or are null, in this sentence.)

---

   [11]The + indicates that the feature is present, e.g., <u>he</u> + refl will be written out by later rules as <u>himself</u>.

(b)

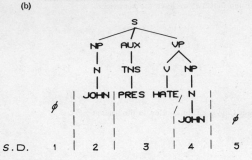

S.D.   1 | 2 | 3 | 4 | 5

Since there is a proper analysis of (a) with respect to <u>Reflexive</u>, namely (b), and since <u>Reflexive</u> is an obligatory rule, the change of the proper analysis of (a) specified in the S.C. of <u>Reflexive</u> <u>must</u> be carried out. This change is shown in:

(c)

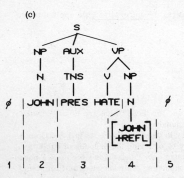

1 | 2 | 3 | 4 | 5

(If the rule we are applying is an optional one, the change specified in the S.C. need not be carried out. We will discuss optional rules later.)

In the following illustrations, we will first give the underlying tree, and underneath it we will state both the S.D. according to which the tree is analyzed and the S.C., in the following manner:

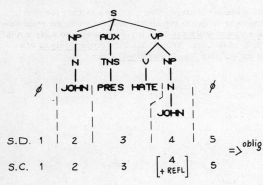

S.D. 1 | 2 | 3 | 4 | 5   => oblig

S.C. 1   2   3   [4]   5
                         [+REFL]

The page following the first diagram will show the tree as it appears after the rule has applied. The changes in the tree will correspond exactly to the S.C. Here, then, is the second diagram of our example, in which the rule of Reflexive has applied to the structure above:

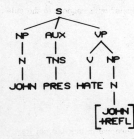

Later rules will apply to change term 4 $\begin{bmatrix} N \\ \\ John \\ +refl \end{bmatrix}$ into <u>himself</u>.

Rules do not always apply to a deep structure. In a number of cases, rules will apply to a structure which is the output of a previous rule. Similarly, a rule may apply to a structure which is the output of several previous rules. The tree to which all the necessary rules have applied is called the <u>final de-rived constituent structure</u>. This is the string of morphemes directly underlying the sounds of the sentence. The phrase structure (PS) rules and transformation (T) rules upon which this study is based are listed at the end of the book. The main purpose of this text is to establish the ordering of these rules.

10

Part I Independent Simplex Sentences

Ordering of Rules to be Presented in Part I[1]

Dative

Passive

Agent Deletion

Reflexive

There Insertion

Tag Formation

Neg-Emp Placement

Imperative

Question Formation

Adverb Preposing

Subject-Verb Inversion

Affix Hopping

Do-Support

[1]Lines connecting two rules indicate that those two rules must be so ordered.

<u>Reflexive</u>

S.D.   X - NP - Y - NP - Z

      1   2   3   4   5

S.C.   1   2   3 $\begin{bmatrix} 4 \\ +\text{refl} \end{bmatrix}$ 5 $\Longrightarrow$ oblig

Condition: 2 = 4, and 2 and 4 are in the same simplex sentence.

Consider the sentence <u>Brahms will wash himself</u>. It has the following deep structure.

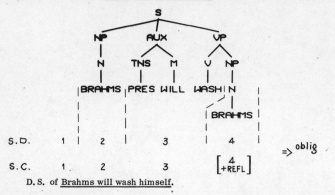

S.D.   1   2   3   4 $\Rightarrow$ oblig

S.C.   1   2   3 $\begin{bmatrix} 4 \\ +\text{REFL} \end{bmatrix}$

      D.S. of <u>Brahms will wash himself</u>.

Q. Can <u>Reflexive</u> apply to this structure?

A. Yes. <u>Reflexive</u> must apply whenever there are two identical NP's within the same sentence.

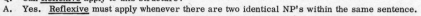

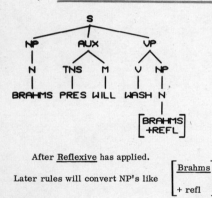

      After <u>Reflexive</u> has applied.

Later rules will convert NP's like $\begin{bmatrix} \text{Brahms} \\ +\text{refl} \end{bmatrix}$ into <u>himself</u>. In what follows, it will be assumed that these rules have applied.

<u>Imperative</u>

S.D. ## Imp - <u>you</u> - Pres - <u>will</u> - X

             1   2   3   4   5

                                  $\Longrightarrow$ oblig

S.C.   1   0   3   0   5

Consider the sentence <u>Come</u>!, which has the following deep structure:

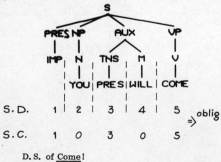

S.D. 1 2   3   4   5

                  $\Rightarrow$ oblig

S.C. 1 0   3   0   5

      D.S. of <u>Come</u>!

Q. Must <u>Imperative</u> apply to this structure?

A. Yes. <u>Imperative</u> must apply when <u>you</u> is the subject NP of the sentence.

12

After _Imperative_ has applied.

Notice that both the subject _you_ and the Modal _will_ have been deleted by the _Imperative_.

Reflexive and _Imperative_

Reflexive

S.D.   X – NP – Y – NP – Z

          1   2   3   4   5
                                          $\implies$ oblig
S.C.   1   2   3 $\left[\begin{smallmatrix} 4 \\ +\text{refl} \end{smallmatrix}\right]$ 5

Imperative

S.D. ## Imp – you – Pres – will – X

          1   2   3   4   5
                                          $\implies$ oblig
S.C.   1   0   3   0   5

To order any two (or more) transformations, we must fund one sentence in which the rules we want to order apply.   Consider the sentence: _Wash yourself!_ which has the following deep structure:

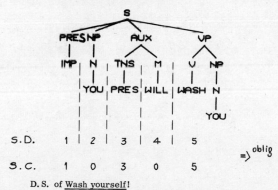

S.D.   1 | 2 | 3 | 4 | 5

S.C.   1   0   3   0   5 $\implies$ oblig

D.S. of _Wash yourself!_

Q.   Which of the above two transformations apply to this deep structure (hereafter D.S.)?
A.   Both _Reflexive_ and _Imperative_ can apply to this structure.   Let us assume _Imperative_ applies first.   (The tree has been analyzed to meet the S.D. of _Imperative._)

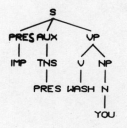

After _Imperative_ has applied.

Notice that the S.D. for _Reflexive_ cannot be met, because after _Imperative_ has applied, there is only one NP left.   _Reflexive_ demands two identical NP's in the same simplex S (sentence).   Therefore, this structure will eventually give us the unacceptable *_Wash you!_ Let us consider the same deep structure again.

13

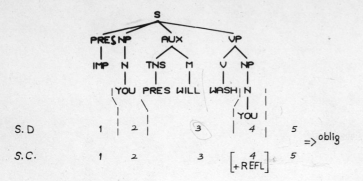

S.D	1		2		3		4		5
S.C.	1		2		3	$\begin{bmatrix} 4 \\ +REFL \end{bmatrix}$			5

$\Rightarrow$ oblig

D. S. of <u>Wash yourself</u>!

Q. Can both <u>Reflexive</u> and <u>Imperative</u> apply to this D. S. ?

A. Yes, but as we have seen from the ungrammatical sentence on p. 13, <u>Reflexive</u> must apply first. (The tree has been analyzed to meet the S.D. for <u>Reflexive</u>.)

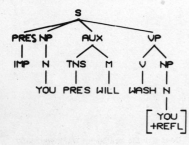

After <u>Reflexive</u> has applied.

Q. Does <u>Imperative</u> apply to this structure?

A. Yes. The S.D. for <u>Imperative</u> can still be met after <u>Reflexive</u> has applied.

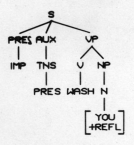

After <u>Imperative</u> has applied.

Q. After both <u>Reflexive</u> and <u>Imperative</u> have applied, must another transformation apply?

A. Yes. <u>Affix Hopping</u>[2] must apply. Let us consider the tree we have so far:

<u>Affix Hopping</u>

S. D.   X - [Affix] - [verb] - Y

        1   2   3   4

$\Longrightarrow$ oblig

S. C.   1   # 3 2   # 4

---

[2]For motivation and discussion of this rule and others in Part I, see N. Chomsky, <u>Syntactic Structures</u>, pp. 38–42.

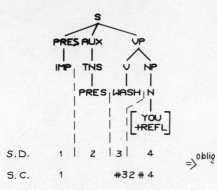

S.D.   1 | 2 | 3 | 4 $\Rightarrow$ oblig

S.C.   1   #3 2 #4

After <u>Imperative</u> has applied.

Q. Must <u>Affix Hopping</u> apply?
A. Yes. <u>Affix Hopping</u> is obligatory. This tree has been analyzed to meet the S. D. for <u>Affix Hopping</u>.

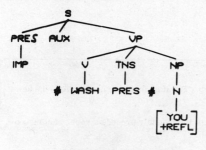

After <u>Affix Hopping</u> has applied.

We now have the sentence <u>Wash yourself</u>! To get this sentence, it is necessary to order <u>Reflexive</u> before <u>Imperative</u>. It is obvious that the order in which these rules are applied is crucial, for if they are ordered <u>Imperative-Reflexive</u>, an unacceptable S (*<u>Wash you</u>) is produced. Only with the reverse order is the correct <u>wash yourself</u>! produced. (By a general convention to be discussed later, the node <u>Aux</u> will be deleted, since it does not dominate any other node after <u>Affix Hopping</u>.)

<u>Neg-Emp Placement</u>

$$\text{S.D.} \quad \#\# \; [\; (\left\{ \begin{matrix} Q \\ Imp \end{matrix} \right\}) \; - \; (Neg)(Emp) \;] \; - \; NP \; - \; \left\{ \begin{matrix} \text{Tense} & & - \; VY \\ \text{Tense} \left\{ \begin{matrix} M \\ \underline{have} \\ \underline{be} \end{matrix} \right\} & - \; X \end{matrix} \right\}$$
$$\text{PreS}\text{PreS}$$

	1	2	3	4	5
	1	2	3	4	5	$\Rightarrow$ oblig
S.C.	1	0	3	4	2	5

Let us now consider the sentence <u>Don't go</u>! which has the following deep structure:

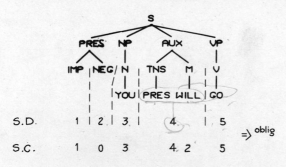

S.D.   1 | 2 | 3 | (4) | 5 $\Rightarrow$ oblig

S.C.   1   0   3   4 2   5

Analysis of tree for <u>Neg-Emp Placement</u>.

This tree has been analyzed to meet the S. D. for <u>Neg-Emp Placement</u>.

Q. Is there any rule that must apply to this tree?
A. Yes. When there is a Neg or an Emp in the Pre-Sentence, <u>Neg-Emp Placement</u> must apply.

15

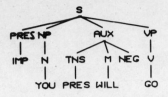

After <u>Neg-Emp Placement</u> has applied.

Q. Must any other transformation apply to this structure?
A. Yes. <u>Imperative</u> must apply.

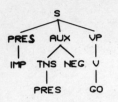

After <u>Imperative</u> has applied.

Q. Can <u>Affix Hopping</u> now apply?
A. No. <u>Affix Hopping</u> cannot now apply because the Tns, which is an affix, does not immediately precede a verb. But if no further rules applied, the ungrammatical *<u>not go</u> would be generated.
Q. Then how can we get <u>don't go</u>?
A. There is a rule called <u>Do-Support</u>, which must apply whenever affixes have been "stranded"—when they do not immediately precede a verb. Let us consider the structure we have so far, to which <u>Do-Support</u> must apply:

<u>Do-Support</u>

S.D.   X – [Affix] – Y

     1   2   3 $\Rightarrow$ oblig

S.C.   1   <u>do</u> + 2   3

Condition: $1 \neq W + [\text{verb}]$[3]

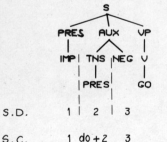

S.D.   1 | 2 | 3   => oblig

S.C.   1 do + 2   3

Analysis of tree for <u>Do-Support</u>.

This structure has been analyzed to meet the S. D. of <u>Do-Support</u>, which must apply here.

---

[3]The condition for <u>Do-Support</u> is that the variable string which precedes the affix cannot end with a [verb], which would have been the case if <u>Affix Hopping</u> had previously applied.

16

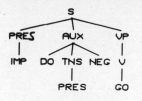

After <u>Do-Support</u> has applied.

Q. What sentence do we have?
A. <u>Don't go!</u>

Affix Hopping and Do-Support

We will now determine the order of <u>Do-Support</u> and <u>Affix Hopping</u>. Consider the sentence <u>The girls have gone</u>. It has the following D.S.:

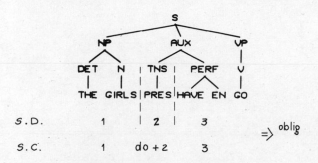

S.D.   1 | 2 | 3   => oblig

S.C.   1   do + 2   3

D.S. of <u>The girls have gone</u>.

Q. Does <u>Do-Support</u> apply to the above deep structure?
A. Yes. Since there is no verb to the left of the Tns, <u>Do-Support</u> must apply. The structure has been so analyzed.

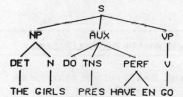

After <u>Do-Support</u> has applied.

Q. What do we have after <u>Affix Hopping</u>?
A. *<u>The girls do have gone</u>.
Q. How can we derive the desired <u>The girls have gone</u>?
A. We must apply <u>Affix Hopping</u> before <u>Do-Support</u>. Let us begin again with the same D.S. as above.

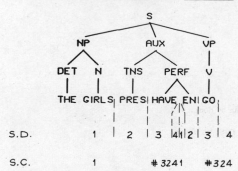

S.D.   1 | 2 | 3 |4|2| 3 | 4

S.C.   1   #3241   #324

Analysis of tree for application of <u>Affix Hopping</u> twice.

17

This structure has now been analyzed to undergo <u>Affix Hopping</u> twice. Although <u>Affix Hopping</u> and <u>Do-Support</u> both apply, we have just seen from the unacceptability of the S on p. 17 that <u>Do-Support</u> cannot apply before <u>Affix Hopping</u>.

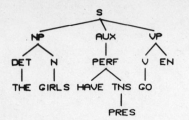

      After <u>Affix Hopping</u> has applied twice.

Q. Can <u>Do-Support</u> now apply?
A. No. There is no Tns which does not have a verb to its left.
Q. What S do we have?
A. <u>The girls have gone.</u> The grammaticality of this S and the ungrammaticality of the one on p. 17 shows that <u>Affix Hopping</u> must precede <u>Do-Support</u>.

<u>Neg-Emp Placement</u> and <u>Do-Support</u>

Let us consider the sentence <u>John does not eat bananas</u>, which has the following D.S.:

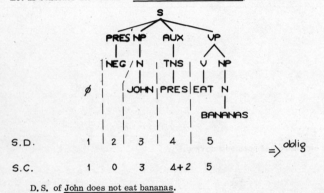

      D.S. of <u>John does not eat bananas</u>.

This D.S. has been analyzed to meet the S.D. of <u>Neg-Emp Placement</u>. Let us assume, contrary to fact, that <u>Do-Support</u> precedes <u>Neg-Emp Placement</u>.

Q. Can <u>Do-Support</u> apply to the above D.S.?
A. Yes, but we have just seen that <u>Affix Hopping</u> must precede <u>Do-Support</u>. After <u>Affix Hopping</u> has necessarily applied, the TNS will be to the right of the verb <u>eat</u>. Then, however, <u>Do-Support</u> can't apply because <u>Do-Support</u> only applies when there is no verb directly to the left of the affix.
Q. Must <u>Neg-Emp Placement</u> apply?
A. Yes. There is a Neg in the PreS.

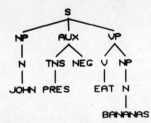

      After <u>Neg-Emp Placement</u> has applied.

Q. What S will this give us?
A. The unacceptable *<u>John not eat bananas</u>. Since we have already passed <u>Do-Support</u>, nothing more can be done.
Q. How can we get the sentence <u>John doesn't eat bananas</u>?
A. We must order <u>Neg-Emp Placement</u> before <u>Do-Support</u>. Let's try again, starting off with the same D.S. as above.

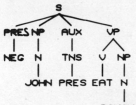

D. S. of <u>John does not eat bananas</u>.

This time we will apply <u>Neg-Emp Placement</u> first.

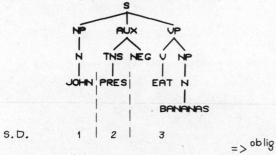

S.D.   1 | 2 | 3   => oblig

S.C.   1 do + 2   3

After <u>Neg-Emp Placement</u> has applied.

Q. Must <u>Do-Support</u> now apply?
A. Yes. The affix Tns now has no verb directly to its left, so <u>Do-Support</u> must apply. (The tree has been analyzed for <u>Do-Support</u>.)

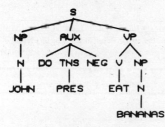

After <u>Do-Support</u> has applied.

Q. What sentence do we have?
A. <u>John does not eat bananas</u>. The grammaticality of this sentence, and the ungrammaticality of the sentence on p. 18 illustrate that the order of <u>Neg-Emp Placement</u> and <u>Do-Support</u> must be:

   <u>Neg-Emp Placement</u>
   <u>Do-Support</u>

(The line between these two rules means that they are necessarily ordered as shown.)

<u>Tag Formation</u>

$$\text{S.D.} \quad \# \begin{Bmatrix} Q \\ Imp \end{Bmatrix} - \begin{Bmatrix} Neg \\ \emptyset \end{Bmatrix} - (Emp) - NP - \begin{Bmatrix} \begin{Bmatrix} Tense \\ Tense \end{Bmatrix} \begin{Bmatrix} M \\ \underline{have} \\ \underline{be} \end{Bmatrix} & - V\ Y \\ & - X \end{Bmatrix}$$

$$\qquad 1 \qquad 2 \qquad\quad 3 \qquad 4 \qquad 5 \qquad\qquad 6$$

$$\text{S.C.} \quad 1 \qquad 2 \qquad 3 \qquad 4 \quad 5 \quad 6 \quad 5 \begin{Bmatrix} \emptyset \\ Neg \end{Bmatrix} \begin{bmatrix} 4 \\ +PRO \end{bmatrix} \Longrightarrow \text{oblig}$$

Consider now the following sentence <u>John does it, doesn't he</u>? This has the following D. S. :

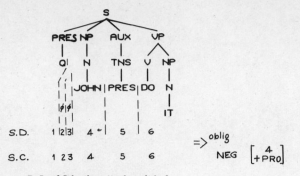

S.D.   1 |2|3| 4 · | 5 | 6

S.C.   1 2 3   4   5   6 $\Rightarrow$ oblig

                               NEG $\begin{bmatrix} 4 \\ +\text{PRO} \end{bmatrix}$

     D. S. of <u>John does it, doesn't he</u>?

This tree has been analyzed to meet the S. D. for <u>Tag-Formation</u>.

Q.   Is <u>Tag-Formation</u> obligatory?
A.   Yes, because there is a Q in the PreS and there is no WH-word elsewhere in the sentence.   (We will come to questions with WH-words shortly.)

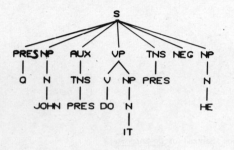

     After <u>Tag Formation</u> has applied.

Q.   What other rules must apply to this structure?
A.   <u>Affix Hopping</u> cannot apply in the tag (although it will apply in the main S), but <u>Do-Support</u> must apply there, because the affix Pres in the tag is stranded.

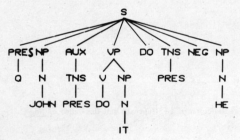

     After <u>Do-Support</u> has applied.

Q.   What does this give us?
A.   <u>John does it, doesn't he</u>?   (We will assume that the rule <u>Contraction</u>, which converts <u>does not</u> $\Longrightarrow$ <u>doesn't</u>, etc., has also applied, although we will not discuss it.)

<u>Tag Formation</u> and <u>Do-Support</u>

We will now determine the order of <u>Tag Formation</u> and <u>Do-Support</u>.   Consider the sentence <u>Churchill hated bagels, didn't he</u>? which has the following deep structure:

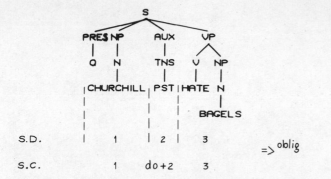

S.D.	1	2	3		
S.C.	1	do+2	3		

=> oblig

D. S. of <u>Churchill hated bagels, didn't he</u>?

The argument to show that <u>Do-Support</u> must follow <u>Tag Formation</u> is indirect. That is, we will show that there is a third rule, <u>Affix Hopping</u>, which must precede <u>Do-Support</u> and, then, that <u>Affix Hopping</u> must follow <u>Tag Formation</u>. It follows naturally that both <u>Affix Hopping</u> and <u>Do-Support</u> would then have to follow <u>Tag Formation</u>. We have already shown (pp. 17-18) that <u>Affix Hopping</u> must precede <u>Do-Support</u>. We now have to show that <u>Affix Hopping</u> must follow <u>Tag Formation</u>. This is quite simple. If we apply <u>Affix Hopping</u> to the structure above, we get the following result:

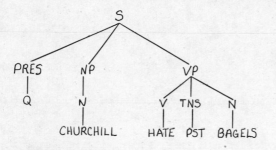

After <u>Affix Hopping</u> has applied.

Q. Can <u>Tag Formation</u> now apply?
A. No, because the order of the verb and tense is not correct. It can be seen from the statement of <u>Tag Formation</u> (p. 19) that tense (term 5), must precede the verb (term 6). Therefore (unless we complicate the rule), <u>Tag Formation</u> cannot apply after we have applied <u>Affix Hopping</u>, so we cannot derive the sentence, <u>Churchill hated bagels, didn't he</u>? Thus, <u>Affix Hopping</u> must follow <u>Tag Formation</u>. We have already seen that <u>Do-Support</u> must follow <u>Affix Hopping</u>, so naturally <u>Do-Support</u> must follow <u>Tag Formation</u>, too. Let us start again, this time applying <u>Tag Formation</u> first.

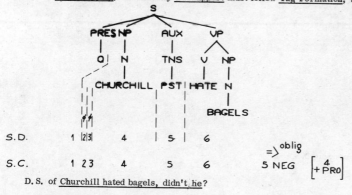

S.D.	1	2 3	4	5	6	
S.C.	1	2 3	4	5	6	

=> oblig

5 NEG $\begin{bmatrix} 4 \\ + PRO \end{bmatrix}$

D. S. of <u>Churchill hated bagels, didn't he</u>?

Q. Can <u>Tag Formation</u> apply?
A. Yes. The tree has been so analyzed.

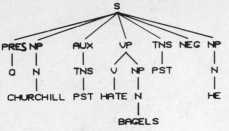

After <u>Tag Formation</u> has applied.

Q. Can <u>Affix Hopping</u> now apply?
A. No, not in the tag (although it will in the main S) because there is no verb to the right of the affix Pst for that affix to hop over.
Q. What must happen?
A. Whenever we have a "stranded" affix, such as we have in the tag, <u>Do-Support</u> must apply.

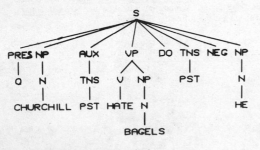

After <u>Do-Support</u> has applied.

Q. What sentence do we have now?
A. After <u>Contraction</u>, we have <u>Churchill hated bagels, didn't he?</u> Since <u>Do-Support</u> cannot apply before <u>Tag Formation</u> has applied, we must order these rules:

> Tag Formation
> Do-Support.

<u>There-Insertion</u>

$$
\text{S.D.} \quad \# \quad (\text{PreS}) \; - \; \text{NP} \; - \; \left\{ \begin{array}{l} \text{Aux} \; - \; \underline{be} \; - \; \text{W} \\[4pt] [\text{X} \; - \; \underline{be} \; - \; \text{Y}] \; - \; \text{Z} \\[4pt] \text{Aux} \end{array} \right\}
$$

	1	2	3	4	5	6

$\Longrightarrow$ opt

S.C.   1   <u>there</u>   3   4 + 2   5   6

Condition: a) 2 has an indefinite determiner.
            b) <u>Be</u> directly follows <u>Tns</u>.

Consider a sentence like <u>There is a devil among us</u>. This sentence has the following D. S. :

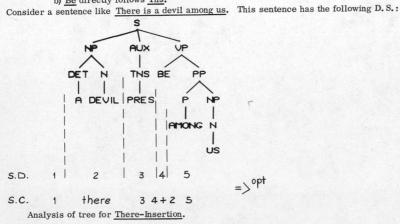

Analysis of tree for <u>There-Insertion</u>.

This tree has been analyzed to meet the S. D. for <u>There-Insertion</u>.

22

Q. Can <u>There-Insertion</u> apply?

A. Yes, optionally. There is an indefinite NP (term 2) and a <u>be</u> directly after <u>Tns</u>. Both of these conditions must be met for the rule to apply. If we choose not to apply <u>There-Insertion</u>, we still get a good sentence, i. e., <u>A devil is among us</u>. This is why the rule is marked <u>optional</u>. Assume that we apply <u>There-Insertion</u>:

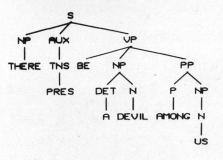

After <u>There-Insertion</u> has applied.

Note that the change in the tree is in accordance with the operation specified in the S. C. of the rule.

Q. What S do we have?

A. After <u>Affix Hopping</u> we will have <u>There is a devil among us</u>. Let us consider again the structure above, but now let us apply both <u>There-Insertion</u> and <u>Tag Formation</u> to it.

<u>There-Insertion</u> and <u>Tag Formation</u>

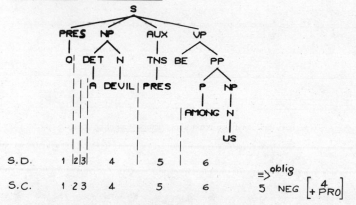

Analysis of tree for <u>Tag Formation</u>.

This tree has been analyzed to meet the S. D. for <u>Tag Formation</u>. Notice that this structure also meets the S. D. for <u>There-Insertion</u>. Let us assume that <u>Tag Formation</u> applies first:

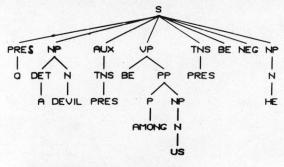

After <u>Tag Formation</u> has applied.

Q. What sentence will this structure give us?

A. After <u>Affix Hopping</u> this will give us the sentence <u>A devil is among us, isn't he?</u>

Q. Can any other rules apply to this tree?

A. Yes. This tree, after <u>Tag Formation</u>, still meets the S. D. for <u>There-Insertion</u>. This will apply (optionally) exactly as above.

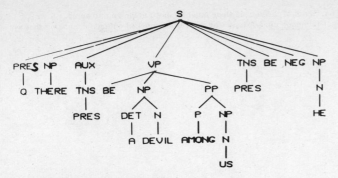

After <u>There-Insertion</u> has applied.

Q. What S will this structure give us?
A. After <u>Affix Hopping</u> this will give us the unacceptable *<u>There is a devil among us, isn't he</u>?
Q. How can this derivation be avoided?
A. By applying the rules in the reverse order, i. e., <u>There-Insertion-Tag Formation</u>. We will start again, using the same structure as on p.

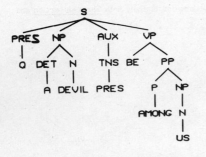

Analysis of tree for <u>Tag Formation</u> and <u>There-Insertion</u>.

This deep structure meets both the S. D. for <u>Tag Formation</u> and <u>There-Insertion</u>. As we have just seen, we must apply <u>There-Insertion</u> first:

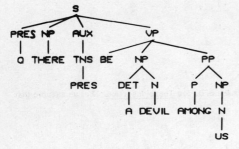

After <u>There-Insertion</u> has applied.

Q. Is it obligatory that <u>Tag Formation</u> now apply?
A. Yes, because there is a Q in the PreS and no WH-word in this structure.

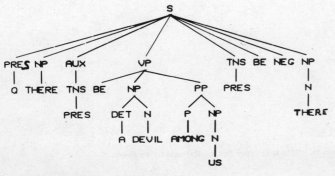

After <u>Tag Formation</u> has applied.

24

Q. What S does this give us?

A. After <u>Affix Hopping</u>, we have <u>There is a devil among us, isn't there</u>? (Again we assume that <u>Contraction</u>, a rule we will not discuss, has already applied.) Thus this sentence and the ungrammaticality of the sentence on p. 24 show the necessity of ordering <u>There-Insertion</u> before <u>Tag Formation</u>.

<u>Question Formation</u>

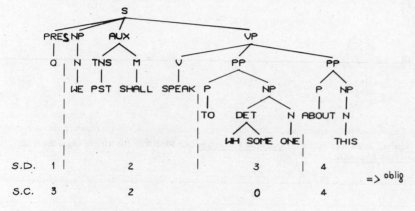

Condition: N = { <u>one</u> / <u>thing</u> / <u>place</u> }

Consider the sentence <u>Whom should we speak to about this</u>? It has the following D.S.:

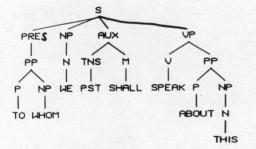

S.D. of <u>Whom should we speak to about this</u>?

Q. What rule can apply to this structure?

A. Since there is a Q in the PreS, either <u>Tag Formation</u> or <u>Question Formation</u> must apply. However, <u>Tag Formation</u> is ruled out because there is a WH-
word in the structure. <u>Tag Formation</u> can only apply when there is no WH-word in the structure. Therefore, we must apply <u>Question Formation</u>. The
tree has been so analyzed.

After <u>Question Formation</u> has applied.[4]

Q. Must any other transformation now apply to this structure?

A. Yes. Note that there is now a PP preceding the subject at the beginning of the sentence. Whenever this happens at the beginning of a main clause, and
the first PP or NP dominates Neg or WH (in our case it dominates WH), then <u>Subject-Verb Inversion</u> must apply.

[4]Again, it will be assumed that low-level rules which convert WH + <u>some</u> + <u>one</u> to <u>who</u> (and the case marking rule which converts <u>to who</u> to <u>to whom</u>)
have applied.

Subject-Verb Inversion

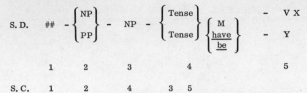

S. D. ## - $\left\{\begin{array}{c} NP \\ PP \end{array}\right\}$ - NP - $\left\{\begin{array}{c} Tense \\ Tense \end{array}\right\}\left\{\begin{array}{c} M \\ \underline{have} \\ \underline{be} \end{array}\right\}$ - V X - Y

	1	2	3	4	5
S. C.	1	2	4	3	5

Condition: a) If 2 = NP, it must dominate WH or Neg.
           b) The transformation applies in main clauses only.

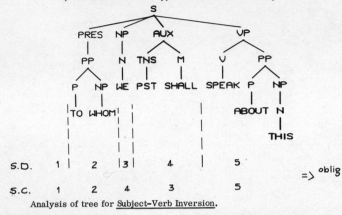

Analysis of tree for Subject-Verb Inversion.

Subject-Verb Inversion must apply to the output of Question Formation, since it is only after Question Formation that PP NP or NP NP can begin the main clause. The tree has been analyzed to meet the S. D. for Subject-Verb Inversion.

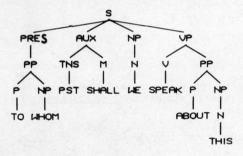

After Subject-Verb Inversion has applied.

Q. What other rule must apply to this structure?
A. Affix Hopping must apply.

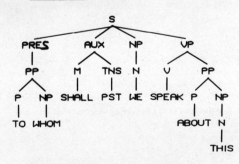

After Affix Hopping has applied.

Q. What sentence will this structure give us?
A. To whom should we speak about this?

26

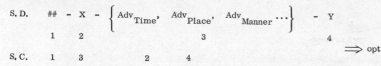

Adverb Preposing

S.D.   ## - X - { Adv$_{Time}$, Adv$_{Place}$, Adv$_{Manner}$ ··· } - Y

     1   2   3   4

                                                      ⟹ opt

S.C.   1   3   2   4

We will now consider the sentence <u>At that time, Willy had his finger in a crevice</u>. It has the following D.S.:

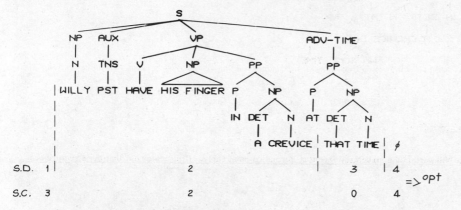

S.D. 1 | 2   3   4

S.C. 3   2   0   4

                                                   ⟹ opt

    D.S. of <u>At that time, Willy had his finger in a crevice</u>.

Q. Must <u>Adverb Preposing</u> apply?

A. No. <u>Adverb Preposing</u> is an optional rule, so we do not have to apply it. However, to show what happens when this tree undergoes this rule, let us apply <u>Adverb Preposing</u>.

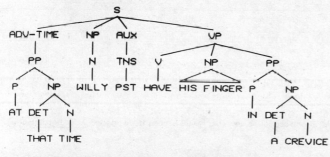

    After <u>Adverb Preposing</u> has applied.

Q. Must any other rule apply to this structure?

A. Yes. <u>Affix Hopping</u> must apply, which will give us <u>At that time, Willy had his finger in a crevice</u>. Now let us consider an adverb with a WH-word in it. <u>Subject-Verb Inversion</u> cannot apply since term 2 (NP) <u>At that time</u> does not dominate WH or Neg.

<u>Question Formation</u>, <u>Subject-Verb Inversion</u>, and <u>Affix Hopping</u>

S.D.   Q - X - [$_{PP}$ (P) [$_{NP}$ [$_{Det}$ WH <u>some</u>]$_{Det}$ N]$_{NP}$]$_{PP}$ - Y

     1   2   3   4

S.C.   3   2   4   ⟹ oblig

Condition: N = { <u>one</u>, <u>thing</u>, <u>place</u> }

Consider the sentence <u>At what time did Willy put his finger in a crevice?</u> This has the following D.S.:

27

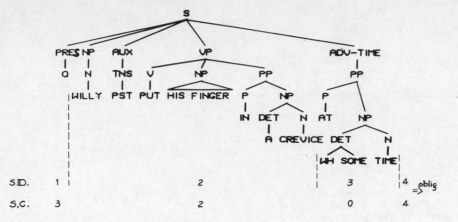

S.D.	1		2		3	4 $_{\text{oblig}}$
S.C.	3		2		0	4

D.S. of <u>At what time did Willy put his finger in a crevice</u>?

Q. What rule must apply to this structure?

A. Since there is a Pre-Sentence dominating Q and a WH-word in the structure, <u>Question Formation</u> must apply. (It is incidental that the structure containing WH is an Adverb.)

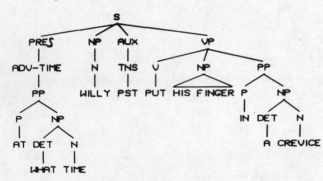

After <u>Question Formation</u> has applied.[5]

Q. Must any other rule now apply?

A. Yes. Since PP NP starts off the sentence, <u>Subject-Verb Inversion</u> must apply. However, let us see what would happen if we applied <u>Affix Hopping</u> now, before <u>Subject-Verb Inversion</u>.

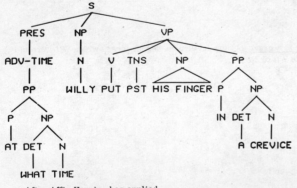

After <u>Affix Hopping</u> has applied.

Q. Can <u>Subject-Verb Inversion</u> now apply?

A. No, because the subject NP is followed by a verb, not by that part of the auxiliary which contains the element <u>Tns</u>, as required in the S.D. of <u>Subject-Verb Inversion</u>. The only S we can get by applying <u>Subject-Verb Inversion</u> now is *At what time put Willy his finger in a crevice?

Q. How can we get <u>At what time did Willy put his finger in a crevice</u>?

A. We must order <u>Subject-Verb Inversion</u> before <u>Affix Hopping</u>. Consider the structure we had above, after <u>Question Formation</u>:

---

[5]Again, we will assume the low level rules which convert WH + <u>some</u> into <u>what</u> have applied.

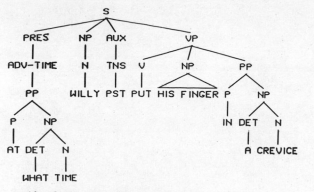

After <u>Question Formation</u> has applied.

We now apply <u>Subject-Verb Inversion</u>.

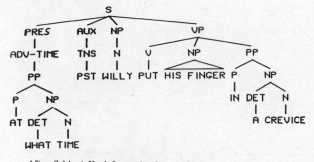

After <u>Subject-Verb Inversion</u> has applied.

Q. Must any other rules apply to this structure?

A. Yes. Since the <u>Tns</u> does not precede a verb, <u>Affix Hopping</u> cannot apply; this situation calls for <u>Do-Support</u>.

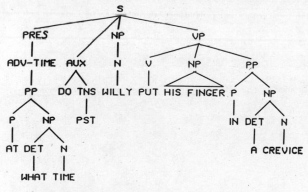

After <u>Do-Support</u> has applied.

This surface structure gives us the desired S <u>At what time did Willy put his finger in a crevice</u>?

Note 1: For certain dialects: Had we taken both Tns and (e.g.) <u>have</u> (rather than just Tns), we would have derived <u>At what time had Willy his finger in a crevice</u>? Notice that here <u>Do-Support</u> would not have applied, since the Tns would not have been stranded without a verb.

Note 2: On p. 27 we noted that when the Adverb <u>at that time</u> is preposed, <u>Subject-Verb Inversion</u> does not apply. But when <u>at what time</u> starts the S, <u>Subject-Verb Inversion</u> must apply because of the presence of WH. If the negative Adverb <u>at no time</u> had been preposed, the presence of the Neg would also trigger <u>Subject-Verb Inversion</u>, and the resulting S would be <u>At no time did Willy put his finger in a crevice</u>.

<u>Question Formation</u>, <u>Neg-Emp Placement</u>, and <u>Subject-Verb Inversion</u>

We will next consider the ordering of <u>Question Formation</u>, <u>Neg-Emp Placement</u>, and <u>Subject-Verb Inversion</u>. Consider the sentence <u>What doesn't John like</u>? This has the following deep structure:

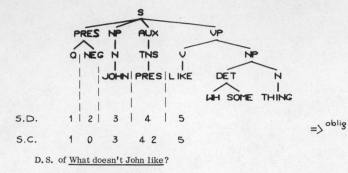

S.D.   1 | 2 | 3 | 4 | 5   => oblig

S.C.   1   0   3   42   5

D. S. of <u>What doesn't John like</u>?

Q.   What rules can apply to this tree?
A.   <u>Neg-Emp Placement</u> and <u>Question Formation</u>.
Q.   Which one must apply first?
A.   Let us apply <u>Neg-Emp Placement</u> first.   The tree has been analyzed to meet the S.D. for <u>Neg-Emp Placement</u>.

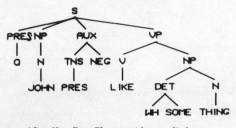

After <u>Neg-Emp Placement</u> has applied.

Q.   Must <u>Question Formation</u> apply to this structure?
A.   Yes, because there is a Q in the PreS and a WH-word in the structure (the NP of term 5).

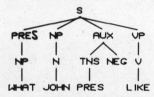

After <u>Question Formation</u> has applied.

Q.   What rule must now apply?
A.   Because we have two NP's at the beginning of a main clause, <u>Subject-Verb Inversion</u> must apply.   After <u>Neg-Emp Placement</u> and <u>Question Formation</u> have applied, the structure we have is analyzed to undergo <u>Subject-Verb Inversion</u>:

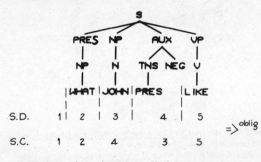

S.D.   1 | 2 | 3 | 4 | 5   => oblig

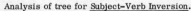

S.C.   1   2   4   3   5

Analysis of tree for <u>Subject-Verb Inversion</u>.

Before we continue this derivation, however, let us start again with the deep structure given on top of this page and apply <u>Question Formation</u> before <u>Neg-Emp Placement</u> this time.

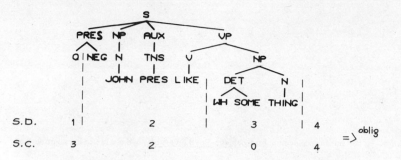

S.D.	1		2		3	4
S.C.	3		2		0	4

$\Rightarrow$ oblig

Analysis of tree for <u>Question Formation</u>.

This deep structure has been analyzed to meet the S. D. of <u>Question Formation</u> which we now apply.

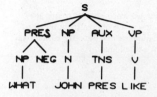

After <u>Question Formation</u> has applied.

Q. Can we now apply <u>Neg-Emp Placement</u>?
A. Yes, we must.

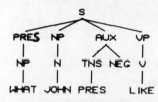

After <u>Neg-Emp Placement</u> has applied.

Notice we now have the same derived structure as on p. 30, which we repeat for convenience:

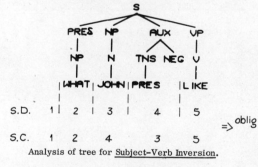

S.D.	1	2	3	4	5
S.C.	1	2	4	3	5

$\Rightarrow$ oblig

Analysis of tree for <u>Subject-Verb Inversion</u>.

Since we get the same structure with either order of <u>Neg-Emp Placement</u> and <u>Question Formation</u>, we say these rules are not ordered with respect to each other. The above tree has been analyzed to meet the S. D. for <u>Subject-Verb Inversion</u>, which must now apply.

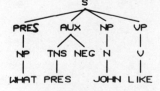

After <u>Subject-Verb Inversion</u> has applied.

Q. What rule must now apply?
A. <u>Affix Hopping</u> cannot apply because the affix <u>Tns</u> has no verb to its right to hop over. Instead, <u>Do-Support</u> must apply.

31

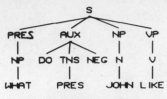

After <u>Do-Support</u> has applied.

Q. What sentence do we have?
A. After <u>Contraction</u> we have <u>What doesn't John like</u>? Note that if the <u>Neg</u> had not been placed before <u>Subject-Verb Inversion</u>, we could not have gotten the <u>Neg</u> to precede <u>John</u> by <u>Subject-Verb Inversion</u>.

Active and Passive Sentences

Let us now consider the relation between active and passive sentences in some detail. In the Introduction we showed how we were able to relate sentences to each other by certain grammatical transformations. By postulating a few sentences as basic, we were able to derive many others from these by applying various rules to the basic sentences. In the following few pages, we will attempt to show that active and passive sentences are actually reflections of one underlying entity and that one is derived from the other by a grammatical rule. To this end, consider first the active sentences:

1) Everyone adores chivalry.
2) Martha took the pill.

and compare them to the corresponding passives:

3) Civalry is adored by everyone.
4) The pill was taken by Martha.

The first fact brought out by this comparison is a semantic one. ~~The active-passive pairs are synonymous. 1) means the same thing as 3) and 2) means the same thing as 4). We can also say something about the syntax of these pairs, and we might begin by comparing:~~

4) The pill was taken by Martha.

to:

5) The girl was proud of Martha.

Outwardly, these sentences appear to be quite similar, and syntactically they are alike in some respects. Let us conjoin 4) with another similar sentence:

The pill was taken by Martha and the cough syrup was taken by Martha.

Analogously, we can do the same with 5):

The girl was proud of Martha and Charlie was proud of Martha.

Moreover, in each case, we may optionally delete the second occurrence of the phrases <u>taken by Martha</u> and <u>proud of Martha</u>, replacing each by <u>too</u>, as follows:

The pill was taken by Martha and the cough syrup was ... too.

and:

The girl was proud of Martha and Charlie was ... too.

Or, if we conjoin sentences like 4) and 5) with slightly different sentences, we get:

The pill was taken by Martha and the cough syrup was taken by Ann.

and:

The girl was proud of Martha and the boy was proud of Mary.

We may then optionally delete <u>was taken</u> and <u>was proud</u> in each case, giving:

The pill was taken by Martha and the cough syrup ... by Ann.

and:

The girl was proud of Martha and the boy ... of Mary.

From the phrase structure rules stated on pp. 243-244, we note that one of the expansions of VP is <u>be</u> + Adj(ective) P(hrase), and that AdjP may expand to Adj + PP. Thus, the structure for the adjectival VP of 5) would be:

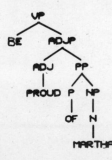

32

Since the passive Part(iciple) P(hrase) in 4) behaves similarly in several respects to the adjectival VP in 5), we might suggest parallel phrase structure rules to generate passive Part P's, like:

    i. VP → be + Part P
   ii. Part P → Part + by P(hrase)
  iii. Part → V + en

The above rules would generate the following structure for 4) <u>The pill was taken by Martha</u>:

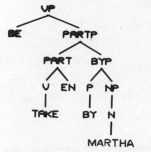

Structure for the passive Part P of 4). [6]

The phrase structure rule which would generate such a configuration is the following: ii. Part P → Part + <u>by</u> P(hrase).

We will assume, for our present purposes, that the above structure is correct for passive Participle Phrases, and the following discussion will deal primarily with structures of this type.

    The similarities between 4) and 5) suggest that these two sentences types should also resemble one another in their phrase structure above. Thus, ~~the sentences with adjectival VP's differ from those with a true passive verb only in that a true passive verb stands in place of the adjective in the latter.~~ We shall, however, show that things are somewhat more complex than this, and that these differences are more basic than might appear at first sight.

    Note first, that in a structure of this form (<u>be</u> + Part P), ~~only transitive verbs~~ (i.e., only those that can take objects) ~~may appear under the node Part.~~ We cannot, for example, replace this V by an intransitive V like <u>sleep</u>, or <u>occur</u>:

    *All day was slept (by John) (compare to John slept all day)

or:

    *The accident <u>was occurred</u> (compare to the accident occurred)

~~It is unclear how a phrase structure framework would encompass this systematic gap properly.~~ To restrict derivations of this type to VP's containing transitive verbs is a very mechanical way out; a less mechanical solution would clearly be welcome. Before proposing a better solution, let us examine some additional difficulties with the phrase structure derivation proposed above.

    Another fact about Part P's is that they may always have <u>by</u>-Phrases at their end. We have only considered one kind of Part P so far, but there are many other types, a few of which we will illustrate below. Of course, to generate each of the other structures, we will need to add the appropriate phrase structure rule necessary for each one. This will be stated below the Part P. Consider now the sentence 6) <u>The booze was begged for by everyone</u>, whose Part P structure is:[7]

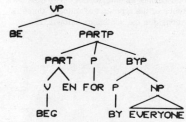

Structure for the Part P of 6).

A second phrase structure rule is required to generate this configuration, namely:

    ii. Part P → Part + P + <u>by</u> P(hrase)

A third kind of Part P appears in sentence 7) <u>The job was attributed to a genius by the cops</u>, whose Part P structure is:

---

[6]<u>Take</u> + en will be spelled out as <u>taken</u> by later rules.
 [7]Actually, this structure is not quite correct, but we will disregard the problem here for the purpose of illustration. (We will correct it in the next structure.)

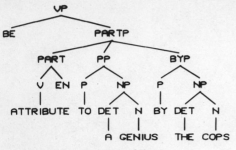

Structure for the Part P of 7).

This type of sentence would require an expansion of Part P:

iii. Part P→Part + PP + by P(hrase)

Still a fourth type of Part P is exemplified by sentence 8) <u>The giant door was boomed shut by Miss Stackpole</u>. The Part P structure of this sentence is something like:

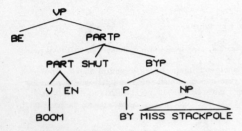

Structure for the Part P of 8).

The associated rule is:

iv. Part P→Part + <u>shut</u> + <u>by</u> P(hrase)

In cases 4)-7), it is quite possible to replace some of the constituents with other constituents of the same kind. Thus, in 4), we can replace the V under the Part node with <u>blast</u>, <u>emulate</u> (i.e., <u>blasted by</u>, <u>emulated by</u>). In 6), we can replace the V dominated by Part with <u>ask</u>, <u>look</u>, etc. (i.e., <u>asked for</u>, <u>looked for</u>); or we may replace the P dominated by the Part P with <u>to</u>, or <u>into</u> (i.e., <u>seen to</u>, <u>looked into</u>). This is also true for 7), where the V <u>attribute</u> may be replaced by <u>give</u> (i.e., <u>given to</u> ...), or the P <u>to</u> may be replaced by <u>into</u> (i.e., <u>turned into</u> ...), or the NP <u>a genius</u> may be replaced by <u>a drape</u> (i.e., <u>turned into a drape by the witch</u>). ~~The fact that certain constituents are substitutes for each other is evidence that they are the same kind of constituents,~~ as we mentioned earlier.

Thus, we see that there is a large variety of passive sentences and that each of these types would require a special phrase structure rule. The disadvantage of this proposal is not that we used a large number of phrase structure rules, but that for every passive sentence of the type just examined, there is a corresponding active sentence for which very similar phrase structure rules are used. To see these similarities, consider the sentences below. The corresponding active VP of 4) (p. 33) is illustrated in sentence <u>4)</u> <u>Mary took the pill</u>, whose VP structure is:

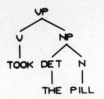

VP structure for <u>4)</u>.

The following rule generates such deep structures:

i. VP→V + NP

The active VP corresponding to 6) (p. 33) is exemplified by the sentence:
6) <u>Everyone begged for the booze</u>, whose VP structure is:[8]

---

[8]See fn. 6, p. 33.

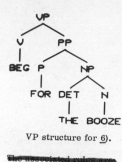

VP structure for 6).

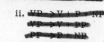

~~The associated rules are:~~

ii. ~~VP → V + P + NP~~
~~VP → V + PP~~
~~PP → P + NP~~

For 7) (p. 34), the corresponding active sentence is 7) <u>The cops attributed the job to a genius</u>, whose VP structure is:

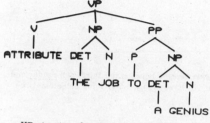

VP structure for 7).

This structure is produced by the rules:

iii. VP → V + NP + PP
PP → P + NP

The active VP corresponding to the Part P in 8) (p. 34) is found in sentence 8) <u>Miss Stackpole boomed the giant door shut</u>, whose VP is diagrammed:

VP structure for 8).

The associated rule is:

iv. VP → V + NP + <u>shut</u>

Compare now the phrase structure rules necessary (stated below each structure) to generate the Part P's 4) and 6)-8) with the VP's 4) and 6)-8).

<u>Passive Part P phrase structure rules</u>

$$\text{Part P} \rightarrow \text{Part} + \begin{cases} \text{i.} \\ \text{ii. P} \\ \text{iii. PP} \\ \text{iv. shut} \end{cases} + \underline{\text{by}} \text{ Phrase.}$$

Part → Verb + en

<u>Active VP phrase structure rules</u>

$$\text{VP} \rightarrow \text{V} + \begin{cases} \text{i. } \underline{\text{NP}} \\ \text{ii. P } \underline{\text{NP}}[9] \\ \text{iii. } \underline{\text{NP}} \text{ PP} \\ \text{iv. } \underline{\text{NP}} \text{ shut} \end{cases}$$

Notice there is partial identity between these rules. The active VP PS rule has one extra NP in each line (they have been underlined), but otherwise the material inside the braces is identical in each case. For example, if we compare Part P 4) (p. 33) to the active VP of 4) (p. 34), we find that once the <u>by</u>-Phrase in the Part P is disregarded, the object of the Part P (i.e., everything which follows the Part) and that of the VP (i.e., everything which follows the V) differ only in the one extra NP present in the object of the VP (p. 35). Or compare Part P 8) (p. 34) to VP 8) (p. 35). Again, the objects of these are identical except for the extra NP in the active VP (p. 35), disregarding the Part P <u>by</u>-Phrase. This is exactly the case with all the other pairs. This is already a remarkable "coincidence." Even if other types of nodes in our PS rules have the same number of expansions, they con't normally correspond to one another, ~~as the expansions of Part P and VP do.~~

Note, moreover, that ~~there is an exact parallelism between the object types which may appear in the passive Part P's and those in the corresponding~~ ~~active VP's.~~ Thus if a verb appearing under a Part takes Part P object #84, the corresponding VP verb takes object <u>#84</u>, and not some other one. For example, Part P 7) (p. 34) takes object #7. (attributed <u>to a genius</u>), and the corresponding active VP in 7) (p. 35) takes object #7 (attribute <u>the job to a genius</u>), but this active VP may not take #8 (*<u>attribute shut</u> by Miss Stackpole) or #6 (*<u>attribute for by everyone</u>). And conversely, if an active VP takes object <u>#8</u>, as in

[9]See fn. 6, p. 33.

boomed <u>the door shut</u>

the corresponding passive Part P also takes #8:

was boomed <u>shut</u>

but not <u>#7</u>

*was boomed <u>the job to a genius</u>

or <u>#6</u>

*was boomed <u>for the booze</u>

or any other object type.

These symmetrical co-occurrence restrictions would have to be stated twice in a phrase structure grammar, once for the active VP and once for the Passive VP. The two lists of restrictions suggest that we are failing to bring out the fact that these co-occurrence restrictions are one and the same thing, for within a phrase structure grammar we have no means of stating the fact that the two lists are identical. As we continue our investigation, we find that additional repetitive lists are required to capture additional co-occurrence restrictions. Thus in the first sentences, the following <u>by</u>-Phrases are acceptable:

John was rendered ineligible by $\left\{\begin{array}{l}\text{the facts}\\ \text{his funny face}\\ \text{old age}\end{array}\right\}$.

However, none of the following makes sense:

John was rendered ineligible by $\left\{\begin{array}{l}\text{*the lamp}\\ \text{*the toothpick}\\ \text{*chocolate covered ants}\\ \text{*Sturbridge, Mass.}\end{array}\right\}$.

To exclude the latter sentences, a complete grammar of English will have to state at least some ~~selectional restrictions~~ between the Part verb <u>render</u> and the NP which may be in the following <u>by</u>-Phrase. However, for the corresponding active VP's, the grammar will have also to state some selectional restrictions between the subject NP and the verb, for while we have:

$\left\{\begin{array}{l}\text{The facts}\\ \text{His funny face}\\ \text{Old age}\end{array}\right\}$ rendered John ineligible.

we do not have:

$\left\{\begin{array}{l}\text{*The lamp}\\ \text{*The toothpick}\\ \text{*Chocolate-covered ants}\\ \text{*Sturbridge, Mass.}\end{array}\right\}$ rendered John ineligible.

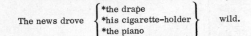 ~~We are aware, of course, that whatever the restrictions are that are placed on the Part P verb and the NP in the following by-Phrase, they are exactly the same restrictions that obtain between the active VP verb and its subject NP.~~ But this is only the beginning.

Consider now the relation between the subject NP's and the verbs which appear under Part in Part P. The subject NP in the context:

_____ was driven wild

may be <u>Henrietta</u>, <u>the announcer</u>, or <u>Johnson</u>. However, the subject NP in this context may not be:

$\left\{\begin{array}{l}\text{*the drape}\\ \text{*his cigarette-holder}\\ \text{*the piano}\end{array}\right\}$ was driven wild.

Again, any complete grammar which has Part P in deep structure will have to state some selectional restrictions between the subject NP and the Part P V. There is also a relation, however, between the object NP and this verb when it appears as an active VP. Thus, in the context

The news drove _____ wild

we may have NP's like <u>Henrietta</u>, <u>the announcer</u>, or <u>Johnson</u>, but none of the following:

The news drove $\left\{\begin{array}{l}\text{*the drape}\\ \text{*his cigarette-holder}\\ \text{*the piano}\end{array}\right\}$ wild.

To exclude these, of course, it will be ~~necessary to state the selectional restrictions which exist between the object NP and the verb appearing in the active VP.~~ But again, these are the same selectional restrictions that obtain between the subject NP and verb when the latter appears in the passive Part P.

As a final bit of evidence, consider the word <u>tabs</u>. This NP occurs in exactly two contexts in English. One is as the object of <u>keep</u> when this verb assumes its active form.

1) The CIA is keeping tabs on you.

The other is as the subject of keep when this verb assumes its passive form:

2) Tabs are being kept on you by the CIA.

If we say both actives and passives are basic, we will need a phrase structure rule for 1), which specifically states that <u>tabs</u> may only occur as the object of the active form of <u>keep</u> (to exclude *<u>the CIA saw tabs</u>, etc.), and a phrase structure rule for 2), which must state that <u>tabs</u> may only occur as the subject of <u>keep</u> when that verb assumes its passive form (to exclude *<u>tabs were seen by the CIA</u>). But this duplication is not necessary if we derive one form from the other by a rule.

We can easily summarize the evidence accrued so far with the help of the table below.

(a) ~~Facts about active VP's~~

1. Certain PS rules are necessary to generate the active VP's (p. 35).
2. The lexicon must state that the object of the VP verb

   <u>attribute</u> is #7 only
   <u>took</u> is #4 only
   <u>beg</u> is #6 only
   <u>boom</u> is #8 only
   etc. (pp. 35-36)

3. There are certain selectional restrictions between the active VP verb and its subject:

   $NP_1 - V - NP_2$

   to exclude: *the toothpick rendered John ineligible but to include: old age rendered John ineligible

4. There are certain selectional restrictions between the active VP verb and its object.

   $NP_2 - V - NP_1$ Adj

   to exclude: *The news drove the drape wild but to include: The news drove Henrietta wild (p. 36).

5. We need a phrase structure which states that the NP <u>tabs</u> may occur only as the object of the active form of <u>keep</u>:
   to exclude: *The CIA saw tabs but to allow: The CIA kept tabs on John (p. 36).

6. The active and passive pairs are synonymous (p. 36).

(b) ~~Facts about passive Part P's~~

1. The PS rules necessary to generate Part P's are partially identical to those necessary for the active VP's (p. 35).
2. The lexicon must state the same restrictions—that the object of the Part P verb

   <u>attribute</u> is #7 only
   <u>took</u> is #4 only
   <u>beg</u> is #6 only
   <u>boom</u> is #8 only
   etc. (pp. 35-36)

3. The same selectional restrictions must be stated, but now between the Part P verb and the <u>by</u>-Phrase NP.

   $NP_2 - V - $ by NP_1

   to exclude: *John was rendered ineligible by the toothpick but to include: John was rendered ineligible by old age

4. The same selectional restrictions must be stated, but now between the Part P verb and its subject.

   $NP^1 - V - $ by NP_2

   to exclude: *The drape was driven wild but to include: Henrietta was driven wild (p. 36).

5. An almost identical phrase structure rule is necessary, but this one states that <u>tabs</u> may occur only as subject of the passive form of <u>keep</u>:
   to exclude: *Tabs were seen by the CIA but to allow: Tabs were kept on John by the CIA (p. 36).

In a grammar having phrase structure rules only, it will be necessary to state all the facts we have been discussing in two places: once for actives and once for passives, as we have done in our table above. Such a grammar assumes that all sentence types are basic, and it has no rules to relate one type of sentence to another. But this need not be the case if a grammar has rules which relate sentences to each other. Since we have already illustrated the need for such rules in some detail (e.g., the rules <u>Reflexive</u> and <u>Imperative</u>, pp. 5-8 and 13-14), will now propose a <u>Passive</u> rule, which relates passive sentences to active ones.

The existence of such a rule means, of course, that we will have to state either just the restrictions given in column (a), or just those given in column (b). Any complete grammar must do this much, at least. That is, if we assume passives to be basic and if we then postulate a rule to derive actives from these, we need only state the restrictions in column (b), and our rule will automatically predict all the corresponding ones in column (a). Or conversely, if we assume that only actives are generated in deep structure and we then postulate a rule which derives passives from these, we need only state the restrictions on actives (given in column (a)). Such a rule will give us all the corresponding restrictions on passives (stated in column (b)). Although either way is conceivable, generative grammarians have assumed actives to be underlying, and passives to be derived from these by the <u>Passive</u> rule. We will not discuss the motivation for this choice, as the arguments are long and complicated.

At this point in our discussion, let us turn to the formal statement of this rule, on which the illustrations in the next section are based:

		## (PreS) - NP -	[X Passive]	V (Prep) -	NP - Y		
			Aux Aux				
S.D.	1	2	3		4	5	
S.C.	1	4	3	5 by 2			$\Rightarrow$

Q. What does this rule explain?

A. ~~The Passive rule explains why the restrictions on passive sentences are identical to those of the corresponding active ones.~~ Or, conversely, the fact that the restrictions on active sentences (in column (a)) are the same as those on passive sentences (in column (b)) justifies the postulation of a rule which relates these two sentence types to each other.[10] Now, let us see how the rule works, and how it relates to other rules in our grammar.

<u>Passive</u>

	## (PreS) - NP -	[X Passive]	V (Prep) -	NP - Y	
S.D.		Aux Aux			
	1 2	3	4 5		
S.C.	1 4	3	5 by 2		$\Rightarrow$

As an example of <u>Passive</u>, consider the sentence <u>Aristotle was pricked in the back by an ant</u>, which has the following D.S.:

[10] For motivation and discussion for this statement of the rule, including the expansion <u>be + en</u> of the auxiliary, see Chomsky, <u>Syntactic Structures</u>, pp. 42-43.

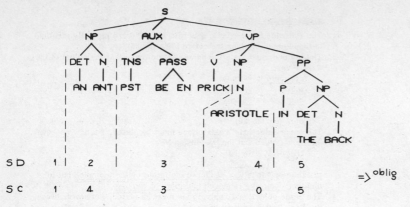

SD   1 | 2 | 3 | 4 | 5

SC   1   4   3   0   5   => oblig

D. S. of <u>Aristotle was pricked in the back by an ant</u>.

Q.   Must <u>Passive</u> apply to this structure?
A.   Yes.   Whenever the constituent <u>Passive</u> appears in the auxiliary, <u>Passive</u> must apply.

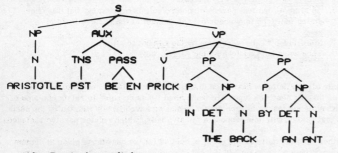

After <u>Passive</u> has applied.

Q.   Since there is still a <u>be + en</u> in the auxiliary, can the <u>Passive</u> apply again?
A.   No.   ~~Cyclic rules~~ (which we will explain later), ~~do not apply to their own output.~~ After <u>Passive</u> has applied to a clause, it may not apply again within that same clause.
Q.   Can any other rule apply to this structure?
A.   There is another rule called <u>Agent Deletion</u> which may apply only when the agent is <u>by someone</u>, <u>by something</u>, etc., which are 'recoverable' and can be deleted.
Q.   Must <u>Affix Hopping</u> apply?
A.   Yes.

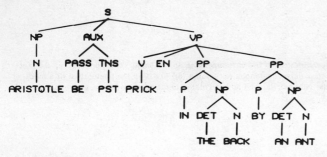

After <u>Affix Hopping</u> has applied.

Q.   What sentence do we have?
A.   <u>Aristotle was pricked in the back by an ant</u>.

<u>Dative</u>

S.D.   XV - NP - NP - Y

         1   2   3   4
                             => opt
S.C.   1   0   3 to 2   4

As an example of <u>Dative</u>, consider the sentence <u>Lucifer sent some B.O. bomb to Jane</u>, which has the following D. S.:

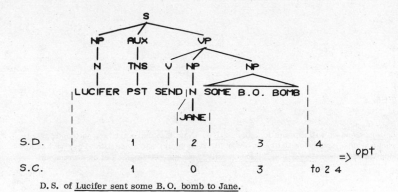

S.D.   1   2   3   4

S.C.   1   0   3   to 2 4 ⟹ opt

D.S. of <u>Lucifer sent some B.O. bomb to Jane.</u>

Q. Must <u>Dative</u> apply to this structure?

A. No. <u>Dative</u> is an optional rule. We get a grammatical sentence either way. If we don't apply <u>Dative</u>, we will have the S <u>Lucifer sent Jane some B.O.</u> <u>bomb</u>. Let us assume, however, that <u>Dative</u> applies.

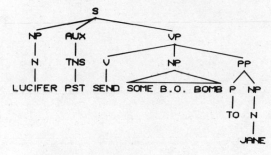

After <u>Dative</u> has applied.

Q. Must any other transformation apply to this tree?

A. Yes. <u>Affix Hopping</u> must apply, giving us the sentence <u>Lucifer sent some B.O. bomb to Jane</u>.

<u>Dative</u> and <u>Passive</u>

Consider again the deep structure above, but with a <u>Passive</u> in the auxiliary and an Adverb-Time, <u>yesterday</u>, at the end:

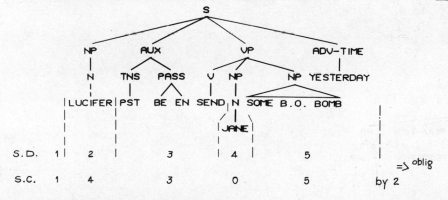

S.D. 1 2   3   4   5

S.C. 1 4   3   0   5   ⟹ oblig

                                       by 2

Q. What transformations apply to this structure?

A. <u>Passive</u> must apply, and <u>Dative</u> and <u>Adverb Preposing</u> may apply optionally. We will apply all three.

Q. In what order should <u>Passive</u> and <u>Dative</u> apply?

A. We will assume that <u>Passive</u> applies before <u>Dative</u>. (The tree has been analyzed to undergo <u>Passive</u>.)

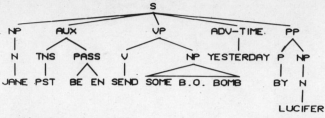

After *Passive* has applied.

This will give us the S <u>Jane was sent some B.O. bomb yesterday by Lucifer</u>. Now we will attempt to apply <u>Dative</u>. Note that there are now no longer two NP's directly following the verb. Since V NP NP is required in the structural description for <u>Dative</u> in order for it to apply, and since after <u>Passive</u> has applied this condition is no longer met, we cannot apply <u>Dative</u>. Conclusion: ~~to apply both Passive and Dative, Dative must apply first~~. Let us start again with the same D.S. as on p. 39.

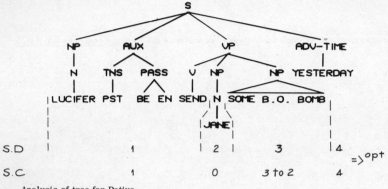

Analysis of tree for <u>Dative</u>.

This tree has been analyzed to undergo <u>Dative</u>, which we now apply.

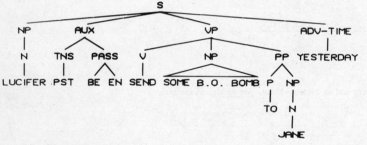

After <u>Dative</u> has applied.

Q. Can we still apply <u>Passive</u>?
A. Yes. The structural description for <u>Passive</u> is still met.

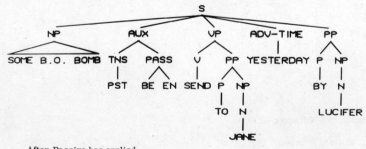

After <u>Passive</u> has applied.

Q. Can any other rule now apply?
A. Yes. <u>Adverb Preposing</u> may optionally apply. If we do not apply it, we will eventually derive <u>Some B.O. bomb was sent to Jane yesterday by Lucifer</u>. Let us assume <u>Adverb Preposing</u> applies. This will give us the following derived structure:

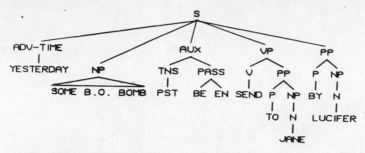

After <u>Adverb Preposing</u> has applied.

Q. What other rules can now apply? Can <u>Subject-Verb Inversion</u> apply?
A. No, because while a constituent precedes the subject NP, this constituent does not dominate WH or Neg, one of which is required if <u>Subject-Verb Inversion</u> is to apply.
Q. Must <u>Affix Hopping</u> apply?
A. Yes, and that will give us <u>Yesterday, some B.O. bomb was sent to Jane by Lucifer</u>. If we want to get the S <u>Yesterday, Jane was sent some B.O. bomb by Lucifer</u>, we do not apply <u>Dative</u> (since it is optional); we apply only <u>Passive</u>. Only the order <u>Dative</u> (opt.)-<u>Passive</u> allows us both possibilities. Conclusion: <u>Dative</u> must precede <u>Passive</u>.

<u>Passive</u> and <u>There-Insertion</u>

We will now order <u>Passive</u> with respect to <u>There-Insertion</u>. Consider the sentence <u>There was a stone thrown by Jupiter</u>. It has the following deep structure:

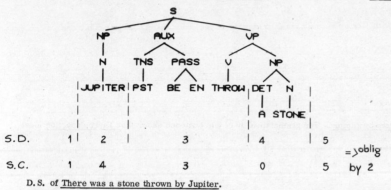

D.S. of <u>There was a stone thrown by Jupiter</u>.

Q. Can <u>There-Insertion</u> apply?
A. No. Although there is a <u>be</u> in the sentence, the subject NP is not indefinite, which is required in the S.D. of <u>There-Insertion</u>. (p. 22)
Q. Must <u>Passive</u> apply?
A. Yes, because the constituent <u>Passive</u> appears in the auxiliary. The tree has been analyzed to undergo <u>Passive</u>.

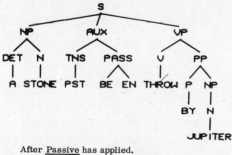

After <u>Passive</u> has applied.

Q. Can <u>There-Insertion</u> now apply?
A. Yes. After <u>Passive</u> has applied there is now an indefinite NP in subject position. Let us consider the tree so far derived, to which we shall apply <u>There-Insertion</u>.

41

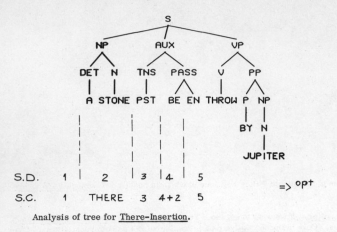

S.D.   1 | 2 | 3 | 4 | 5   => opt

S.C.   1   THERE   3   4+2   5

Analysis of tree for <u>There-Insertion</u>.

This structure has now been analyzed to undergo <u>There-Insertion</u>, which we apply optionally:

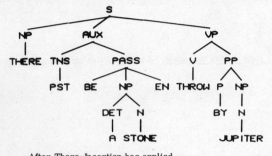

After <u>There-Insertion</u> has applied.

Q. What else can apply to this structure?

A. <u>Affix Hopping</u> will apply to produce the S <u>There was a stone thrown by Jupiter</u>. The grammaticality of this sentence shows that <u>There-Insertion</u> must follow <u>Passive</u>.

<u>Passive</u> and <u>Tag Formation</u>

We will now order <u>Passive</u> with respect to <u>Tag Formation</u>. Consider the sentence <u>An arrow was shot by Paris, wasn't it</u>? It has the following deep struc-

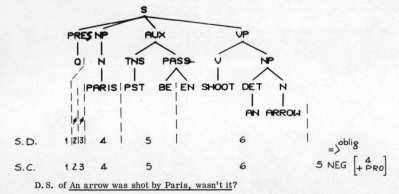

S.D.   1 |2|3| 4 | 5 | 6 | =>^oblig

S.C.   1 2 3   4   5   6   5 NEG $\begin{bmatrix} 4 \\ +PRO \end{bmatrix}$

D.S. of <u>An arrow was shot by Paris, wasn't it</u>?

Q. Can both <u>Tag Formation</u> and <u>Passive</u> apply to this structure?

A. Yes. Both are obligatory. Suppose we apply <u>Tag Formation</u> first. (The tree has been analyzed to meet the S.D. for <u>Tag Formation</u>.)

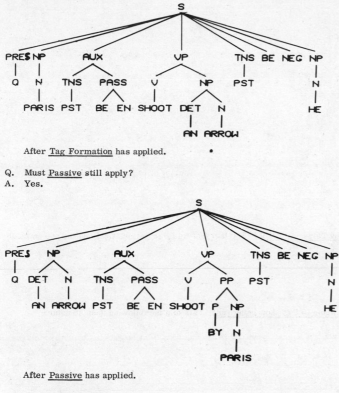

After <u>Tag Formation</u> has applied.

Q. Must <u>Passive</u> still apply?
A. Yes.

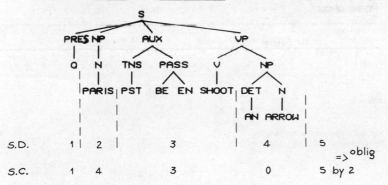

After <u>Passive</u> has applied.

Q. What S do we get?
A. *<u>An arrow was shot by Paris, wasn't he?</u>
Q. How can we prevent this sentence?
A. We must order <u>Passive</u> before <u>Tag Formation</u>. Consider the deep structure of p. 42 again.

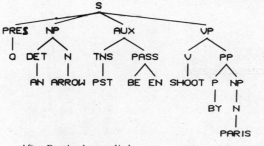

S.D.	1	2		3		4		5
S.C.	1	4		3		0		5 by 2

=> oblig

Analysis of tree for <u>Passive</u>.

This structure has been analyzed to meet the S. D. of <u>Passive</u>, which we now apply.

After <u>Passive</u> has applied.

43

Q. Does this structure still meet the S. D. for <u>Tag Formation</u>?
A. Yes, and we must apply it.

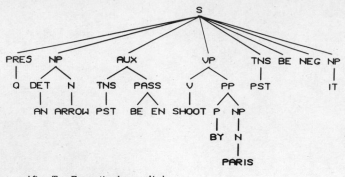

After <u>Tag Formation</u> has applied.

Q. Must any other rule apply to this derived structure?
A. Yes. <u>Affix Hopping</u> must apply to give us the sentence <u>An arrow was shot by Paris, wasn't it</u>? The fact that this S is grammatical and the one on p. 43 is not shows that <u>Passive</u> must precede <u>Tag Formation</u>.

<u>Passive</u> and <u>Question Formation</u>

We will now order <u>Passive</u> and <u>Question Formation</u>. Consider the sentence <u>By whom is this show being run</u>? This has the following deep structure:

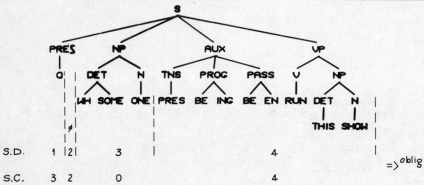

D. S. of <u>By whom is this show being run</u>?

Q. Must both <u>Passive</u> and <u>Question Formation</u> apply to this deep structure?
A. Yes. Both must apply.
Q. In what order?
A. Let's say <u>Question Formation</u> applies before <u>Passive</u>. The tree has been analyzed accordingly.

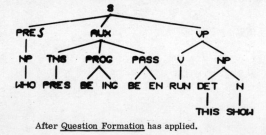

After <u>Question Formation</u> has applied.

Note that if there were no <u>Passive</u> auxiliary in this structure, we would get the sentence <u>Who is running this show</u>?

Q. Can the <u>Passive</u> now apply?
A. Yes, it must.

44

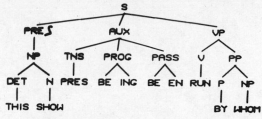

After _Passive_ has applied.

Q. What sentence do we get?
A. *<u>This show is being run by whom</u>? This sentence is an acceptable echo question, but it is ungrammatical if taken to be a normal question.
Q. How can we obtain the desired <u>(By) who is this show being run (by)</u>?
A. The rules of Passive and Question Formation must apply in that order. Using the same deep structure as on p. 44 we start again.

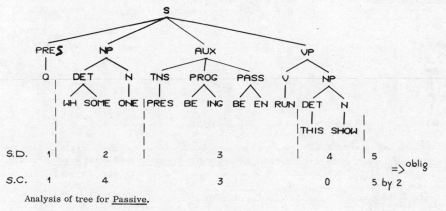

S.D.	1	2	3	4	5	
S.C.	1	4	3	0	5 by 2	$\Rightarrow$ oblig

Analysis of tree for _Passive_.

This deep structure has now been analyzed to meet the structural description of _Passive_. Let us apply this rule.

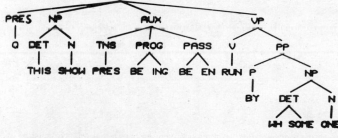

After _Passive_ has applied.

Q. Must we now apply <u>Question Formation</u>?
A. Yes.

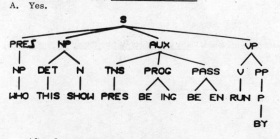

After <u>Question Formation</u> has applied.

Note that we may optionally take the <u>by</u> to the front with <u>who</u>, or we may leave it, as we have done. Either way, we have a good sentence.

Q. Must another transformation now apply?
A. Yes. Notice that after <u>Question Formation</u> has applied, there are two NP's at the beginning of a main clause. This is the structural index of <u>Subject-Verb Inversion</u>, which must apply. The following is the tree as it appears after <u>Passive</u> and <u>Question Formation</u>, the same as the one above.

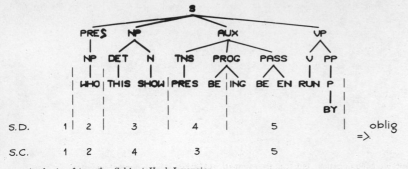

S.D.	1	2		3		4		5			

$$\Rightarrow \text{oblig}$$

S.C.	1	2	4	3	5

Analysis of tree for <u>Subject-Verb Inversion</u>.

This tree has been analyzed to meet the S. D. for <u>Subject-Verb Inversion</u>, which we now apply.

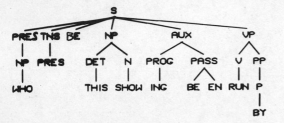

After <u>Subject-Verb Inversion</u> has applied.

Note that since <u>Subject-Verb Inversion</u> must follow <u>Question Formation</u> and, as we have illustrated, since <u>Question Formation</u> must follow <u>Passive</u>, clearly <u>Subject-Verb Inversion</u> must also follow <u>Passive</u>.

Q. What other rule must apply to this structure?
A. <u>Affix Hopping</u> must now apply.

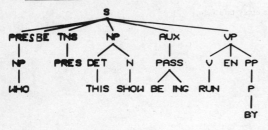

After <u>Affix Hopping</u> has applied.

Q. What sentence do we have?
A. The desired S <u>Who is this show being run by</u>? The grammaticality of this S and the ungrammaticality of the one on p. 45 shows that <u>Passive</u> must be ordered before <u>Question Formation</u>.

<u>Passive</u>, <u>Tag Formation</u>, and <u>Neg-Emp Placement</u>

We will now order <u>Passive</u> with respect to both <u>Tag Formation</u> and <u>Neg-Emp Placement</u>. Consider the sentence <u>Mary wasn't cooked by the chief, was she</u>? It has the following deep structure:

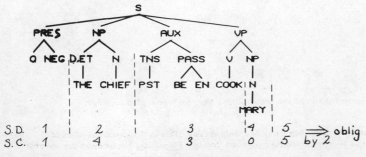

S.D.	1		2			3		4	5	

$$\Rightarrow \text{oblig}$$

S.C.	1	4	3	0	5	by 2

D. S. of <u>Mary wasn't cooked by the chief, was she</u>?

46

Q. Can <u>Passive</u>, <u>Tag Formation</u>, and <u>Neg-Emp Placement</u> all apply to this deep structure?
A. Yes. All three must apply. We have already seen that <u>Passive</u> must precede <u>Tag Formation</u>. We will therefore apply <u>Passive</u> first. (The tree has been analyzed to undergo <u>Passive</u>.)

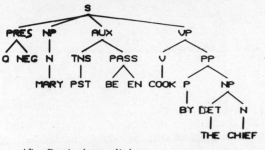

After <u>Passive</u> has applied.

Q. Should we now apply <u>Tag Formation</u> or <u>Neg-Emp Placement</u>?
A. Notice that if we apply <u>Neg-Emp Placement</u> first, the <u>Neg</u> in the PreS will be deleted because it will be moved into the auxiliary (see pp.15-16 for <u>Neg-Emp Placement</u>). If we then applied <u>Tag Formation</u>, we would get a <u>Neg</u> in the tag, since there would no longer be <u>Neg</u> in the PreS. We do not want *<u>Mary wasn't cooked by the chief, wasn't she</u>? Therefore, <u>Tag Formation</u> must precede <u>Neg-Emp Placement</u>. Following is the tree so far derived. It is exactly as the one above, to which <u>Passive</u> has applied:

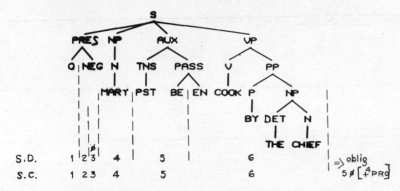

Analysis of tree for <u>Tag Formation</u>.

This structure has now been analyzed to meet the S.D. for Tag Formation, which we apply:

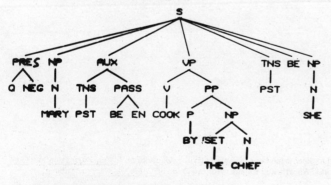

After <u>Tag Formation</u> has applied.

Q. Must we now apply <u>Neg-Emp Placement</u>?
A. Yes.

47

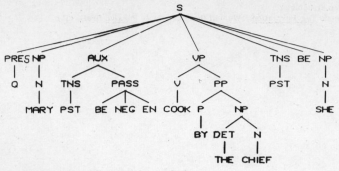

After <u>Neg-Emp Placement</u> has applied.

Q. What S do we have?

A. After <u>Affix Hopping</u> we derive <u>Mary wasn't cooked by the chief, was she</u>? This sentence shows that the rules of <u>Passive</u>, <u>Tag Formation</u>, and <u>Neg-Emp Placement</u> must apply in that order.

<u>Tag Formation</u> and <u>Imperative</u>

We will now order <u>Tag Formation</u> and <u>Imperative</u>. Consider the sentence <u>Come, won't you</u>? It has the following deep structure:

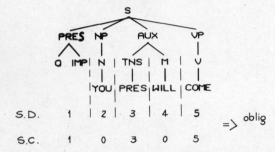

S.D.   1 | 2 | 3 | 4 | 5

S.C.   1   0   3   0   5   => oblig

D.S. of <u>Come, won't you</u>?

Q. Must both <u>Tag Formation</u> and <u>Imperative</u> apply to this deep structure?

A. <u>Imperative</u> must, and <u>Tag Formation</u> may. (<u>Tag Formation</u> is optional with <u>Imperative</u>.) Let us assume that <u>Imperative</u> applies first. (The tree has been analyzed to undergo <u>Imperative</u>.)

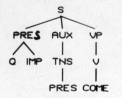

After <u>Imperative</u> has applied.

Q. Can <u>Tag Formation</u> now apply?

A. No. There is now no longer any subject NP for <u>Tag Formation</u> to repeat. It has been wiped out by <u>Imperative</u>. Conclusion: If <u>Tag Formation</u> and <u>Imperative</u> are both to apply within the same clause, <u>Tag Formation</u> must be first. We will start again with the D.S. of <u>Come, won't you</u>? above.

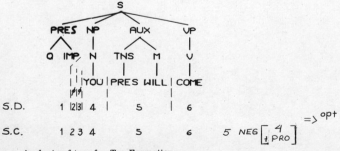

S.D.   1 |2|3| 4 | 5 | 6

S.C.   1 2 3 4   5   6   5 NEG $\begin{bmatrix} 4 \\ + PRO \end{bmatrix}$ => opt

Analysis of tree for <u>Tag Formation</u>.

This structure has been analyzed to meet the S. D. for Tag Formation, which we now apply.

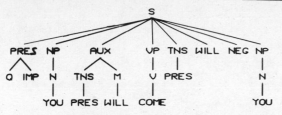

After Tag Formation has applied.

Q. Can Imperative now apply?

A. Yes. Tag Formation has safely copied over the subject NP which Imperative will now delete:

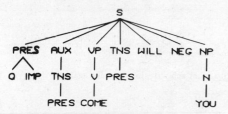

After Imperative has applied.

Q. What sentence will this generate?

A. After Affix Hopping and Contraction, we will have Come, won't you? This S can be generated only if we assume the ordering: Tag Formation-Imperative.

There-Insertion and Question Formation

We will next order There-Insertion and Question Formation. Let's take the sentence What is there in the drink? which has the following deep structure:

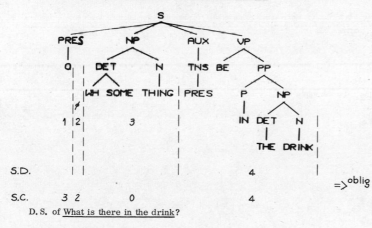

D. S. of What is there in the drink?

Q. Can both There-Insertion and Question Formation apply here?

A. Yes. Question Formation is obligatory, and There-Insertion is optional. Suppose that Question Formation applies before There-Insertion. The tree has been so analyzed.

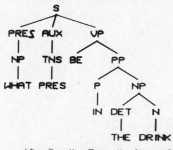

After Question Formation has applied.

49

Q. What would this give us, if no further rules besides <u>Affix Hopping</u> were to apply?
A. <u>What is in the drink</u>?
Q. Can <u>There-Insertion</u> now apply?
A. Yes. We may optionally apply <u>There-Insertion</u> (see p. 22).

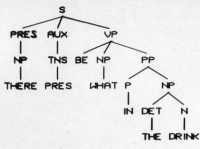

After <u>There-Insertion</u> has applied.

Q. What do we have?
A. *<u>There is what in the drink</u>? which is acceptable only as an echo question, just as was the case with the sentence on p.45.
Q. How can we get <u>What is there in the drink</u>?
A. When both <u>There-Insertion</u> and <u>Question Formation</u> are to apply within the same clause, <u>There-Insertion</u> must apply first. Consider again the deep structure:

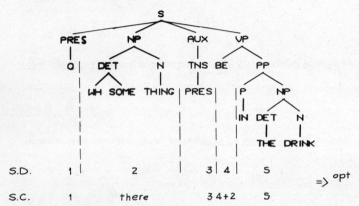

S.D.	1	2		3	4	5	=> opt
S.C.	1	there		3 4+2		5	

Analysis of tree for <u>There-Insertion</u>.

This structure has now been analyzed to meet the S. D. for <u>There-Insertion</u>. Let us apply it.

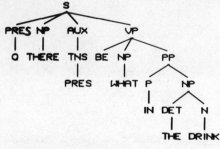

After <u>There-Insertion</u> has applied.

Q. Must <u>Question Formation</u> now apply?
A. Yes.

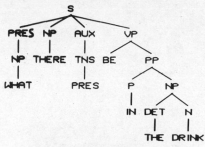

After <u>Question Formation</u> has applied.

Q. Must another transformation now apply?

A. Yes. <u>Subject-Verb Inversion</u> must apply, since two NP's begin the main clause. This can be seen from the following tree which shows the structure derived so far, exactly as the one above, after <u>There-Insertion</u> and <u>Question Formation</u> have been applied.

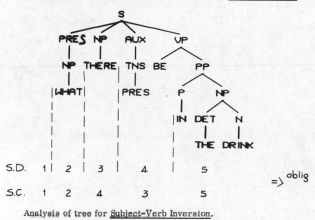

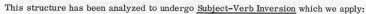

S.D.   1   2   3   4   5   =⟩ oblig

S.C.   1   2   4   3   5

Analysis of tree for <u>Subject-Verb Inversion</u>.

This structure has been analyzed to undergo <u>Subject-Verb Inversion</u> which we apply:

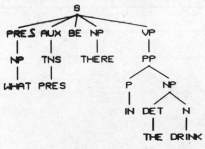

After <u>Subject-Verb Inversion</u> has applied.

Q. Must any other rule now apply?

A. Yes. <u>Affix Hopping</u> must apply, giving the S <u>What is there in the drink</u>? This S, in contrast to the ungrammatical sentence on p. 50, shows that <u>There-Insertion</u> must precede <u>Question Formation</u>, as well as <u>Subject-Verb Inversion</u>.

<u>There-Insertion</u> and <u>Reflexive</u>

We will now order <u>There-Insertion</u> and <u>Reflexive</u>. Consider the sentence <u>There is a boy washing himself</u>. This has the following D.S.:

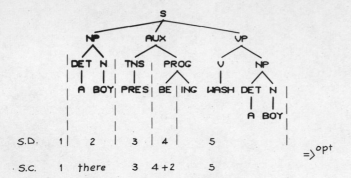

S.D.   1 | 2 | 3 | 4 | 5 | =>^{opt}

S.C.   1   there   3   4 + 2   5

> D. S. of <u>There is a boy washing himself</u>.

Q.   Can both <u>Reflexive</u> and <u>There-Insertion</u> apply to this deep structure?
A.   Yes.   <u>Reflexive</u> is obligatory, and <u>There-Insertion</u> is optional.
Q.   What order must these two rules have if we apply both in one clause?
A.   Let's suppose <u>There-Insertion</u> applies first.   (The tree has been so analyzed.)

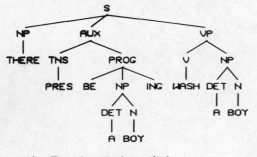

> After <u>There-Insertion</u> has applied.

Q.   Can <u>Reflexive</u> now apply?
A.   Yes.   There are two identical NP's within the same simplex sentence, so the second NP will become reflexive.   Consider the tree derived after <u>There-Insertion</u> (which is exactly as the one above).

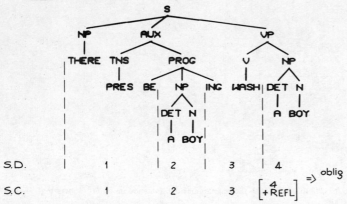

S.D. | 1 | 2 | 3 | 4

S.C.   1   2   3 $\left[\begin{array}{c} 4 \\ +\text{REFL} \end{array}\right]$ => ^{oblig}

> Analysis of tree for <u>Reflexive</u>.

This tree has been analyzed to meet the S.D. for <u>Reflexive</u> (see p. 11).   The conditions for <u>Reflexive</u> (p. 11) are met, and we must apply it.

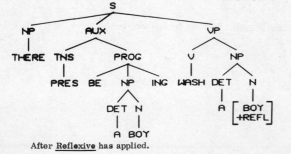

> After <u>Reflexive</u> has applied.

52

Q. Will this give us an acceptable sentence?
A. Yes. After <u>Affix Hopping</u> we will have <u>There is a boy washing himself</u>. Let's try the other order—first <u>Reflexive</u> and then <u>There-Insertion</u>. We will use the same D. S. as on p. 52:

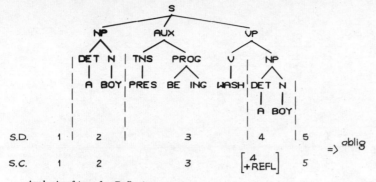

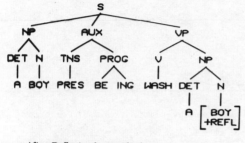

Analysis of tree for <u>Reflexive</u>.

Q. Can both <u>Reflexive</u> and <u>There-Insertion</u> apply to this structure?
A. Yes. <u>Reflexive</u> will apply first, since the tree has been analyzed accordingly.

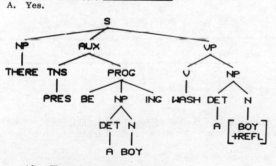

After <u>Reflexive</u> has applied.

Q. Can we now apply <u>There-Insertion</u>?
A. Yes.

After <u>There-Insertion</u> has applied.

Q. Will this give us an acceptable sentence?
A. Yes. After <u>Affix Hopping</u>, we have <u>There is a boy washing himself</u>.
Conclusion: <u>There-Insertion</u> and <u>Reflexive</u> are not ordered with respect to each other. With either order, we get an acceptable sentence.

<u>Passive</u> and <u>Agent Deletion</u>

We will now order <u>Passive</u> and <u>Agent Deletion</u>. Consider the sentence <u>The spirit was felt</u>. It has the following deep structure:

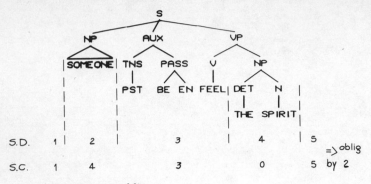

S.D.	1		2		3		4		5	
S.C.	1		4		3		0		5	

⇒ oblig
by 2

D. S. of <u>The spirit was felt</u>.

Q. Can both <u>Passive</u> and <u>Agent Deletion</u> apply to this tree?

A. No. Only <u>Passive</u> can apply. <u>Passive</u> creates the agent which may be deleted by <u>Agent Deletion</u>. One cannot delete what has not yet been created. Therefore, we must apply <u>Passive</u> first. The tree has been analyzed to meet the S. D. for <u>Passive</u>.

<u>Agent Deletion</u>

S. D. X Passive V – by NP – Y

                    1   2   3   ⟹ opt

S. C.   1   0   3

Condition: 2 = <u>by</u> + <u>some</u> { <u>one</u> / <u>thing</u> }

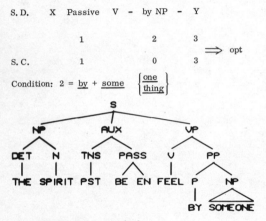

After <u>Passive</u> has applied.

Q. Can <u>Agent Deletion</u> now apply?

A. Yes. Now that <u>Passive</u> has created an agent which may be deleted, <u>Agent Deletion</u> may optionally apply. The rules <u>Passive</u> and <u>Agent Deletion</u> are said to be "intrinsically" ordered. That is, the formal structure of the rules in question determine their order. We now apply <u>Agent Deletion</u>:

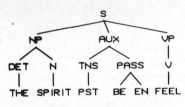

After <u>Agent Deletion</u> has applied.

Q. Must <u>Affix Hopping</u> now apply?

A. Yes. After <u>Affix Hopping</u>, we have <u>The spirit was felt</u>.

<u>Affix Hopping</u> and <u>Agent Deletion</u>

Q. Could <u>Affix Hopping</u> have applied before <u>Agent Deletion</u>?

A. Yes. Consider the structure above, which results after <u>Passive</u> has applied:

54

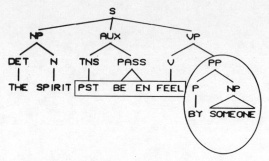

After <u>Passive</u> rule has applied.

Q. Can both <u>Affix Hopping</u> and <u>Agent Deletion</u> apply?

A. Yes. Both can apply—at once, or in either order. The rectangle includes the constituents of <u>Affix Hopping</u> (which occurs in two places) and the circle includes what is involved in <u>Agent Deletion</u>. These processes apply to different parts of the tree, and are therefore unordered with respect to each other.

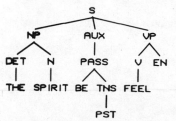

After both <u>Affix Hopping</u> and <u>Agent Deletion</u> have applied.

As noted earlier, this produces the sentence <u>The spirit was felt</u>.

Extrinsic Ordering

We will now consider an example of "extrinsic" ordering, using the rules of <u>Question Formation</u> and <u>There-Insertion</u>. Consider the sentence <u>Who is there watching the show</u>? which has the following D. S.:

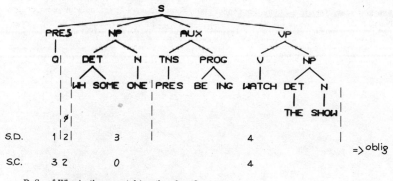

D. S. of <u>Who is there watching the show</u>?

Q. Can <u>Question Formation</u> and <u>There-Insertion</u> both apply to the above structure?

A. Yes. Both can apply, but the order in which they apply will make a difference in the outcome. Let's try <u>Question Formation</u> first.

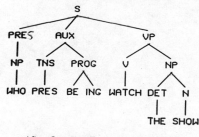

After <u>Question Formation</u> has applied.

Q. What would we have if no other rule besides <u>Affix Hopping</u> were to apply?

55

A. <u>Who is watching the show</u>?
Q. Can <u>There-Insertion</u> now apply to this structure?
A. Yes. It can apply optionally. Let's apply it.

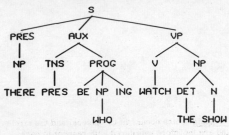

After <u>There-Insertion</u> has applied.

Q. What do we have?
A. *<u>There is who watching the show</u>? (This sentence is unacceptable in the same way the sentences on pp. 45 and 50 are.)
Q. How can we avoid this sentence?
A. We can apply <u>There-Insertion</u> before <u>Question Formation</u>. Let us use the D. S. on p. 55 again:

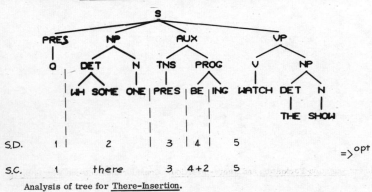

S.D.   1 | 2 | 3 | 4 | 5   =>\ opt

S.C.   1   there   3 4+2   5

Analysis of tree for <u>There-Insertion</u>.

Both <u>There-Insertion</u> and <u>Question Formation</u> can apply. As we have just seen, <u>Question Formation</u> cannot apply first, or we will end up with an unacceptable S. <u>There-Insertion</u> applies first. (The tree has been so analyzed.)

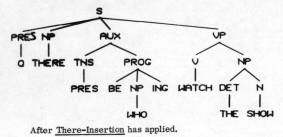

After <u>There-Insertion</u> has applied.

Q. Can <u>Question Formation</u> now apply?
A. Yes. It must apply to the above structure. Let us analyze the structure accordingly:

56

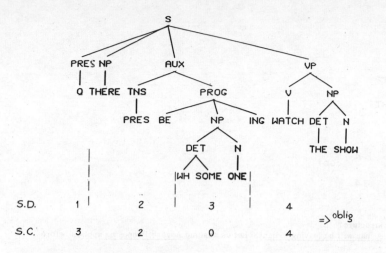

S.D.	1	2	3	4
S.C.	3	2	0	4

$\Rightarrow$ oblig

Analysis of tree for <u>Question Formation</u>.

When <u>Question Formation</u> applies to this tree, the following changes occur:

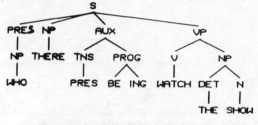

After <u>Question Formation</u> has applied.

Q. What rule must now apply?

A. Since two NP's start off a main clause, <u>Subject-Verb Inversion</u> must apply to this structure.

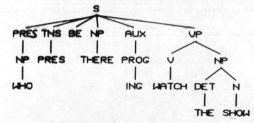

After <u>Subject-Verb Inversion</u> has applied.

Q. What sentence do we have?

A. After <u>Affix Hopping</u> we will have <u>Who is there watching the show</u>? This sentence provides an example of extrinsic ordering. Both <u>There-Insertion</u> and <u>Question Formation</u> apply to the deep structure on p. 55, but only the ordering: <u>There-Insertion</u>-<u>Question Formation</u> will give us the desired result. The rules of <u>Reflexive</u> and <u>Imperative</u> are likewise extrinsically ordered, as discussed on

<u>There-Insertion</u> and <u>Adverb Preposing</u>

We will next order <u>There-Insertion</u> and <u>Adverb Preposing</u>. We will derive the sentence <u>Tonight, there will be a man leaving</u>, which has the following deep structure:

57

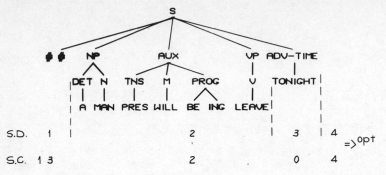

S.D.	1		2		3	4
S.C.	1	3	2		0	4

$\Rightarrow$ opt

D. S. of <u>Tonight, there will be a man leaving.</u>

Q. Can both <u>There-Insertion</u> and <u>Adverb Preposing</u> apply to this deep structure?

A. Yes. Both apply optionally. If we applied neither, we would have <u>A man will be leaving tonight</u>. Let us assume <u>Adverb Preposing</u> applies before <u>There-Insertion</u>.

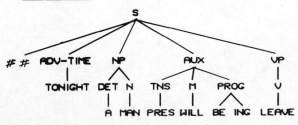

After <u>Adverb Preposing</u> has applied.

Q. Can <u>There-Insertion</u> now apply?

A. No, because there is a constituent other than PreS directly preceding the subject NP. The S. D. for <u>There-Insertion</u> does not allow an Adverb to precede the subject NP, so we cannot apply <u>There-Insertion</u>. The only sentence we can obtain now is <u>Tonight a man will be leaving</u>.

Q. How can we obtain <u>Tonight there will be a man leaving</u>?

A. We must order <u>There-Insertion</u> before <u>Adverb Preposing</u>.

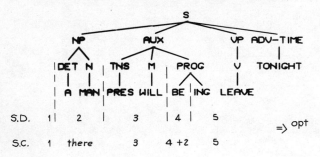

S.D.	1	2	3	4	5	
S.C.	1	*there*	3	4 +2	5	

$\Rightarrow$ opt

Analysis of tree for <u>There-Insertion</u>.

This structure has now been analyzed to meet the S. D. for <u>There-Insertion</u>, which we will apply:

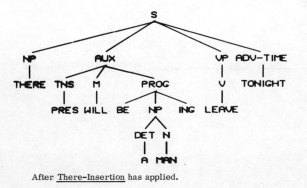

After <u>There-Insertion</u> has applied.

Q. Can <u>Adverb Preposing</u> now apply?
A. Yes.

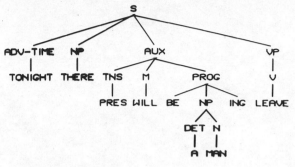

After <u>Adverb Preposing</u> has applied.

Q. Must another rule now apply to this structure?
A. Yes. <u>Affix Hopping</u> must apply.

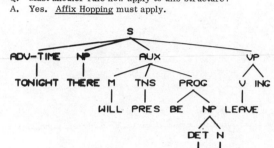

After <u>Affix Hopping</u> has applied.

Q. What do we have now?
A. The sentence <u>Tonight there will be a man leaving</u>. This sentence can be derived only if the rules are ordered so that <u>There-Insertion</u> precedes <u>Adverb Preposing</u>.

Review I

Suppose we now want to get the following sentence: <u>At no time were there many obscene pictures being sent to us</u>. It has the following deep structure:

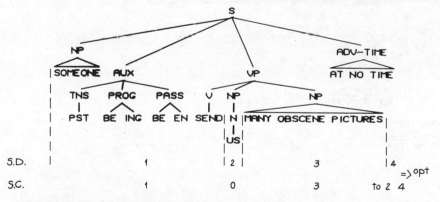

D. S. of <u>At no time were there many obscene pictures being sent to us</u>.

Q. What transformations apply to this tree?
A. <u>Dative</u> may apply; <u>Passive</u> must apply; <u>Agent Deletion</u> may apply; <u>There-Insertion</u> may apply; <u>Adverb Preposing</u> may apply; and if <u>Adverb Preposing</u> applies, <u>Subject Verb Inversion</u> must also apply; and <u>Affix Hopping</u> must apply.
Q. Which of these must apply first?
A. As we have seen (pp. 41–54), <u>Dative</u> and <u>Passive</u> apply before any of the others. Of these, <u>Dative</u> applies first. (See pp. 39–41.)

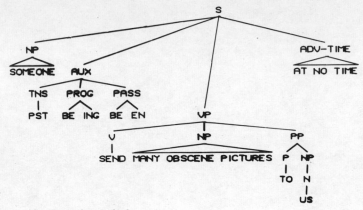

After _Dative_ has applied.

Passive will now obligatorily apply to the following tree, which is the output of _Dative_:

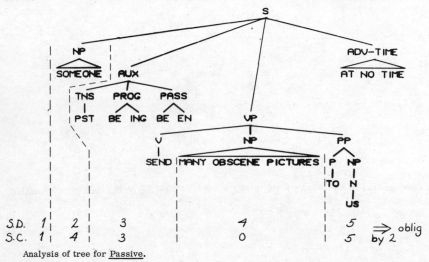

S.D.	1	2	3	4	5	
S.C.	1	4	3	0	5	$\Rightarrow$ oblig

$\Rightarrow$ oblig
by 2

Analysis of tree for _Passive_.

Passive now applies (before _Agent Deletion_, pp. 53-54, and before _There-Insertion_, pp. 41-42) to produce the following tree:

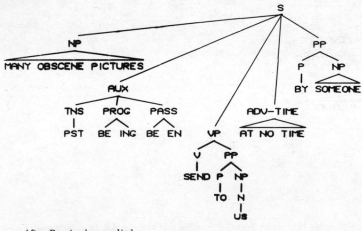

After _Passive_ has applied.

Now _Agent Deletion_ may apply:

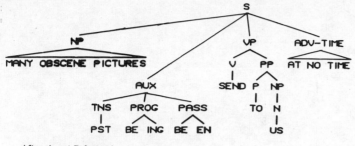

After <u>Agent Deletion</u> has applied.

<u>There-Insertion</u> may now optionally apply to the structure so far derived:

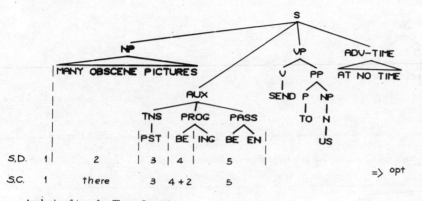

S.D.	1	2	3	4	5	
S.C.	1	there	3	4 + 2	5	

=> opt

Analysis of tree for <u>There-Insertion</u>.

This derived structure (after <u>Dative</u>, <u>Passive</u>, and <u>Agent Deletion</u> have applied) has now been analyzed to meet the S. D. for <u>There-Insertion</u>, which we optionally apply:

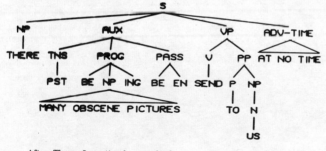

After <u>There-Insertion</u> has applied.

Now <u>Adverb Preposing</u> may apply optionally (see p. 27):

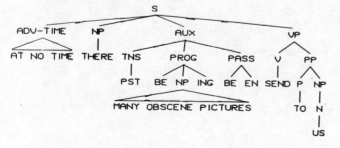

After <u>Adverb Preposing</u> has applied.

Since we have preposed a negative Adverb, we must now apply <u>Subject-Verb Inversion</u> to the output of <u>Adverb Preposing</u> (see pp. 28-29). So far, the following structure has been derived:

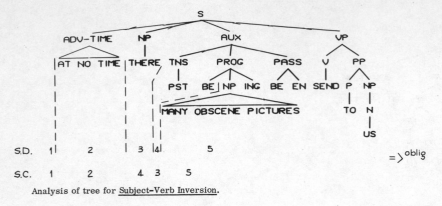

S.D.   1 | 2 | 3 |4| 5   =⟩ oblig
S.C.   1   2   4 3   5

      Analysis of tree for <u>Subject–Verb Inversion</u>.

<u>Subject–Verb Inversion</u> must apply, since the preposed Adverb is dominated by <u>Neg</u>:

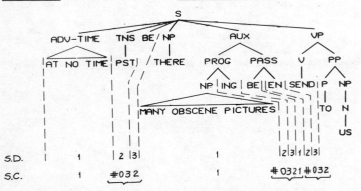

      After <u>Subject–Verb Inversion</u> has applied.

<u>Affix Hopping</u> must apply to the output of <u>Subject–Verb Inversion</u>. Let us analyze the tree accordingly:

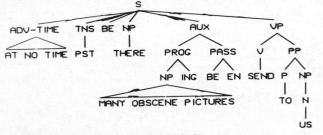

S.D. | 1 | 2 |3| 1 |2|3|1|2|3|
S.C.   1   #032   1   #0321#032

      Analysis of tree for <u>Affix Hopping</u>.

<u>Affix Hopping</u> will now apply in these three places with the following effect:

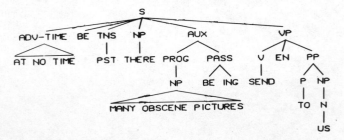

      After <u>Affix Hopping</u> has applied.

The above final derived constituent structure is the result.

Review II

We shall now derive the following sentence: <u>There was not a banana being given to an idiot by a moron, was there</u>? This has the following deep structure:

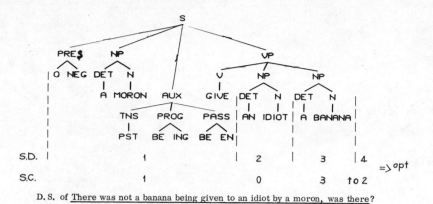

S.D.		1			2	3	4	=> opt
S.C.		1			0	3	to 2	

D. S. of <u>There was not a banana being given to an idiot by a moron, was there</u>?

Q. What transformations can apply to this structure?

A. <u>Dative</u> (opt.), <u>Passive</u> (oblig.), <u>There-Insertion</u> (opt.), <u>Tag Formation</u> (oblig.), <u>Neg-Emp Placement</u> (oblig.), and <u>Affix Hopping</u> (oblig.). We have already given examples to show the necessity for ordering these in the order given. In this example, we will apply all the rules listed above. We begin with <u>Dative</u>. (The tree has been analyzed to undergo <u>Dative</u>.)

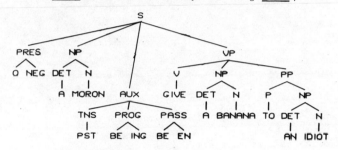

After <u>Dative</u> has applied.

We must now apply <u>Passive</u> to the output of <u>Dative</u>.

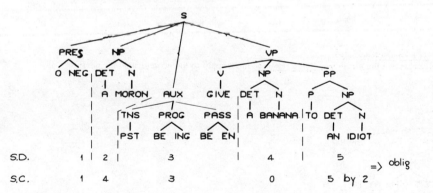

S.D.	1	2	3		4	5	=> oblig
S.C.	1	4	3		0	5 by 2	

Analysis of tree for <u>Passive</u>.

This tree has been analyzed to undergo <u>Passive</u>, which we must now apply.

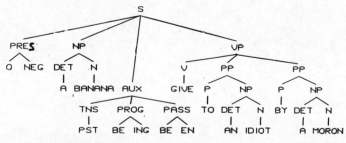

After <u>Passive</u> has applied.

63

The output of <u>Dative</u> and <u>Passive</u> (as above) is analyzed to undergo <u>There-Insertion</u>:

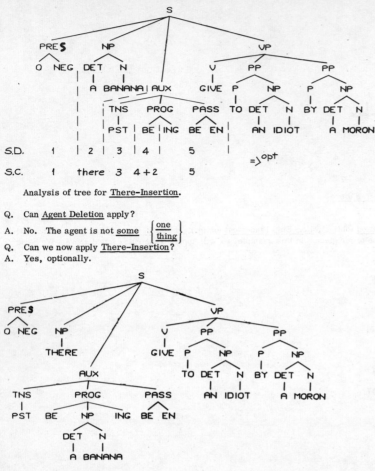

S.D.   1 | 2 | 3 | 4 | 5 |
                                        $=\!\!>$ opt
S.C.   1   there   3   4 + 2   5

Analysis of tree for <u>There-Insertion</u>.

Q. Can <u>Agent Deletion</u> apply?
A. No. The agent is not <u>some</u> $\left\{ \frac{\text{one}}{\text{thing}} \right\}$
Q. Can we now apply <u>There-Insertion</u>?
A. Yes, optionally.

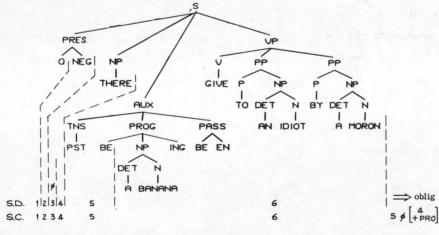

After <u>There-Insertion</u> has applied.

Q. Continuing through the list given on p. 63, we ask—can <u>Tag Formation</u> apply?
A. Yes. Since there is a Q in the PreS and no WH-word elsewhere in the structure, <u>Tag Formation</u> must apply to the structure so far derived:

S.D. 1|2|3|4| 5 | 6 | $\Longrightarrow$ oblig
S.C. 1 2 3 4   5   6   5 $\emptyset$ $\begin{bmatrix} 4 \\ +\text{PRO} \end{bmatrix}$

Analysis of tree for <u>Tag Formation</u>.

This structure has been analyzed to undergo <u>Tag Formation</u>, which we now apply:

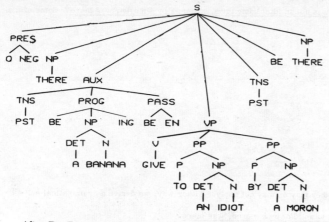

After <u>Tag Formation</u> has applied.

Let us now apply the next ordered rule, <u>Neg-Emp Placement</u>:

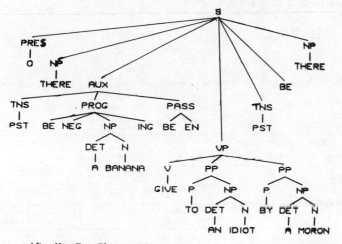

After <u>Neg-Emp Placement</u> has applied.

Now <u>Affix Hopping</u> must apply in four places.

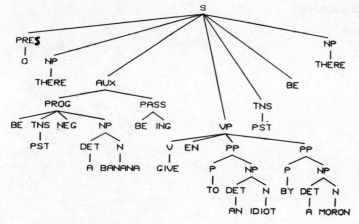

After <u>Affix Hopping</u> has applied.

This is the final derived constituent structure after <u>Dative</u>, <u>Passive</u>, <u>There-Insertion</u>, <u>Tag Formation</u>, and <u>Affix Hopping</u> have applied.

Q. What does this give us?
A. <u>There was not a banana being given to an idiot by a moron, was there?</u>

Note that if we had not applied the optional <u>Dative</u>, we would have obtained <u>There was not an idiot being given a banana by a moron, was there</u>? Some of the other possibilities can be diagramed in the following manner:

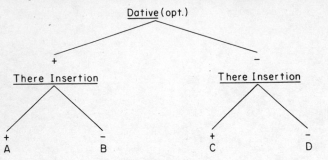

Dative (opt.)

<pre>
              +   −
      There Insertion   There Insertion

   +   −   +   −
   A   B   C   D
</pre>

The above rules were the only optional rules in our last derivation. This means they may or may not apply. Either way, we derive a grammatical sentence. A, B, C, and D represent the four possibilities which we will list below.

A = <u>Dative</u> applied, <u>There-Insertion</u> applied: <u>There was not a banana being given to an idiot by a moron, was there</u>?
B = <u>Dative</u> applied, <u>There-Insertion</u> did not apply: <u>A banana was not being given to an idiot by a moron, was it</u>?
C = <u>Dative</u> did not apply, <u>There-Insertion</u> did apply: <u>There was not an idiot being given a banana by a moron, was there</u>?
D = <u>Dative</u> did not apply, <u>There-Insertion</u> also did not apply: <u>An idiot was not being given a banana by a moron, was he</u>?
<u>Passive</u>, <u>Tag Formation</u>, <u>Neg-Emp Placement</u>, and <u>Affix Hopping</u> all obligatorily apply in A, B, C, and D.

Ordering of rules presented in Part I

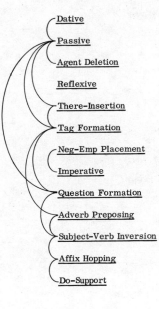

<u>Dative</u>

<u>Passive</u>

<u>Agent Deletion</u>

<u>Reflexive</u>

<u>There-Insertion</u>

<u>Tag Formation</u>

<u>Neg-Emp Placement</u>

<u>Imperative</u>

<u>Question Formation</u>

<u>Adverb Preposing</u>

<u>Subject-Verb Inversion</u>

<u>Affix Hopping</u>

<u>Do-Support</u>

66

Part II Relative Clauses and Related Structures

<u>New Rules and their Ordering to be Presented in Part II</u>

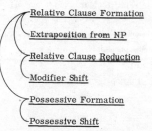

Relative Clause Formation

Extraposition from NP

Relative Clause Reduction

Modifier Shift

Possessive Formation

Possessive Shift

<u>Relative Clauses</u>

Thus far, we have been considering only simplex sentences, that is, sentences which have no other sentences embedded in them. In Parts II-IV, we will consider more complex sentence forms—sentences which have one or more sentences embedded in them.

In general, there are three types of complex sentences in English. One type of complex sentence is a sentence with a relative clause. For example, <u>The boy who left was tall</u> has one relative clause embedded in it, <u>the boy whom I knew who left was tall</u> has two embedded relative clauses, and <u>the boy whom you saw whom I knew who left was tall</u> has three. A second type of complex sentence contains <u>complement structures</u>, such as <u>everyone knows that you're a square</u> (with one embedded complement structure), <u>I believe that everyone knows that you're a square</u> (with two embedded complement structures), or <u>it is crazy for me to believe that everyone knows that you're a square</u> (with three embedded complement structures). The third type of complex sentence is characterized by <u>coordinate structures</u>, such as <u>John and Mary are cool</u>, or <u>John and Mary are cool and like pot</u>, or <u>John and Mary are cool and like pot and live in the Village</u>.

In this section we will briefly consider simple relative clauses of the type given above and some structures related to them. In Parts III and IV, we will be concerned with various complement structures. Coordinate structures, however, take us beyond the bounds of this elementary work and will not be considered here.

Let us begin by considering the following three sentences with relative clauses. In each case, a single relative clause is embedded in the main sentence. (For clarity, we have italicised the relative clauses in these examples. What remains is called the "matrix," or "main" clause.)

1) The boy <u>who left</u> is cute
2) The boy <u>whom you will see</u> is cute
3) The boy <u>to whom you were speaking</u> is cute

We see that each embedded relative clause has a WH-word followed by the rest of the relative clause. (In 1) the rest of the relative clause is <u>left</u>, in 2) <u>you will see</u>, and in 3) <u>you were speaking</u>.)

Q. If we had no grammatical transformations, what kind of phrase structure rules would we need to generate the above structures?

A. We might suggest the following two:

NP → (Det) + (Adj) N (Modifier)
Modifier → WH-word S

To see what kind of structures these rules give, let us take the two sentences:

4) Bill invited the women.
5) Henrietta slew a dragon

Now we can make the object NP in each of these into the head of a relative clause:

4a) <u>The women whom Bill invited</u> (caused his downfall).
5a) <u>The dragon which Henrietta slew</u> (had flames coming out of his mouth and a thick dark fog rising from his tail).

The structure given to the relative clause in 4a) (italicized) by our two PS rules is as follows:[1]

(a)

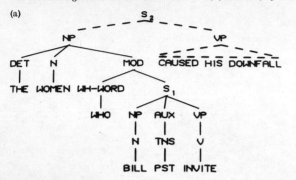

This looks acceptable at first glance. But this structure says that the verb <u>invite</u> (and also <u>slay</u>) need not have objects (S_1). We know this is not so, for we do not have, in isolation:

*Bill invited

or

*Henrietta slew.

These intransitive forms show up only in relative clauses. Thus, if we accept the above structure, it will be necessary to state in the grammar that every transitive verb has an intransitive cognate verb which shows up only in relative clauses (as in our S_1). Let us call this cognate verb V+. Now consider the sentence:

6) Everyone thought the boy cooked the genie.

We can make the NP, <u>the boy</u>, into a relative clause, to get the following phrase:

<u>The boy whom everyone thought cooked the genie</u> (was the king's son).

The structure of this relative NP given by the two PS rules at the top of this page is as follows:

(b)

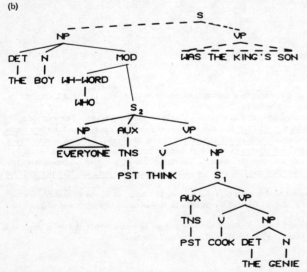

Again, (b) seems to reflect the correct surface structure of 6). But notice that this structure says the verb <u>cook</u> in S_1 does not need a subject. This is true only if the verb occurs in a relative clause, for we do not have, in isolation:

---

[1]From here on, we will number the S's in the trees for easy reference.

68

*cooked the genie
*invited the women

So this time, given (b), we will have to state that every verb has a cognate verb which has no subject, and which occurs only in relative clauses. We will call this subjectless cognate verb +V. But there are some complications with these cognate verbs.

There must be at least one V+ or one +V present in every relative clause. For example, in structure (a) (p. 68), the verb <u>invite</u> in S_1 is that intransitive cognate V+ which occurs only in relative clauses. And it <u>must</u> be intransitive there, for we could not have the structure:

(a^1)

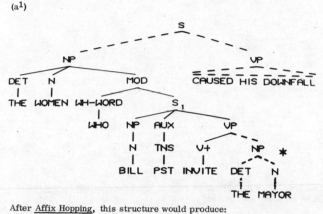

After <u>Affix Hopping</u>, this structure would produce:

   *<u>The women whom bill invited the mayor</u> (caused his downfall).

In a structure like (b) (p. 68), the verb cook in S_1 is that subjectless cognate, +V, which occurs only in relative clauses. Again, it <u>must</u> be subjectless, for we cannot have a structure like (b^1):

(b^1)

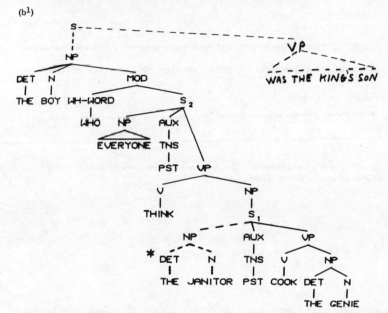

This would eventually give us the unacceptable:

   *<u>The boy whom everyone thought the janitor cooked the genie</u> (was the king's son).

Thus, we must also state that there must be at least one V+ or one +V present in every relative clause. However, in certain cases there may be no more than one V+ or one +V in a structure containing relative clauses. To see this, consider the following structure:

(c)

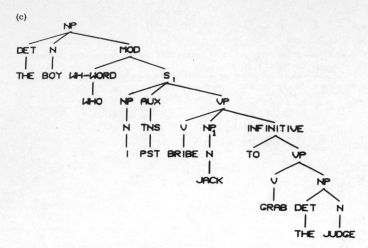

The structure as it now stands will give us the unacceptable:

*The boy whom I bribed Jack to grab the judge.

This is because the relative clause (S_1) contains neither a V+ nor a +V. However, if we make bribe the objectless cognate V± of the transitive bribe (which must have an object in isolation, for we do not have *I bribed) by removing NP_1, we have the acceptable phrase:

the boy whom I bribed to grab the judge (was the son of a gondolier).

This contains a V+ in the relative clause and a +V (i.e., grab) in the infinitive. But we can also make grab an objectless V+. (This V too, must have an object in isolation, for we do not have *Jack grabbed). Then, however, bribe may not also assume its V+ form. Rather, bribe must keep its object NP:

the boy who I bribed Jack to grab

But if both bribe and grab assume their V+ form, we get the unacceptable phrase:

*the boy who I bribed to grab

If we assume that the structures generated by the PS rules on p.67 are correct, we will also have to state that in certain cases, more than one V+ may not occur.

Our final observations which illustrate the implausibility of a theory of grammar which postulates only phrase structure rules, deal with selectional restrictions between certain verbs and their subjects. Thus we have:

1) The group dispersed.
2) The herd scattered.

because a group can disperse, and a herd can scatter. But we do not have:

3) *Malcolm dispersed.
4) *The fly scattered.

because Malcolm cannot disperse, and a fly cannot scatter. Any grammar will have to state this much. These same selectional restrictions, however, manifest themselves in relative clauses. Thus, we can make the subject NP of 1) into a relative clause:

the group which dispersed

or the subject NP of 2):

the herd which scattered

but not the subject NP of 3):

*Malcolm, who dispersed

nor that of 4):

*the fly which scattered.

Thus, a phrase structure grammar will have to state the restrictions operating between the head noun and the verb in its relative clause as well as between the subject NP and verb in a simplex sentence. However, if relative clauses are derived by a rule which relates simplex sentences to relative clauses, these restrictions will have to be stated only once—between the subject and verb of the simplex sentence.

Phrase structure grammars have one more problem to solve. It will be necessary to state selectional restrictions between the head noun and the verb in the relative clause, even when the verb in the relative clause is indefinitely far away. Consider, for example, the sentence

5) *the boy whom Tom thinks everyone hopes you know dispersed comes from Baghdad.

Very roughly, this has the following structure:

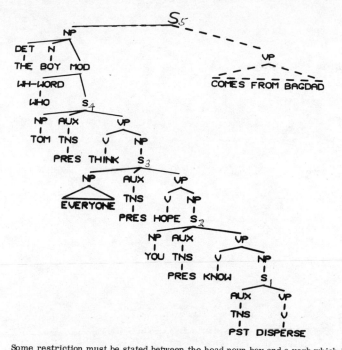

Some restriction must be stated between the head noun <u>boy</u> and a verb which is four sentences away. Clearly, the verb in the relative clause (⁺V in this case) might be any number of sentences away from the head noun, and each time we must find it in order to state the correct restrictions between it and the head noun to exclude sentences like 5). On the other hand, if relative clauses are derived by a rule from simplex sentences, we need state these selectional restrictions only once, and they will automatically apply to the derived relative clauses, no matter how far apart the subject and verb.

The Relative Clause Formation rule is stated below; let us now see how it works.

Relative Clause Formation

S. D.   X = [NP [Y - (P) - NP - W]] - Z
              NP   S   S NP

         1   2   3   4   5   6   7
                                              $\Longrightarrow$ oblig

S. C.   1   2   4 $\begin{bmatrix} 5 \\ +PRO \\ +WH \end{bmatrix}$ 3   6   7

Condition: 2 = 5

The NP structure for <u>Relative Clause Formation</u> is as follows:

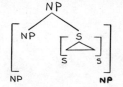

As our first example of <u>Relative Clause Formation</u>, consider the sentence <u>The nut whom I was kissing laughed</u>. It has the following deep structure.

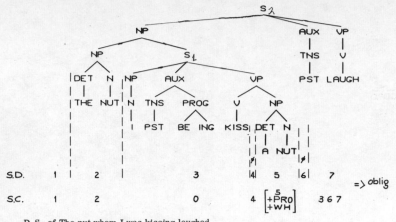

```
S.D.    1  |  2  |           3        |4| 5 |6| 7
S.C.    1     2              0         4  ⎡ 5 ⎤   3 6 7
                                          ⎢+PRO⎥
                                          ⎣+WH⎦
```
=> oblig

. D. S. of <u>The nut whom I was kissing laughed</u>.

Q.   Must <u>Relative Clause Formation</u> apply to this structure?
A.   Yes. <u>Relative Clause Formation</u> is an obligatory transformation.

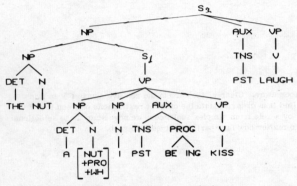

After <u>Relative Clause Formation</u> has applied.

Q.   What other rule must still apply?
A.   <u>Affix Hopping</u> must still apply, and it will give us <u>The nut whom I was kissing laughed</u>.[2]

<u>Extraposition from NP</u>

```
S.D.    Y -  [ NP-S ] - Y
             NP    NP

         1    2 3   4                  ⟹ opt
S.C.     1    2 0   4 + 3
```

This rule applies to structures of the form:

```
⎡      NP-S    ⎤
NP           NP
```

Consider the sentence <u>A performer will appear shortly who is dressing now</u>. It has the following deep structure:

---

[2]As on p.25 , it will be assumed that low-level rules have applied to convert <u>who</u> to <u>whom</u>.

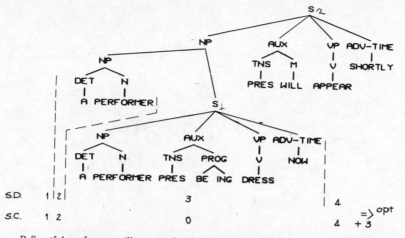

S.D.	1	2		3		4	
S.C.	1	2		0		4 + 3	$\Rightarrow$ opt

D.S.   of <u>A performer will appear shortly who is dressing now</u>.

Q.   Can <u>Extraposition from NP</u> apply to this structure?

A.   Yes, optionally. This tree has been analyzed to meet the S.D. for <u>Extraposition from NP</u>.

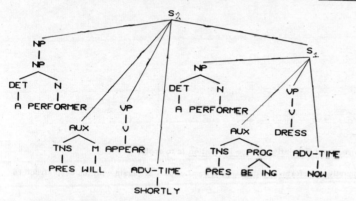

After <u>Extraposition from NP</u> has applied.

<u>Relative Clause Formation</u> and <u>Extraposition from NP</u>

Q. Can <u>Relative Clause Formation</u> apply to the structure on p. 73?
A. No, because the extraposed sentence is no longer within an NP, which is required if <u>Relative Clause Formation</u> is to apply.
Q. What S do we have?
A. After <u>Affix Hopping</u> we have the unacceptable *<u>A performer will appear shortly a performer is dressing now</u>. Let us start again with the deep structure on p. 73:

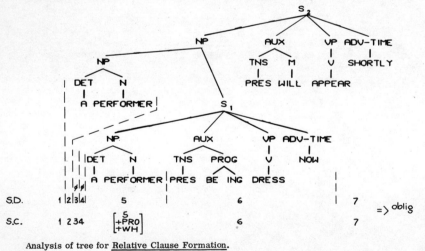

Analysis of tree for <u>Relative Clause Formation</u>.

This structure has now been analyzed to meet the S. D. for <u>Relative Clause Formation</u>. As the ungrammaticallity of the sentence above shows, <u>Relative Clause Formation</u> must precede <u>Extraposition from NP</u>.

74

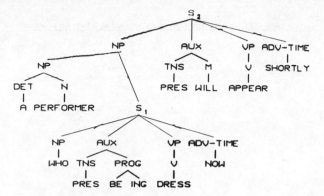

After <u>Relative Clause Formation</u> has applied.

Q. Can <u>Extraposition from NP</u> now apply to this structure?

A. Yes. optionally. If we don't apply it, we will have <u>A performer who is dressing now will appear shortly</u>. However, let us apply <u>Extraposition from NP</u>. Following is the structure derived after <u>Relative Clause Formation</u> (exactly as above):

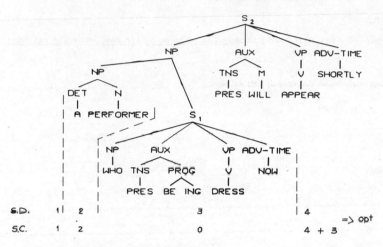

Analysis of tree for <u>Extraposition from NP</u>.

Since this tree has been analyzed to undergo <u>Extraposition from NP</u>, we may now apply it optionally.

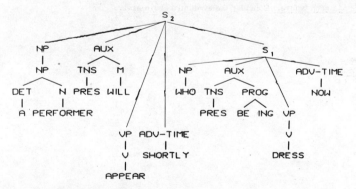

After <u>Extraposition from NP</u> has applied.

Q. What is the result?

A. After <u>Affix Hopping</u>, we have <u>A performer will appear shortly who is dressing now</u>. Note also that we may optionally apply <u>Adverb Preposing</u> to S_2, giving <u>Shortly, a performer will appear who is dressing now</u>. The grammaticality of the last two sentences and ungrammaticality of the one on p. 74, show that <u>Relative Clause Formation</u> must precede <u>Extraposition from NP</u>.

Let us now consider a sentence having two clauses which may be extraposed by Extraposition from NP. A man who was dying jumped up whom no one had seen before. This has the following deep structure:[3]

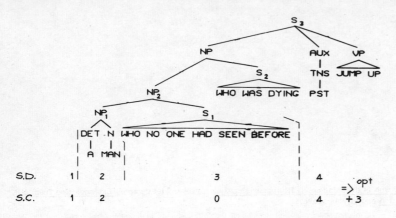

S.D.   1| 2 | 3 | 4   => opt

S.C.   1   2   0   4   +3

       D. S. of A man who was dying jumped up whom no one had seen before.

Relative Clause Formation has already been applied to the above structure. The tree as is would give us: A man whom no one had seen before who was dying jumped up.

Q. Can we apply Extraposition from NP more than once?
A. Yes. It can apply to S_1 or to S_2 or to both. The above tree has been analyzed so that only S_1 will extrapose.

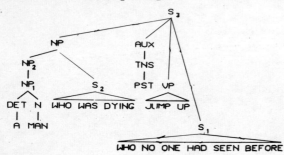

       After Extraposition from NP has applied (S_1).

Q. What is the result after S_1 has been extraposed?
A. After Affix Hopping we have A man who was dying jumped up whom no one had seen before. Consider the structure above again.

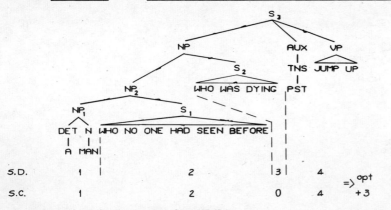

S.D.   1 | 2 |3| 4   => opt

S.C.   1   2   0   4   +3

       Analysis of tree for Extraposition from NP (S_2).

This structure has now been analyzed so that S_2 will be extraposed by Extraposition from NP.

---

[3]The numbers on the S's refer to the like-numbered NP's which the S's are modifying.

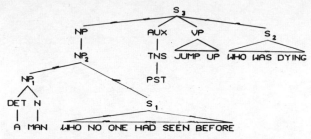

After <u>Extraposition from NP</u> has applied.

Q. What will this give us?
A. After <u>Affix Hopping</u> we will have <u>A man whom no one had seen before jumped up, who was dying</u>. This sentence is acceptable for some dialects.
Q. Can we apply <u>Extraposition from NP</u> so that both S_1 and S_2 will extrapose at once?
A. Yes. Consider again the structure of p. 76.

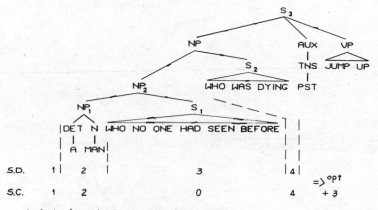

Analysis of tree for <u>Extraposition from NP</u> (S_1).

This tree has been analyzed so that S_1 will extrapose. It can be analyzed simultaneously so that S_2 will extrapose:

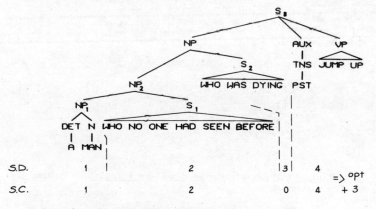

Analysis of tree for <u>Extraposition from NP</u> .

This tree has been analyzed so that S_2 will be extraposed.

Q. Can S_2 and S_1 both be extraposed?
A. Yes, and in either order. We will extrapose S_1 and then S_2.

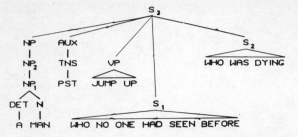

After both S_1 and S_2 have been extraposed by <u>Extraposition from NP</u>.

Q. What do we get?

A. After <u>Affix Hopping</u> we have <u>A man jumped up, whom no one had seen before, who was dying</u>. If we had first extraposed S_2 and then S_1, we would have had <u>A man jumped up who was dying, whom no one had seen before</u>.

<u>Relative Clause Reduction</u>

$$
\text{S.D.} \quad X - \left[NP - \left[\begin{matrix} NP \\ [\ +PRO\ ]Tns\ \underline{be}\ - VP \\ +WH \end{matrix} \right]_S \right]_{NP} - Y
$$

	1	2	3	4	5	
S.D.	1	2	3	4	5	$\Longrightarrow$ opt
S.C.	1	2	0	2	5	

As an example of <u>Relative Clause Reduction</u>, consider the sentence <u>Alfred would like something normal</u>. This has the following deep structure:

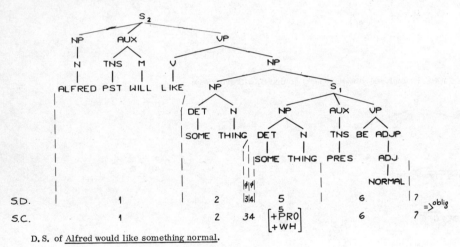

D. S. of <u>Alfred would like something normal</u>.

Q. Can <u>Relative Clause Reduction</u> apply to this tree?

A. No, because there has been no relative clause formed yet. <u>Relative Clause Reduction</u> can apply only after <u>Relative Clause Formation</u> has applied. The above tree has been analyzed to undergo <u>Relative Clause Formation</u>, which we must now apply.

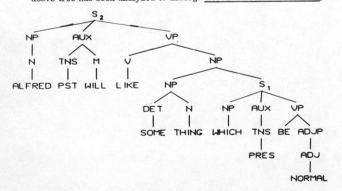

After <u>Relative Clause Formation</u> has applied.

78

Q. Can <u>Relative Clause Reduction</u> now apply?

A. Yes, optionally. If we don't apply it, we have <u>Alfred would like something which is normal</u>. If we apply <u>Relative Clause Reduction</u> to the output of <u>Rela-</u>
<u>tive Clause Formation</u>, we have:

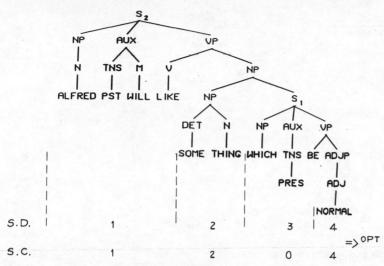

S.D. and S.C. table (OPT):

	1		2		3	4	
S.D.								$\Rightarrow$ OPT
S.C.	1		2		0	4	

Analysis of tree for <u>Relative Clause Reduction</u>.

The tree is exactly the same as the one on p. 78, but it has been analyzed to meet the S.D. for <u>Relative Clause Reduction</u>, which we now apply:

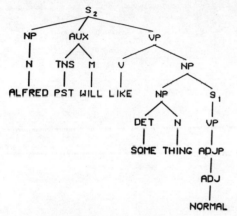

After <u>Relative Clause Reduction</u> has applied.

Q. What sentence have we?

A. After <u>Affix Hopping</u> we have <u>Alfred would like something normal</u>.

Modifier Shift

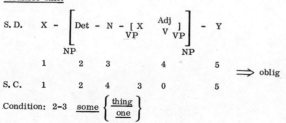

$$\text{S. D.} \quad X - \left[\text{Det} - N - \left[\begin{matrix} X \\ VP \end{matrix} \right. \left. \begin{matrix} \text{Adj} \\ V \end{matrix} \right]_{VP} \right]_{NP} - Y$$

	1	2	3	4	5	
						$\Rightarrow$ oblig
S.C.	1	2	4	3	0	5

Condition: 2-3 <u>some</u> $\left\{ \begin{matrix} \text{thing} \\ \underline{\text{one}} \end{matrix} \right\}$

We next come to <u>Modifier Shift</u>. To see how this rule works, consider the sentence <u>A pink panther wobbled by</u>. It has the following deep structure:

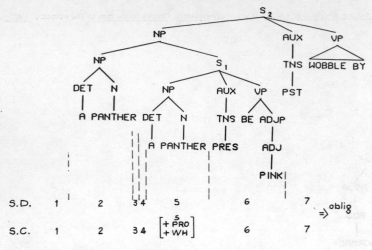

S.D.   1   2   3 4   5   6   7   => oblig

S.C.   1   2   3 4   [+ PRO / + WH (5)]   6   7

D. S. of <u>A pink panther wobbled by</u>.

Q. What transformation must apply to this structure?
A. Only <u>Relative Clause Formation</u> must apply. The tree has been analyzed accordingly.

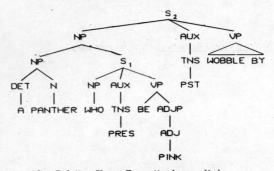

After <u>Relative Clause Formation</u> has applied.

Q. Can <u>Relative Clause Reduction</u> now apply?
A. Yes, optionally. If we don't apply it, we have <u>A panther who was pink wobbled by</u>. But let us apply this rule.

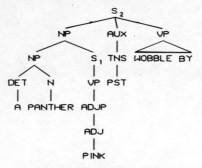

After <u>Relative Clause Reduction</u> has applied.

Q. What kind of structure do we have now?
A. See next page.

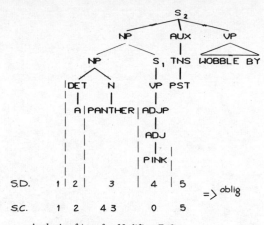

S.D.   1 | 2 | 3 | 4 | 5   =⟩ oblig

S.C.   1   2   4 3   0   5

Analysis of tree for <u>Modifier Shift</u>.

Q. What sentence would we get from this structure if no further rules except <u>Affix Hopping</u> applied?
A. *<u>A panther pink wobbled by</u>.
Q. What do we do in order to get the desired sentence <u>A pink panther wobbled by</u>?

A. <u>Modifier Shift</u> applies when the NP modified by an S is not <u>some</u> $\left\{\begin{array}{c}\text{thing}\\\text{one}\end{array}\right\}$. In our case, a panther is not <u>some</u> $\left\{\begin{array}{c}\text{one}\\\text{thing}\end{array}\right\}$, so this structure must undergo <u>Modifier Shift</u>. The tree has been analyzed accordingly.

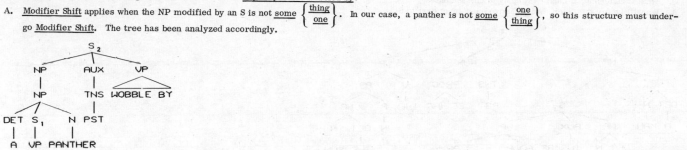

After <u>Modifier Shift</u> has applied.

Q. What sentence does this structure generate?
A. After <u>Affix Hopping</u> we have <u>A pink panther wobbled by</u>.

Restrictions on <u>Modifier Shift</u>

Consider the sentence <u>A man who was pleased with himself was lying in the sun</u>. This has the following deep structure:

81

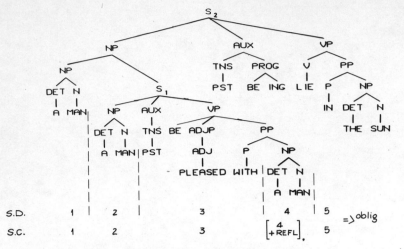

S.D.	1	2	3	4	5	$\Rightarrow$ oblig
S.C.	1	2	3	$\begin{bmatrix} 4 \\ +REFL \end{bmatrix}$,	5	

D. S. of <u>A man who was pleased with himself was lying in the sun</u>.

Q. What transformation must first apply to this sentence?
A. We will justify this later, but <u>Reflexive</u> must apply first to S_1.

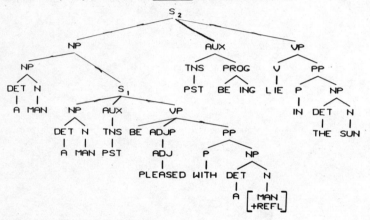

After <u>Reflexive</u> has applied.

Q. Must <u>Relative Clause Formation</u> apply to this structure?
A. Yes. <u>Relative Clause Formation</u> is obligatory.

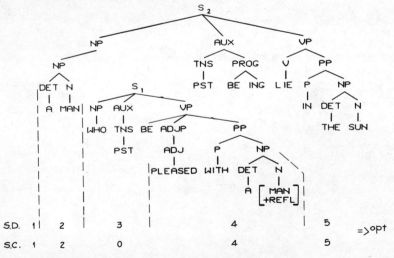

S.D.	1	2	3	4	5	$\Rightarrow$ opt
S.C.	1	2	0	4	5	

After <u>Relative Clause Formation</u> has applied.

82

Q. Can we now apply <u>Relative Clause Reduction</u>?

A. Yes, optionally. Without it, we have <u>A man who was pleased with himself was lying in the sun</u>. The structure above is analyzed to undergo <u>Relative Clause Reduction</u>, which we now apply:

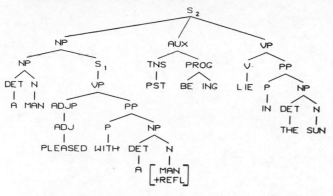

After <u>Relative Clause Reduction</u> has applied.

Q. What do we have?

A. After <u>Affix Hopping</u> we have <u>A man pleased with himself was lying in the sun</u>.

Q. Could we now apply <u>Modifier Shift</u>?

A. No, because something other than an Adj ends the VP, i.e., the PP <u>with himself</u> ends the VP in S_1. Were we now to apply <u>Modifier Shift</u>, we would get *<u>A pleased with himself man was lying in the sun</u>.

Conclusion: The application of <u>Modifier Shift</u> is restricted to cases where an Adj ends the VP. Note that just as the PP <u>with himself</u> may not end the VP if <u>Modifier Shift</u> is to apply, the Agent "by someone" also may not be present if <u>Modifier Shift</u> is to apply, e.g., *<u>the murdered by someone man</u>. This means that Agent Deletion must apply before we can apply <u>Modifier Shift</u> to get <u>the murdered man</u>.

Further Restrictions on <u>Modifier Shift</u>

We shall now consider another restriction on <u>Modifier Shift</u>. Consider the sentence <u>The roller coaster which was plummeting wildly swerved off the track</u>. This has the following deep structure:

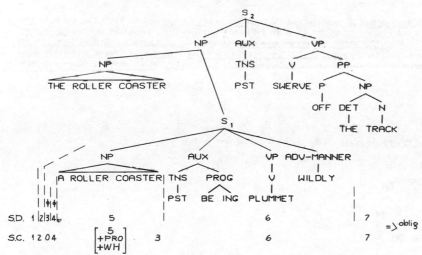

D. S. of <u>The roller coaster which was plummeting wildly swerved off the track</u>.

Q. What rule must apply to this tree?

A. <u>Relative Clause Reduction</u> can't apply because there is no relative clause, yet; and <u>Modifier Shift</u> applies only to the output of <u>Relative Clause Reduction</u>. But <u>Relative Clause Formation</u> must apply. (The tree has been so analyzed.)

83

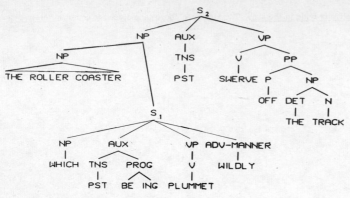

After <u>Relative Clause Formation</u> has applied.

Q. Can <u>Relative Clause Reduction</u> now apply?
A. Yes, optionally. If we do not apply it, we have <u>The roller coaster which was plummeting wildly swerved off the track.</u>

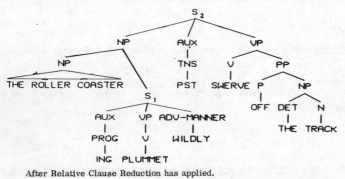

After Relative Clause Reduction has applied.

Q. Can <u>Modifier Shift</u> apply to this structure?
A. No, because there is an Adv ending the VP in S_1. The <u>Modifier Shift</u> S.D. requires that either a <u>verb</u> or an <u>adjective</u> end the VP. If we did apply <u>Modifier Shift</u>, we would get *<u>The plummeting wildly roller coaster swerved off the track</u>. If we don't apply <u>Modifier Shift</u>, we get the desired <u>The roller coaster, plummeting wildly, swerved off the track</u>. The sentence <u>The wildly plummeting roller coaster swerved off the track</u> is derived by applying a rule we will not discuss in detail. This rule converts sentences like <u>The roller coaster was plummeting wildly</u> to <u>The roller coaster was wildly plummeting</u>. The VP in the sentence now ends with a verb, and if this VP were to appear post-nominally as a reduced relative clause, application of <u>Modifier Shift</u> would produce the desired sentence.

Extraposition from NP and Relative Clause Reduction

Consider now the following sentence: <u>Someone must have done this who is crazy.</u> This has the following deep structure.

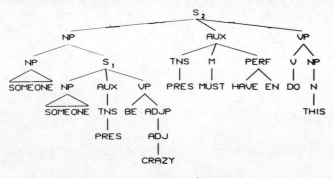

D.S. of <u>Someone must have done this who is crazy.</u>

Q. What transformation must apply to this structure?
A. Only <u>Relative Clause Formation</u> must apply.

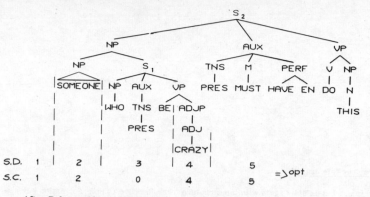

S.D.	1		2		3		4		5	
S.C.	1		2		0		4		5	$\Rightarrow$ opt

After <u>Relative Clause Formation</u> has applied.

Q. Can <u>Relative Clause Reduction</u> now apply to this structure?

A. Yes, optionally. If it doesn't, we have <u>Someone who is crazy must have done this</u>. This structure has been analyzed to meet the S. D. for <u>Relative Clause Reduction</u>, and we will apply it.

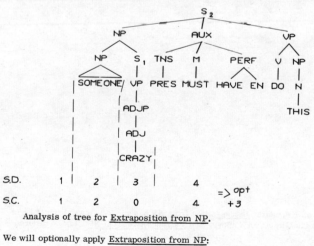

After <u>Relative Clause Reduction</u> has applied.

Q. Can <u>Extraposition from NP</u> apply now?

A. Yes. Consider the structure we have so far, now analyzed to undergo <u>Extraposition from NP</u>:

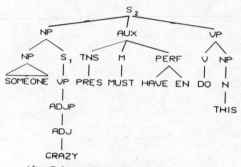

S.D.	1		2		3		4	
S.C.	1		2		0		4	$\Rightarrow$ opt +3

Analysis of tree for <u>Extraposition from NP</u>.

We will optionally apply <u>Extraposition from NP</u>:

85

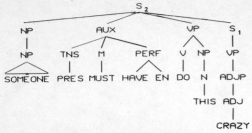

After <u>Extraposition from NP</u> has applied.

Q. What S do we have now?
A. After <u>Affix Hopping</u> we have the ungrammatical *<u>Someone must have done this crazy</u>.
Q. How can we prevent this ungrammatical sentence?
A. We must order <u>Extraposition from NP</u> before <u>Relative Clause Reduction</u>. Let us start again with the structure after <u>Relative Clause Formation</u> has applied.

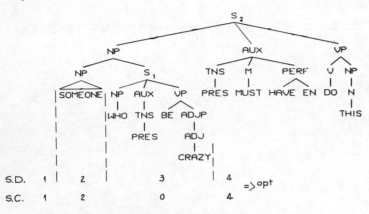

After application of <u>Relative Clause Formation</u>.

Q. Can <u>Extraposition from NP</u> apply now?
A. Yes, optionally. The tree has been analyzed to undergo it. If we do not apply <u>Extraposition from NP</u>, we get <u>Someone who is crazy must have done this</u>.

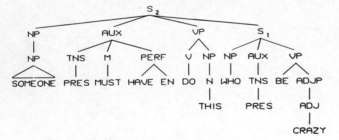

After <u>Extraposition from NP</u> has applied.

Q. What sentence would we have after <u>Affix Hopping</u>?
A. <u>Someone must have done this who is crazy</u>.
Q. Can we now apply <u>Relative Clause Reduction</u>?
A. No, because the S. D. for <u>Relative Clause Reduction</u> (p. 78) requires an S within an NP. After <u>Extraposition from NP</u> has applied, the extraposed S is no longer within an NP. It can be seen from this example and from the ungrammaticality of the S above, that <u>Extraposition from NP</u> must be ordered before <u>Relative Clause Reduction</u>.

<u>Relative Clause Reduction</u> and <u>Modifier Shift</u>

Consider now the following sentence: <u>The dinky professor lost his cool</u>. This has the following deep structure:

86

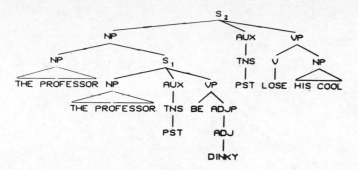

D.S. of <u>The dinky professor lost his cool</u>.

Q. What rule must first apply to this structure?
A. <u>Relative Clause Formation</u>.

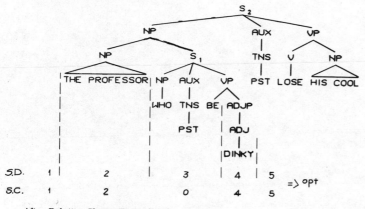

S.D.   1   2   3   4 5

S.C.   1   2   0   4   5   => opt

After <u>Relative Clause Formation</u> has applied.

Q. Can <u>Modifier Shift</u> now apply?
A. No, because the subject and auxiliary of S_1 must be eliminated before <u>Modifier Shift</u> can apply. So first <u>Relative Clause Reduction</u> must apply to provide the environment for <u>Modifier Shift</u>.

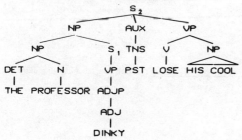

After <u>Relative Clause Reduction</u> has applied.

Q. Must <u>Modifier Shift</u> now apply?
A. Yes. The NP modified by the Adj is not <u>some</u> $\left\{ \begin{array}{c} \text{thing} \\ \hline \text{one} \end{array} \right\}$, so <u>Modifier Shift</u> must apply to the output of <u>Relative Clause Reduction</u> which follows. (The structure is exactly as the one above, but has been analyzed to undergo <u>Modifier Shift</u>.

87

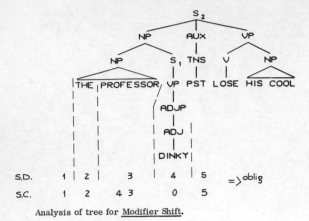

S.D.   1 | 2 | 3 | 4 | 5   =⟩oblig

S.C.   1   2   4 3   0   5

     Analysis of tree for <u>Modifier Shift</u>.

We now apply <u>Modifier Shift</u>:

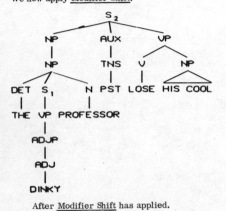

     After <u>Modifier Shift</u> has applied.

Q.   After <u>Affix Hopping</u>, what sentence do we have?

A.   <u>The dinky professor lost his cool</u>.   Note that since <u>Relative Clause Reduction</u> provides the environment for <u>Modifier Shift</u>, the rules are intrinsically ordered that way.

<u>Question Formation</u> and <u>Extraposition from NP</u>

We will now order <u>Question Formation</u> and <u>Extraposition from NP</u>.   Consider the sentence <u>Whom do we know who is unfair</u>? which has the following deep structure to which <u>Relative Clause Formation</u> has already applied:

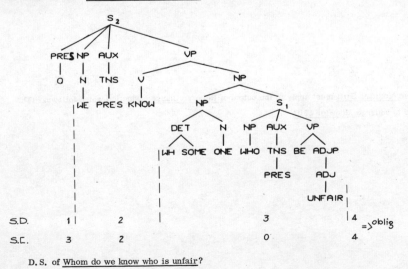

S.D.   1 | 2 | 3 | 4   =⟩oblig

S.C.   3   2   0   4

     D.S. of <u>Whom do we know who is unfair</u>?

88

Q. Can both <u>Question Formation</u> and <u>Extraposition from NP</u> apply to this structure?

A. Yes. <u>Question Formation</u> is obligatory, and <u>Extraposition from NP</u> is optional. If we assume <u>Extraposition from NP</u> is first, nothing will happen because the clause to be extraposed is already at the end, and the S.C. of <u>Extraposition from NP</u> won't affect it. Now we come to <u>Question Formation</u> which is obligatory. The tree has been analyzed to undergo <u>Question Formation</u>.

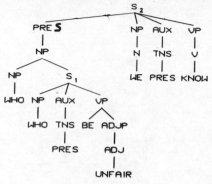

After <u>Question Formation</u> has applied.

Q. What rule must now apply?

A. Since there are two adjacent NP's at the beginning of a main clause, <u>Subject-Verb Inversion</u> must apply.

Note that the entire NP (including the S$_1$ within it) is moved up to the front in <u>Question Formation</u> by a process called <u>Pied Piping</u>. This is discussed in John R. Ross's dissertation, "Constraints on Variables in Syntax" (Massachusetts Institute of Technology, 1967).

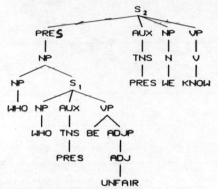

After <u>Subject-Verb Inversion</u> has applied.

Q. Can <u>Affix Hopping</u> now apply?

A. No, because there is no verb to the right of Pres for that affix to hop over.

Q. What must happen?

A. <u>Do-Support</u> must apply.

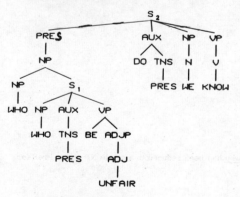

After <u>Do-Support</u> has applied.

Q. What will this give us?

A. <u>Whom, who is unfair, do we know</u>? But now there is no way to obtain <u>Whom do we know who is unfair</u>? because we have already passed <u>Extraposition from NP</u>.

Q. What must we do to get the second sentence?
A. We must order <u>Question Formation</u> before <u>Extraposition from NP</u>. Consider again the structure we had on p. 88.

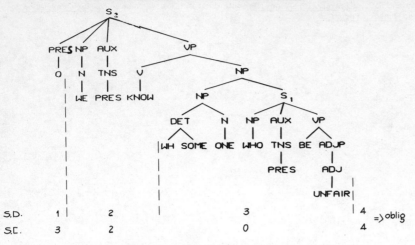

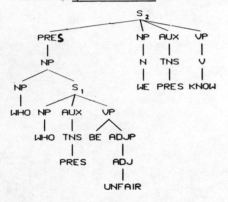

S.D.	1	2		3		4	=) oblig
S.C.	3	2		0		4	

Analysis of tree for <u>Question Formation</u>.

We now order <u>Question Formation</u> first. The structure above has been analyzed to meet the S. D. for <u>Question Formation</u>.

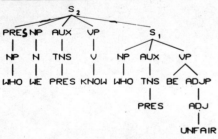

After <u>Question Formation</u> has applied.

If we now chose to do <u>Subject-Verb Inversion</u> and <u>Do-Support</u>, we would get <u>Whom, who is unfair, do we know</u>? However, we may also optionally apply <u>Extraposition from NP</u>.

After <u>Extraposition from NP</u> has applied.

Q. What must now apply?
A. With two NP's beginning a main clause, <u>Subject-Verb Inversion</u> must apply. (The double NP over <u>who</u> has been reduced to a single NP under PreS for reasons we will discuss later.)

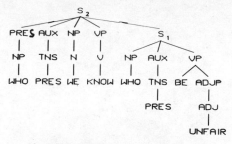

After <u>Subject-Verb Inversion</u> has applied.

Q. Can <u>Affix Hopping</u> now apply?
A. No, because there is no verb for the affix Pres to hop over. This state of affairs calls for <u>Do-Support</u>.

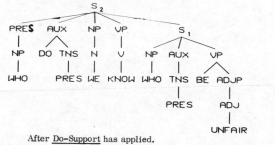

After <u>Do-Support</u> has applied.

Q. What sentence do we have now?
A. <u>Whom do we know who is unfair?</u> This sentence can be derived only if <u>Question Formation</u> precedes <u>Extraposition from NP</u> in the ordering.

Possessive Formation

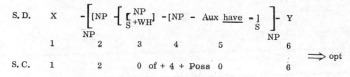

As our first example of <u>Possessive Formation</u>, consider the sentence <u>John rides his horse masterfully</u>. It has the following deep structure:

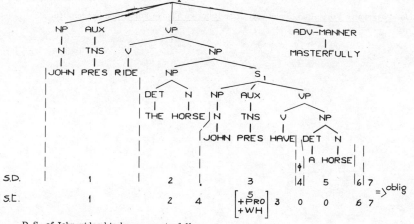

D. S. of <u>John rides his horse masterfully</u>.

This structure has been analyzed to meet the structural description of <u>Relative Clause Formation</u> and must undergo it.

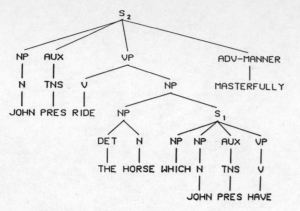

After <u>Relative Clause Formation</u> has applied.

Q. Can <u>Possessive Formation</u> now apply?
A. Yes. The output of <u>Relative Clause Formation</u> is analyzed to undergo Possessive Formation in the following structure:

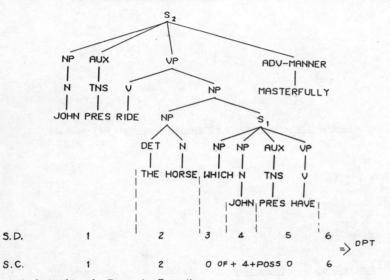

S.D.	1		2	3	4	5	6	

$\Rightarrow$ OPT

| S.C. | 1 | | 2 | 0 OF + 4+POSS 0 | | | 6 | |

Analysis of tree for <u>Possessive Formation</u>.

We now optionally apply <u>Possessive Formation</u>. Note the S.D. for <u>Possessive Formation</u> is met only after <u>Relative Clause Formation</u> has applied.

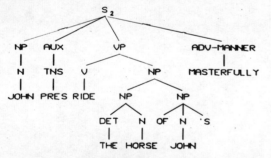

After <u>Possessive Formation</u> has applied.

Q. What would this give us after <u>Affix Hopping</u>?
A. *<u>John rides the horse of John's masterfully.</u>
Q. How can we prevent this sentence and get <u>John's horse</u> instead?
A. <u>Possessive Shift</u> must apply to the output of <u>Possessive Formation</u>.

The following structure represents the output of <u>Possessive Formation</u> (exactly as the one above), but it has been analyzed to undergo <u>Possessive Shift</u>.

Possessive Shift

S.D.   X $\left[\underset{NP}{- [Det] - N - of - NP\ Poss}\right]_{NP}$ - Y

      1   2   3   4   5   6 $\Longrightarrow$ oblig

S.C.   1   5   3   0   0   6

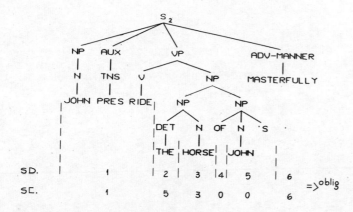

Analysis of tree for Possessive Shift.

This structure, the output of Possessive Formation, has now been analyzed to meet the S.D. for Possessive Shift, which we must apply. Note that the determiner (term 2 in the S.D.) must be definite.

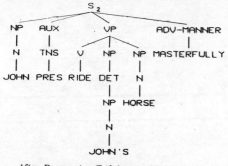

After Possessive Shift has applied.

Q. What do we have now?

A. After Pronominalization (a new rule which changes John's into his) and Affix Hopping, we have John rides his horse masterfully.

Ordering of Rules Presented in Part II

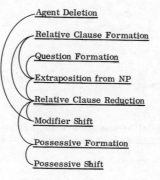

Agent Deletion

Relative Clause Formation

Question Formation

Extraposition from NP

Relative Clause Reduction

Modifier Shift

Possessive Formation

Possessive Shift

93

Part III Simple Complement Structures

New Rules and Their Ordering to be Presented in Part III

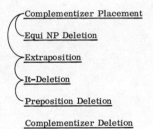

Complementizer Placement

Equi NP Deletion

Extraposition

It-Deletion

Preposition Deletion

Complementizer Deletion

Extraposition

S. D.   X [- it - S] - Y
         NP   NP

         1   2   3   4
                               ⟹ opt
S. C.   1   2   0   4+3

Condition: Applies only with <u>that</u> and <u>for-to</u> complementizers.

Let us now consider synonymous sentence pairs of the following sort:

1) It is clear that we will lose the war.
2) That we will lose the war is clear.

These and many similar pairs have the same meaning, and we shall assume that both have (one) deep structure. In particular, the deep structure for both 1) and 2) is as follows: (let us assume that the rule of <u>Complementizer Placement</u>, which inserts the complementizer <u>that</u>, has already applied):

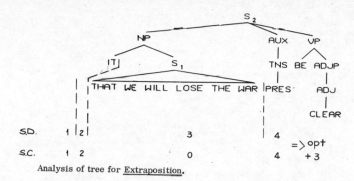

S.D.	1	2		3		4	=> opt
S.C.	1	2		0		4 + 3

Analysis of tree for Extraposition.

Q. Can Extraposition apply to this tree?
A. Yes, optionally. The tree has been analyzed to undergo Extraposition.

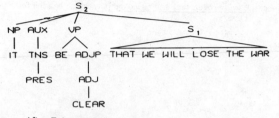

After Extraposition has applied.

Note that with Extraposition we extrapose to the end of the S complement sentences which follow the abstract pronoun it, whereas with Extraposition from NP, we extrapose relative clauses from a full NP.

Q. What would have happened if we had not applied the optional rule of Extraposition?
A. We would have the same structure as above. If no further rules apply to this structure, we will eventually have the unacceptable *It that we will lost the war is clear.
Q. What do we do then, if we choose not to apply Extraposition?
A. We must then apply It-Deletion.

It-Deletion

S.D.   X - [it - S] - Y
               NP   NP

         1   2   3   4

S.C.   1   0   3   4   ==>/ oblig

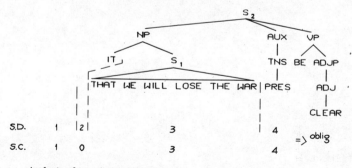

S.D.	1	2		3		4	=> oblig
S.C.	1	0		3		4	

Analysis of tree for It-Deletion.

The above structure has now been analyzed to meet the S.D. for It-Deletion, which we now apply:

95

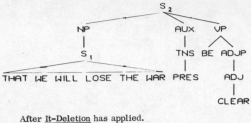

After <u>It-Deletion</u> has applied.

Q. What do we have after <u>Affix Hopping</u>?
A. <u>That we will lose the war is clear.</u>

Passive and Extraposition

We will now show that <u>Passive</u> must precede <u>Extraposition</u>. Let us consider the following sentence: <u>It was proven that Andy smoked pot</u>, which has the following D.S.:

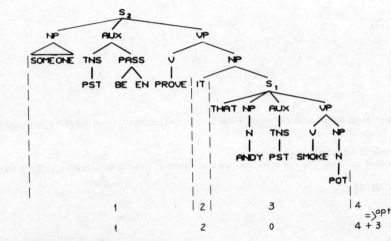

S.D.	1	2	3	4
S.C.	1	2	0	4 + 3

$$=\rangle^{opt}$$

D.S. of <u>It was proven that Andy smoked pot.</u>

We again assume that <u>Complementizer Placement</u>, which places the complementizer <u>that</u>, has already applied.

Q. Can both <u>Passive</u> and <u>Extraposition</u> apply to this tree?
A. Yes. <u>Passive</u> must apply, and <u>Extraposition</u> may. Let us assume, contrary to fact, that <u>Extraposition</u> applies before <u>Passive</u>. Since the clause S_1, which is to be extraposed, is already at the end of the structure, nothing will happen to S_1. It stays right where it is after <u>Extraposition</u> optionally applies.

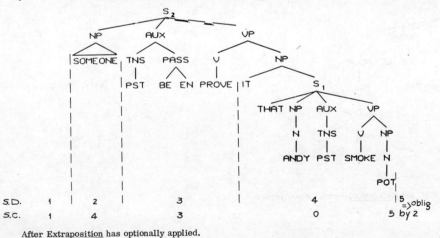

S.D.	1	2	3	4	5
S.C.	1	4	3	0	5 by 2

$$=\rangle^{oblig}$$

After <u>Extraposition</u> has optionally applied.

Note that nothing has happened to the structure.

Q. Must <u>Passive</u> now apply?
A. Yes. It must apply because the constituent <u>Passive</u> is in the auxiliary of S_2. We have seen before that one of the operations of <u>Passive</u> is to move the object NP to the front of the sentence. In our example, the object NP of S_2 contains S_1 within it. When <u>Passive</u> applies, this whole object NP, clause included, will be moved to the front of S_2. (The tree has been so analyzed.)

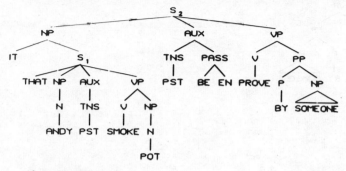

After <u>Passive</u> has applied.

Q. What rule must now apply?
A. Since an <u>it</u> directly precedes S_1 (now in subject position), <u>It-Deletion</u> must apply.

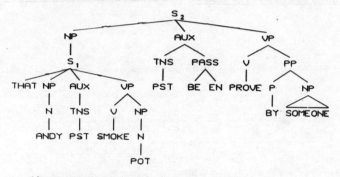

After <u>It-Deletion</u> has applied.

Q. What S do we have?
A. After <u>Affix Hopping</u> we have <u>That Andy smoked pot was proven by someone</u>. After <u>Agent Deletion</u> we derive <u>That Andy smoked pot was proven</u>.
Q. How can we obtain the sentence we originally wanted: <u>It was proven that Andy smoked pot</u>?
A. We cannot get it now because <u>Extraposition</u> has already applied, and we cannot go backwards to apply a rule ordered earlier in the ordering.
Q. What do we do?
A. We must order <u>Passive</u> before <u>Extraposition</u>. We will start again, with the same deep structure as on p. 96:

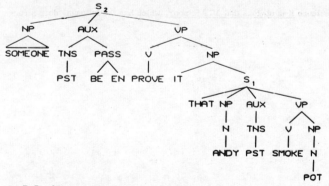

D.S. of <u>It was proven that Andy smoked pot</u>.

Assume that the complementizer <u>that</u> has already been introduced. This time we will apply <u>Passive</u> first. Again, the entire object NP of S_2, which includes all of S_1, will be moved to the front of S_2:

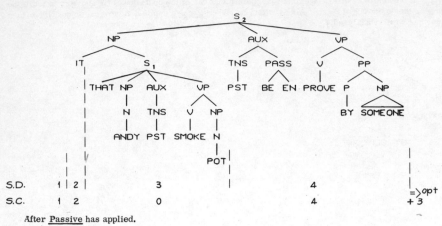

S.D.	1	2		3		4	=⟩opt
S.C.	1	2		0		4	+ 3

After <u>Passive</u> has applied.

Q. May <u>Extraposition</u> now apply?

A. Yes, optionally. If we don't apply it, we will eventually derive <u>That Andy smoked pot was proven by someone</u>. (The tree has been analyzed to undergo <u>Extraposition</u>.)

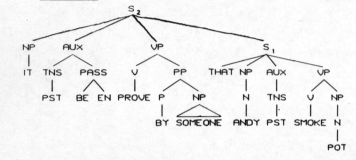

After <u>Extraposition</u> has applied.

Q. What S do we have?

A. After <u>Agent Deletion</u> and <u>Affix Hopping</u> we have <u>It was proven that Andy smoked pot</u>. This S can be derived only if <u>Passive</u> precedes <u>Extraposition</u>.

<u>Extraposition</u> and <u>It-Deletion</u>

Let us consider another example illustrating <u>Extraposition</u>. We will derive the sentence <u>It is obvious that MIT is poor</u>, which has the following deep structure:

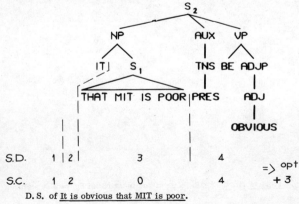

S.D.	1	2	3	4	=⟩ opt
S.C.	1	2	0	4	+ 3

D. S. of <u>It is obvious that MIT is poor</u>.

In this structure, details have been excluded (that is, the complementizer, <u>that</u>, has already been introduced into the structure).

Q. Can both <u>Extraposition</u> and <u>It-Deletion</u> apply to this structure?

A. Yes. Let's assume, contrary to fact, that <u>It-Deletion</u> applies first and is optional, and that <u>Extraposition</u> is second and optional. Let's say we don't apply <u>It-Deletion</u>. If we don't apply <u>It-Deletion</u>, then <u>Extraposition</u> must apply. The tree has been analyzed to undergo <u>Extraposition</u>.

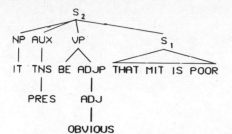

After <u>Extraposition</u> has applied.

Q. What do we have?
A. After <u>Affix Hopping</u>, we have <u>It is obvious that MIT is poor</u>. With this example, it happens that we can order <u>It-Deletion</u> before <u>Extraposition</u>. But let us consider another example.

Consider the sentence <u>I think that this may be difficult</u>, which has the following deep structure:

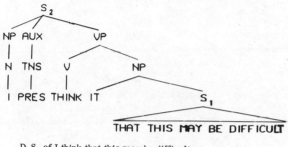

D. S. of <u>I think that this may be difficult</u>.

Again, we assume that the complementizer <u>that</u> has already been placed.

Q. Can both <u>It-Deletion</u> and <u>Extraposition</u> apply to this structure?
A. Yes. Let's assume, again, that <u>It-Deletion</u> is first and optional and that <u>Extraposition</u> is second and obligatory. Since <u>It-Deletion</u> is optional, we will not apply it. We now come to <u>Extraposition</u>, which is obligatory. As we have seen before (p. 96), the clause S$_1$ is already at the end, so nothing will happen when <u>Extraposition</u> applies:

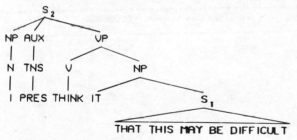

After <u>Extraposition</u> has applied.

Nothing has happened to the structure.

Q. Now what S do we have?
A. After <u>Affix Hopping</u> we have the unacceptable *<u>I think it that this may be difficult</u>.
Q. What should we do now?
A. We could allow another rule of <u>It-Deletion</u> to apply, which would give us the S <u>I think that this may be difficult</u>. But it is atypical to have two rules of <u>It-Deletion</u>.
Q. What can we conclude from this example?
A. We must apply <u>Extraposition</u> first, optionally, and <u>It-Deletion</u> must follow, obligatorily. Let's start again, with the same deep structure as on p. 98:

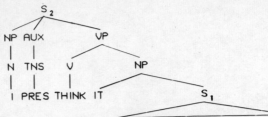

D. S. of <u>I think that this may be difficult</u>.

Q. Can both <u>Extraposition</u> and <u>It-Deletion</u> apply to the above structure?
A. Yes, but as we have just seen, <u>Extraposition</u> must apply first and optionally. Since S_1 is already at the end of S_2, whether we choose to apply <u>Extraposition</u> or not, nothing will happen to the above structure:

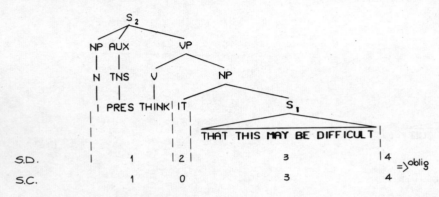

After <u>Extraposition</u> has applied.

Nothing has happened to the structure.

Q. Must <u>It-Deletion</u> now apply?
A. Yes, since an <u>it</u> directly precedes S_1 in the NP which is the direct object of <u>think</u>. The tree has been analyzed to undergo <u>It-Deletion</u>.

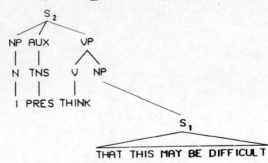

After <u>It-Deletion</u> has applied.

Q. What sentence do we have?
A. After <u>Affix Hopping</u> we have the grammatical sentence that we want (<u>I think that this may be difficult</u>), and we have avoided generating the ungrammatical *<u>I think it that this may be difficult</u>, which could result if an optional rule of <u>It-Deletion</u> were to precede an obligatory rule of <u>Extraposition</u>. Therefore, the correct ordering must be <u>Extraposition</u> (opt.), then <u>It-Deletion</u> (oblig.).

Consider now the sentence <u>That this was unreal was thought by everyone</u>. It has the following deep structure:

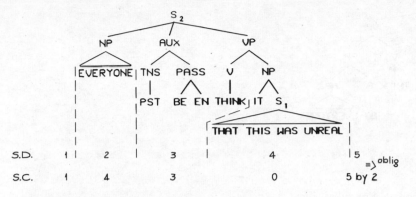

S.D.	1	2		3		4	5	$\Rightarrow$ oblig
S.C.	1	4		3		0	5 by 2

D. S. of <u>That this was unreal was thought by everyone</u>.

This structure has been analyzed to meet the S. D. of <u>Passive</u>.

Q. How do we know an <u>it</u> must be in the D. S. ?
A. Because in passive sentences like <u>It was thought that this was unreal</u>, the pronoun <u>it</u> shows up in subject position. This can be accounted for naturally if the above D. S. is assumed.
Q. What rule must apply first to this structure?
A. <u>Passive</u> must apply first, as was seen on p.

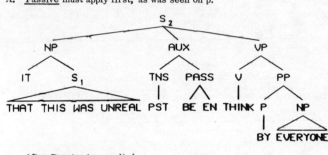

After <u>Passive</u> has applied,

Note that the entire NP ($\overset{\text{NP}}{\underset{\text{it} \quad \text{S}_1}{\triangle}}$) has been moved to the front.

Q. Can <u>Extraposition</u> apply?
A. Yes, but since it is optional, we will not do it this time.
Q. What must now apply?
A. <u>It-Deletion</u> must apply if we do not apply <u>Extraposition</u>.

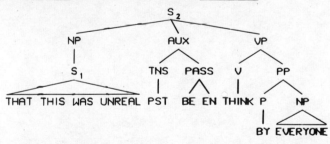

After <u>It-Deletion</u> has applied.

Q. What do we have?
A. After <u>Affix Hopping</u> we have <u>That this was unreal was thought by everyone</u>.
Q. What would happen if we chose to apply <u>Extraposition</u>?
A. Let us start with the structure derived after <u>Passive</u> (as above).

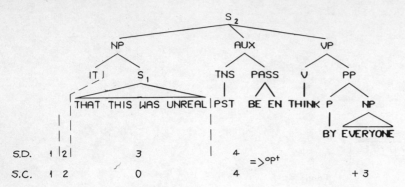

S.D.   1 |2| 3   4 $\Rightarrow^{opt}$

S.C.   1 2   0   4   + 3

     Analysis of tree for <u>Extraposition</u>.

The tree has now been analyzed to meet the S. D. for <u>Extraposition</u>, which we optionally apply.

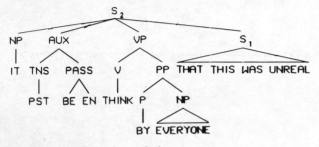

     After <u>Extraposition</u> has applied.

Q. What sentence do we have?

A. After <u>Affix Hopping</u> we have <u>It was thought by everyone that this was unreal</u>. The fact that the deep structure <u>it</u> shows up in surface structure is evidence that this <u>it</u> must be in the deep structure.

<u>Extraposition</u> and <u>Relative Clause Formation</u>

We will now show that <u>Extraposition</u> must precede <u>Relative Clause Formation</u>. Let us consider the following sentence: <u>The hat which it is obvious that Tom bought is made of gold</u>. Excluding details, it has the following D. S. :

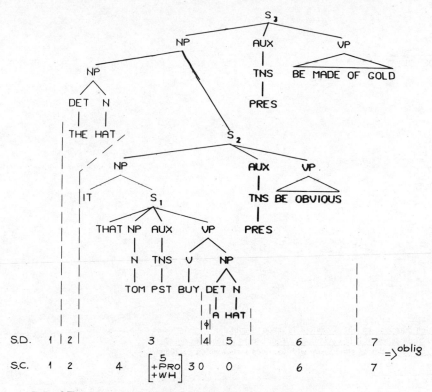

S.D.	1	2		3		4	5		6		7	
S.C.	1	2	4	$\begin{bmatrix} 5 \\ +PRO \\ +WH \end{bmatrix}$ 3 0			0		6		7	

$\Rightarrow$ oblig

D. S. of The hat which it is obvious that Tom bought is made of gold.

We will assume, contrary to fact, that Relative Clause Formation precedes Extraposition. As we have said before, Relative Clause Formation is obligatory, so we must apply it. The above structure has been analyzed to undergo Relative Clause Formation.

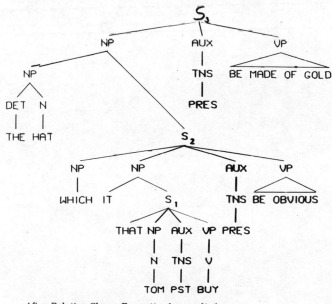

After Relative Clause Formation has applied.

Q. Can Extraposition now apply (i.e., can S_1 be extraposed)?

A. Yes, but since Extraposition is optional, we will choose not to apply it. Since an it directly precedes an S (our S_1) within an NP, It-Deletion must apply.

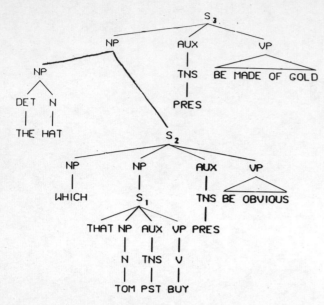

After <u>It-Deletion</u> has applied.

Q. What S do we have?

A. After <u>Affix Hopping</u> we get the unacceptable *<u>The hat which that Tom bought is obvious is made of gold</u>.

Q. How can we prevent this sentence and derive the desired <u>The hat which it is obvious that Tom bought is made of gold</u>?

A. We must order <u>Extraposition</u> before <u>Relative Clause Formation</u>. Let us start again with the deep structure on p. 103.

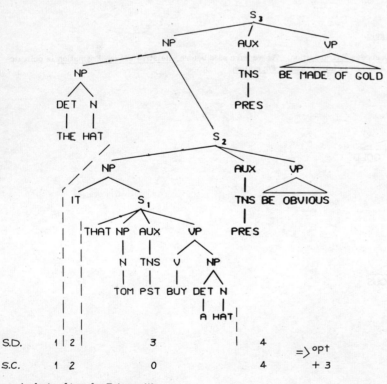

Analysis of tree for <u>Extraposition</u>.

Q. Can <u>Extraposition</u> apply to this structure?

A. Yes, optionally. Let us apply this rule. (The tree has been analyzed to undergo <u>Extraposition</u>.)

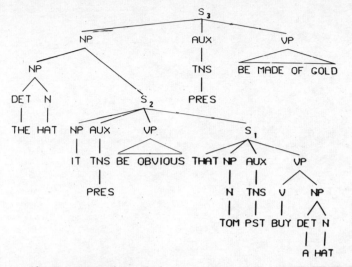

After <u>Extraposition</u> has applied.

S_1 has been extraposed to the end of S_2.

Q. Can <u>Relative Clause Formation</u> now apply?

A. Yes, it must apply. Let us consider the structure we have derived so far (exactly as above, but analyzed to undergo <u>Relative Clause Formation</u>):

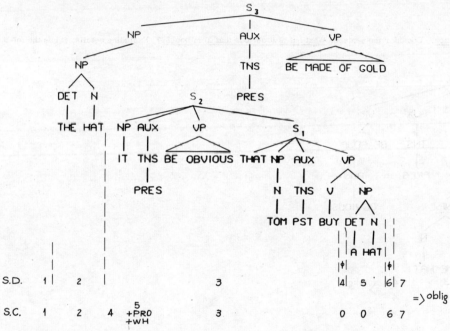

Analysis of tree for <u>Relative Clause Formation</u>.

We must now apply <u>Relative Clause Formation</u>.

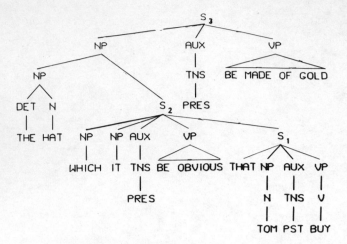

After <u>Relative Clause Formation</u> has applied.

Q. What S do we have?

A. After <u>Affix Hopping</u> we have <u>The hat which it is obvious that Tom bought is made of gold</u>. (<u>It-Deletion</u> can no longer apply since <u>it</u> no longer precedes an S within an NP.) The above sentence can only be derived if <u>Extraposition</u> precedes <u>Relative Clause Formation</u>. And only with this order can we prevent the ungrammatical S on p. 104.

<u>Extraposition</u> and <u>Question Formation</u>

We will now order <u>Extraposition</u> and <u>Question Formation</u>. Consider the sentence <u>What hat is it obvious that Tom bought?</u> Excluding details, it has the following D. S.:

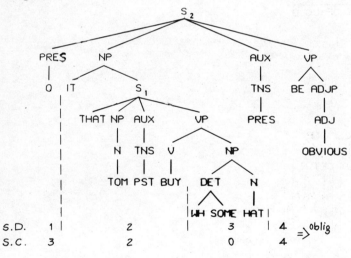

| S.D. | 1 | | 2 | | 3 | | 4 | $\Rightarrow$ oblig |
| S.C. | 3 | | 2 | | 0 | | 4 | |

D. S. of <u>What hat is it obvious that Tom bought?</u>

Again, the complementizer <u>that</u> has already been inserted by a rule we will discuss later. Let us assume, contrary to fact, that <u>Question Formation</u> precedes <u>Extraposition</u>. The above tree has been analyzed to undergo <u>Question Formation</u>, which we will now apply.

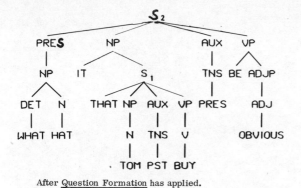

After <u>Question Formation</u> has applied.

Q. What rule must now apply?

A. Since there are now two NP's beginning a main clause, <u>Subject-Verb Inversion</u> must apply. Let us consider the structure we have so far (exactly as above, but analyzed to undergo <u>Subject-Verb Inversion</u>):

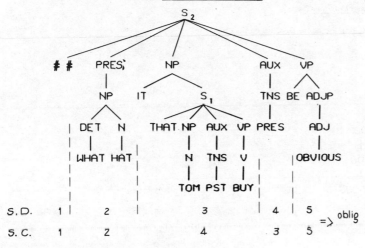

Analysis of tree for <u>Subject-Verb Inversion</u>.

This structure has now been analyzed to undergo <u>Subject-Verb Inversion</u>, which we must now apply. Notice that the NP of term 3 includes all of S_1 within it, so that the NP and the clause within it (S_1) will be permuted with the <u>Tns</u> and <u>be</u> of S_2.

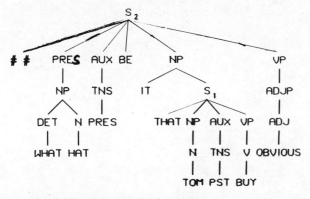

After <u>Subject-Verb Inversion</u> has applied.

Q. Can <u>Extraposition</u> now apply?

A. Yes, but as it is an optional rule, we will choose not to apply it.

Q. What rule must now apply?

A. <u>It-Deletion</u> must apply, because <u>it</u> directly precedes an S (S_1) within an NP.

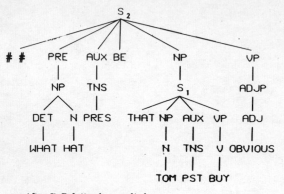

After <u>It-Deletion</u> has applied.

Q. What S do we have?
A. After <u>Affix Hopping</u> we have the unacceptable *<u>What hat is that Tom bought obvious</u>?
Q. How can we prevent this sentence?
A. We must order <u>Extraposition</u> before <u>Question Formation</u>.   Let us consider the same D. S. as on p. 106:

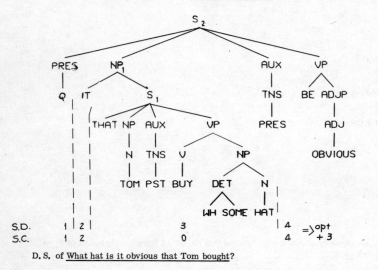

S.D.   1 | 2 | 3 | 4   =⟩ opt
S.C.   1   2   0   4   + 3

D. S. of <u>What hat is it obvious that Tom bought</u>?

This structure has now been analyzed to undergo <u>Extraposition</u>, which we optionally apply:

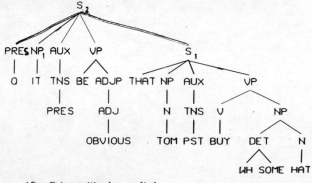

After <u>Extraposition</u> has applied.

Q. Must <u>Question Formation</u> now apply?
A. Yes.

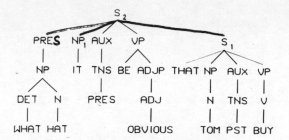

After <u>Question Formation</u> has applied.

Q. What rule must now apply?

A. Since two NP's start off a main clause, <u>Subject-Verb Inversion</u> must apply. Note that S_1 has now been extraposed out of NP_1, so S_1 will not be involved in <u>Subject-Verb Inversion</u>.

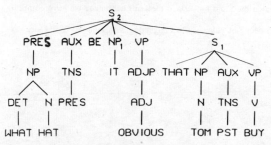

After <u>Subject-Verb Inversion</u> has applied.

Q. What S do we have?

A. After <u>Affix Hopping</u> we have <u>What hat is it obvious that Tom bought?</u> This sentence can be derived only if <u>Extraposition</u> precedes <u>Question Formation</u>. That order will also prevent the ungrammatical sentence on p. 108. Therefore, the rules must apply in this order.

<u>Cyclic Transformations</u>

There is an ordered group of transformations which are said to apply "cyclically." This simply means that if we have a structure with embedded sentences (as we have when we apply <u>Relative Clause Formation</u> or <u>Extraposition</u>), this ordered group applies in their order to each sentence, starting with the most deeply embedded one (the S that has no other sentences embedded in it). Now, suppose we have a structure with three embedded sentences like this:

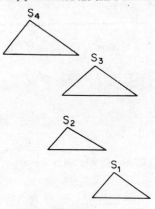

and suppose we have three transformations, A, B, and C, which are ordered as given. 1-A, 2-B, 3-C.

The principle of the transformation cycle says that we start with the most deeply embedded S, which is S_1 in our diagram. We first attempt to apply rule A. Let's say it applies. We will use the following diagram to represent abstractly the structure which would result after rule A has applied to S_1 on the first pass through the cyclically ordered rules.

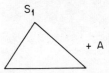

We now see if rule B applies. Let's say it does not apply (a plus sign will mean that the rule has applied, and a minus sign, that it hasn't):

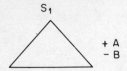

Now we try rule C. Let's say it applies:

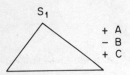

After we have attempted to apply all the transformational rules of this group, in the order given, on the most embedded (bottom) sentence, we have completed the cycle (the group of ordered, cyclic, rules) on the first pass through the cycle.

We now proceed to S_2 (the next most embedded, or lowest, S). We start over with the same group of rules again, beginning with rule A. Let's say rule A does not apply on S_2:

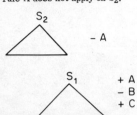

Now we attempt to apply B. We'll say it applies.

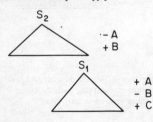

Now we try rule C. Let's say it does not apply:

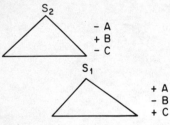

We have now finished with the second pass through the cycle (the group of cyclic, ordered, rules) and can now proceed to S_3, starting with the first rule in the cycle again—rule A.

Let's say rule A applies on S_3 (the third pass through this ordered block of rules):

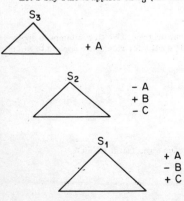

We now try rule B on S_3. We will say that it also applies:

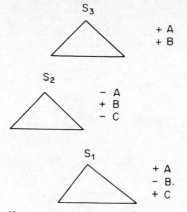

S_3 + A
    + B

S_2 − A
    + B
    − C

S_1 + A
    − B.
    + C

Now we come to rule C. Let's say it does not apply on S_3 (the third pass through the ordered block of cyclic rules):

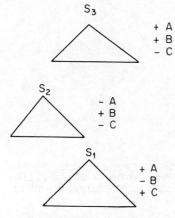

S_3 + A
    + B
    − C

S_2 − A
    + B
    − C

S_1 + A
    − B
    + C

We employ this same process on S_4 (the fourth pass through this ordered block of rules, i.e., A, B, and C) and so on, _ad infinitum_, for as many embedded sentences as there are.

Complementizer Placement[1]

S. D.   X $\left[\begin{array}{c} \text{NP} \end{array}\right.$ − $\begin{array}{c}[\text{Tns(M)} \\ \text{Aux}\end{array}$ − $\left.\begin{array}{c}\text{X}] \\ \text{Aux}\end{array}\right.$ $\left.\begin{array}{c}\text{VP Y}\end{array}\right]$ − Z

     1   2   3   4   5

$\Longrightarrow$ oblig

S. C.   1 $\left\{\begin{array}{c}\underline{\text{that}} \\ \underline{\text{for}} \\ \underline{\text{poss}}\end{array}\right\}$ +2 $\left\{\begin{array}{c} 3 \\ \underline{\text{to}} \\ \underline{\text{ing}}\end{array}\right\}$ 4   5

Condition: <u>Complementizer Placement</u> does not apply to relative clauses.

The first cyclic rule to apply to the structures we will deal with is called <u>Complementizer Placement</u>. <u>Complementizer Placement</u> never applies unless there is at least one sentence embedded in another. The reason for this is quite simple. We have the following three complements:

    that
    for-to
    poss-ing

If we placed any one of these when there was only one S, we would be making an invalid claim. Consider the D.S. for the sentence <u>I like you</u>.

---

[1]<u>That</u> goes by itself, <u>for</u> goes with <u>to</u>, and <u>poss</u> goes with <u>ing</u>.

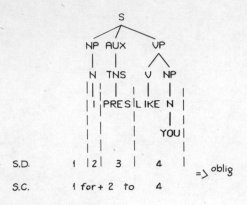

S.D.   1   2   3   4
                                  => oblig
S.C.   1 for + 2 to   4

D. S. of <u>I like you</u>.

Let's place a <u>for-to</u> complement in the structure:

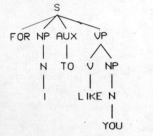

After <u>for-to Complementizer Placement</u> has applied.

By placing this complement, we would be claiming that the string *<u>for me to like you</u> is a good S, as it stands. Similarly, if we placed a <u>poss-ing</u> complement, we would be claiming that *<u>my liking you</u> is also acceptable, as it stands. If we placed a <u>that</u> complement, we would be saying that *<u>that I like you</u> is grammatical. All of the above are only acceptable if they are embedded in another clause, as in <u>Everyone knows that for me to like you is difficult</u>, <u>everyone knows my liking you is only temporary</u>, and <u>everyone knows that I like you</u>.

Complementizer Placement, Extraposition, and It-Deletion

The preceding example means that although in principle we start applying cyclical transformations with the lowest sentence, some cyclic rules will never apply on the lowest cycle, since they affect only embedded sentences. However, in the following examples we will always ask if <u>Complementizer Placement</u> can apply on the lowest sentence (the most deeply embedded one) although it will never apply there. Later, we will discuss some cyclic rules which do apply on the lowest S.

Consider now the pair of sentences <u>It worries me that we are criminals</u> and <u>That we are criminals worries me</u>. Both of these have the following deep structure:

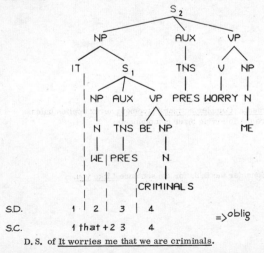

S.D.   1   2   3   4
                                  => oblig
S.C.   1 that + 2 3   4

D. S. of <u>It worries me that we are criminals</u>.

This tree has been analyzed to meet the S. D. for <u>Complementizer Placement</u>.

112

Q. Can <u>Complementizer Placement</u> apply on S_1 (on the S_1 cycle)?

A. No. S_1 does not "know" it is embedded. If we applied <u>Complementizer Placement</u> on S_1, we would be saying that *<u>that we are criminals</u> is a good sentence. We must go to S_2.

Q. Can <u>Complementizer Placement</u> apply on S_2 (on the S_2 cycle)?

A. Yes. We will choose a <u>that</u> complementizer.

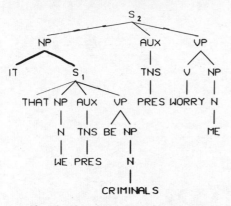

After <u>that</u> <u>Complementizer Placement</u> has applied on the S_2 cycle in S_1.

Q. What sentences could we get with this complement?

A. With a <u>that</u> complementizer we can apply <u>Extraposition</u> and have <u>It worries me that we are criminals</u>. Or, if we do not apply <u>Extraposition</u>, then <u>It-Deletion</u> is obligatory, and we have <u>That we are criminals worries me</u>. Now consider the structure again (without complements).

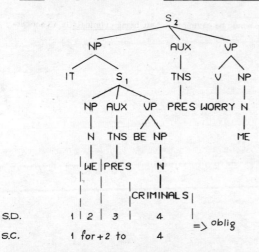

Analysis of tree for <u>Complementizer Placement</u>.

Q. Can <u>Complementizer Placement</u> apply on the S_1 cycle?

A. No. If it did apply, we would be claiming that *<u>for us to criminals</u> is a good sentence all alone. We now go to S_2.

Q. Can <u>Complementizer Placement</u> apply on S_2?

A. Yes. On the S_2 cycle, we may place <u>for-to</u> complements <u>in</u> S_1 because when the cyclic rules can "look at" S_2, they can "see" that S_1 is an embedded clause.

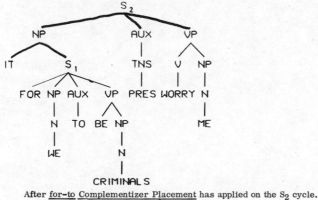

After <u>for-to</u> <u>Complementizer Placement</u> has applied on the S_2 cycle.

Note that <u>to</u> replaces the <u>Tense</u> and Modal (if there is a Modal).

Q. What sentences can we get with complements?
A. If we apply <u>Extraposition</u>, we get <u>It worries me for us to be criminals</u>. If we do not apply <u>Extraposition</u>, then <u>it</u> directly precedes an S (S₁) within an NP, and <u>It-Deletion</u> obligatorily applies, producing <u>For us to be criminals worries me</u>. Consider now the D.S. on p. 112 again.

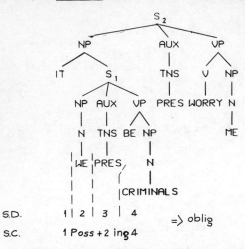

S.D.   1 | 2 | 3 | 4   => oblig

S.C.   1 Poss + 2 ing 4

Analysis of tree for <u>Complementizer Placement</u>.

Q. Can <u>Complementizer Placement</u> apply on S₁?
A. No. If we placed complements on S₁, the rules cannot "see" that it is embedded at all, so we would be saying that *<u>our being criminals</u> is an acceptable sentence, as it stands. We now proceed to S₂.
Q. Can we place complements on S₂?
A. Yes. This time, we will choose <u>poss-ing</u> complements.

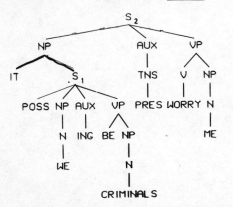

After <u>poss-ing</u> Complementizer Placement has applied on the S₂ cycle.

Q. What sentences can we get with these complements?
A. We will first try <u>Extraposition</u>, as we did with <u>that</u> and <u>for-to</u> complements.

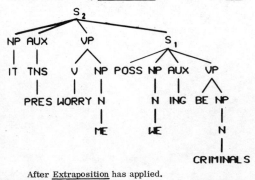

After <u>Extraposition</u> has applied.

Q. What is the result?

A. The unacceptable *It worries me our being criminals.[2] (with no pause between me and our).

Q. What does this mean?

A. We must place a condition on Extraposition, so that it will not apply with poss-ing complements. Since Extraposition will not be able to apply, we must apply It-Deletion. Consider again the structure on p. 114 (after poss-ing complements have been placed on S_2).

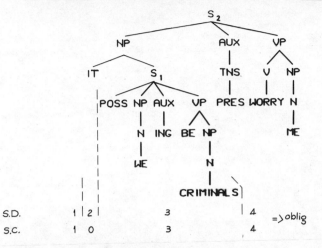

S.D.	1	2	3	4	
S.C.	1	0	3	4	$\Rightarrow$ oblig

Analysis of tree for It-Deletion.

This tree has been analyzed to undergo It-Deletion, which we must apply because we cannot apply Extraposition with poss-ing complements.

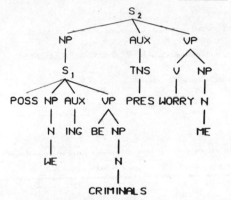

After It-Deletion has applied.

Q. What S do we have?

A. After Affix Hopping, we have Our being criminals worries me. Worry is a verb which takes all three complementizers, but this is not the case with all other verbs. It should be obvious that since the applicability of Extraposition depends on the complementizers, the complements must be placed first. So far, then, we have three cyclic rules ordered:

> Complementizer Placement
> Extraposition (opt)
> It-Deletion (oblig)

Complementizer Placement is cyclic, since if we have ten embedded S's, complements must be placed in each when the rules process the sentence directly above it. For now, we will assume that Extraposition and It-Deletion are cyclic.

Preposition Deletion

$$\text{S.D.} \quad X - [\underset{PP}{\ } P - S] - Y$$

	1	2	3	4	
					$\Longrightarrow$ oblig
S.C.	1	0	3	4	

Condition: Applies only with for-to and that complementizers.

[2]Later low level rules, which we will not discuss, will change poss+we into our, poss+she into her, etc.

We will now consider another cyclic transformation, called <u>Preposition Deletion</u>. This operates in sentences like <u>Everyone is afraid that Linguistics is cool</u>. Note that the following Phrase Structure rules have been applied:

$$VP \rightarrow \underline{be} \; \text{Adj P}$$
$$\text{Adj P} \rightarrow \text{adj} \; \left(\; \left\{ \begin{array}{c} PP \\ NP \end{array} \right\} \; \right)$$

The D. S. of this sentence is as follows:

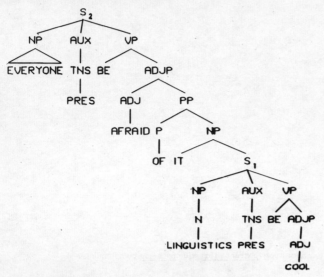

D.S. of <u>Everyone is afraid that Linguistics is cool</u>.

Q. Can we apply on the lowest sentence (S_1) any of the cyclic rules so far considered?

A. No. <u>Complementizer Placement</u> can never apply on the first cycle (the first pass through the cyclic rules which is on S_1). We cannot apply <u>Extraposition</u> or <u>It-Deletion</u> either, because <u>it</u> is in S_2. So we move to S_2.

Q. Can <u>Complementizer Placement</u> apply on S_2?

A. Yes. We will place the complementizer <u>that</u>.

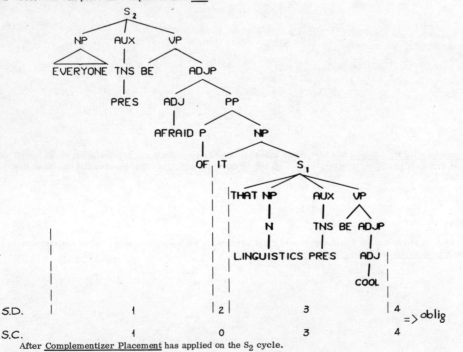

S.D.

S.C.

After <u>Complementizer Placement</u> has applied on the S_2 cycle.

Q. According to the list of cyclic rules on p. 115, we must try <u>Extraposition</u> next.

A. Yes, but nothing will happen, since the complement sentence which would be extraposed is already at the end of the structure. We now come to <u>It-Deletion</u>.

Q. Must <u>It-Deletion</u> now apply?

A. Yes, because there is an <u>it</u> directly preceding an S. The tree has been analyzed to undergo <u>It-Deletion</u>.

116

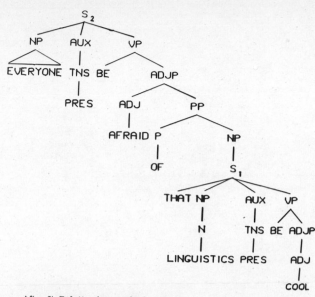

After <u>It-Deletion</u> has applied on S_2.

Q. What does this give us?
A. The unacceptable *<u>Everyone is afraid of that Linguistics is cool</u>.
Q. How can we produce an acceptable sentence?
A. There is a rule called <u>Preposition Deletion</u>, which applies whenever a preposition directly precedes an S within a PP. Note that the preposition is not directly before an S until <u>It-Deletion</u> has applied. Consider the structure we have so far (exactly as above, but analyzed to undergo <u>Preposition Dele-tion</u>).

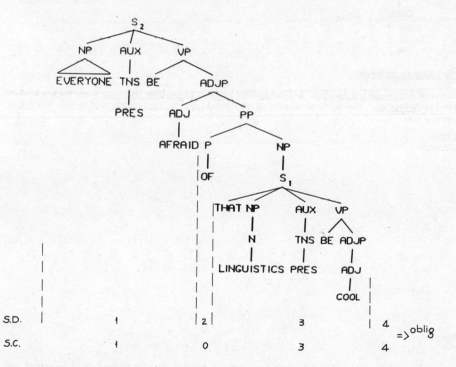

Analysis of tree for <u>Preposition Deletion</u>.

We must now apply <u>Preposition Deletion</u> to the above structure:

Ordering of rules:

Complementizer Placement

Extraposition

It-Deletion

Preposition Deletion

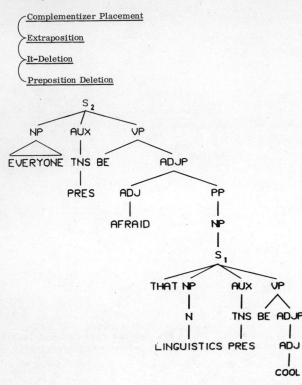

After <u>Preposition Deletion</u> has applied on S₂.

Q. What do we have?
A. After <u>Affix Hopping</u> we have <u>Everyone is afraid that Linguistics is cool</u>.

Since the application of <u>It-Deletion</u> provides the environment for <u>Preposition Deletion</u>, <u>It-Deletion</u> must precede <u>Preposition Deletion</u>, i.e., the preposition does not directly precede S₁ until the <u>it</u> has been deleted by <u>It-Deletion</u>. (See the order of rules given above.) <u>Preposition Deletion</u> applies only with <u>for-to</u> and <u>that</u> complements, but <u>not</u> with <u>poss-ing</u> complements, e.g.,

with <u>that</u>:   <u>I am afraid that Linguistics is cool.</u>
                 *<u>I am afraid of that Linguistics is cool.</u>
with <u>for-to</u>:   <u>I am afraid for him to lose.</u>
                 *<u>I am afraid of for him to lose.</u>
with <u>poss-ing</u>: <u>I am afraid of his losing.</u>
                 *<u>I am afraid his losing.</u>

<u>Equi NP Deletion</u>

Consider now sentences of the form:

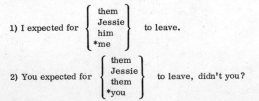

1) I expected for { them / Jessie / him / *me } to leave.

2) You expected for { them / Jessie / them / *you } to leave, didn't you?

Note that with the verb <u>expect</u> (and others, like <u>want</u>, <u>prefer</u>, etc.) the subject NP of the embedded sentence may not equal the subject NP of the matrix sentence. (The matrix sentence is the one directly above the embedded one.) This is illustrated in 1) and 2). But now consider sentences like 3) and 4):

3) We bribed { the captain / everyone / a junkie } to take a bath.

4) The cops forced { us / the horse / the intellectuals } to move back.

118

Q. What is the subject of the embedded S in 3) (to take a bath), which is not overtly present?

A. With the verb bribe, the subject of the embedded S must be the same as the object of the main (matrix) sentence.

Thus, in the matrix S:

5) We bribed the captain

note that if this is followed by to take a bath, the subject of this latter, embedded S can only be the captain, but no other NP. Thus, 5) could not mean:

We bribed the captain for $\begin{Bmatrix} \text{*the horse} \\ \text{*everyone} \\ \text{*the president} \end{Bmatrix}$ to take a bath. [3]

It can only mean:

We bribed the captain for the captain to take a bath.

Additional evidence for this is the fact that only one reflexive form shows up in the complement S of a sentence like 5), and this reflexive agrees with the object NP of the matrix S. Thus, we have:

We bribed the captain to shoot himself

but not:

We bribed the captain to shoot $\begin{Bmatrix} \text{*herself} \\ \text{*myself} \\ \text{*yourself} \\ \text{*themselves} \\ \text{*itself} \end{Bmatrix}$.

The above is also true for the verb force, which belongs to the same class as bribe. Thus:

The cops forced us to move back

can only mean:

The cops forced us for us to move back

but not:

The cops forced us for $\begin{Bmatrix} \text{*the chief} \\ \text{*the kittens} \\ \text{*the world} \end{Bmatrix}$ to move back.

The same facts obtain for the occurrence of reflexives in the complement S:

The cops forced us to shoot $\begin{Bmatrix} \text{ourselves} \\ \text{*themselves} \\ \text{*yourself} \\ \text{*myself} \\ \text{*itself} \end{Bmatrix}$.

To explain the situation presented in examples 1) and 2) on p. 118, there is a transformation called Equi NP Deletion, which deletes the subjects of embedded sentences under two conditions:

i) the verb of the directly higher sentence must belong either to the class of expect, want, etc., or to the class of force, bribe, etc.

ii) the subject NP of the embedded sentence must equal either the subject NP of the matrix sentence, or the object NP of the matrix sentence.

The first sentence we will consider is This little Indian expects to be chief next year. But before we show how Equi NP Deletion affects the deep structure of this sentence, we will look at how the rule Pronominalization operates on the same deep structure:

Pronominalization

Following is the deep structure for the sentence This little Indian expects that he will be chief next year.

---

[3]The rule of Complementizer Deletion will delete the complementizer for.

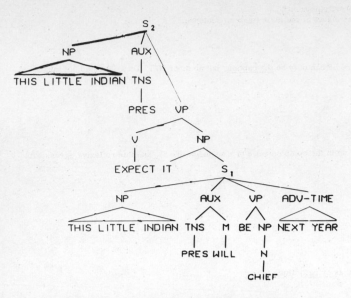

D. S. of <u>This little Indian expects that he will be chief next year</u>.

Q. Will any cyclic rules we have so far (p. 118) apply on S$_1$?
A. No. None of these rules will apply on the lowest S (S$_1$) for the reasons stated on p. 116. We go to S$_2$.
Q. Can <u>Complementizer Placement</u> apply on S$_2$?
A. Yes. We will choose a <u>that</u> complementizer.

Note that evidence for <u>it</u> being in the deep structure is that it shows up in the surface structure's related passive sentence <u>It was expected that this little Indian would be chief next year</u>.

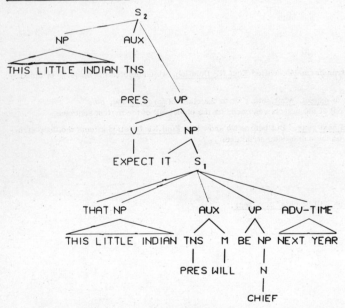

After <u>that</u> Complementizer Placement on the S$_2$ cycle.

Q. Can the next rule on our list, <u>Extraposition</u>, apply?
A. Yes, but nothing will happen since S$_1$ is already at the end. We come to <u>It-Deletion</u>.
Q. Must <u>It-Deletion</u> apply?
A. Yes, since an <u>it</u> directly precedes an S within an NP.

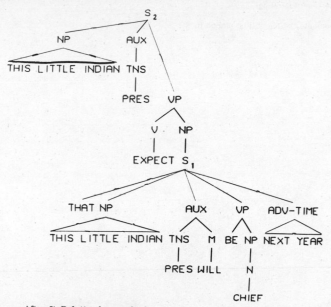

After <u>It–Deletion</u> has applied on S_2.

Q. Running down our list we come to <u>Preposition Deletion</u>. Can it apply?

A. No, because there is no preposition directly before an S.

Q. What sentence do we have?

A. <u>Pronominalization</u> (which we have not mentioned yet) will change the subject NP of S_1 into <u>he</u>, since it is identical with the subject NP of S_2. Then <u>Affix Hopping</u> will apply to produce <u>This little Indian expects that he will be chief next year</u>.

Application of <u>Equi NP Deletion</u>

$$\text{S.D.} \quad X \; - \; (NP) \; - \; Y \; - \; [\left\{\begin{matrix} for \\ poss \end{matrix}\right\} \; - \; NP \; - \; Z] \; - \; W \; - \; (NP) \; - \; R$$

$$\qquad\qquad\qquad\qquad\qquad\quad {}_S \qquad\qquad\qquad {}_S$$

$$\qquad 1 \qquad 2 \qquad 3 \qquad 4 \qquad 5 \qquad 6 \quad 7 \qquad 8 \qquad 9$$

$$\text{S.C.} \quad 1 \qquad 2 \qquad 3 \qquad 4 \qquad \emptyset \qquad 6 \quad 7 \qquad 8 \qquad 9 \qquad \Longrightarrow \text{oblig}$$

Condition: $2 = 5$ or $5 = 8$

$\qquad\qquad$ 2 and 8 may not both be null.

Now consider the sentence <u>This little Indian expects to be chief next year</u>. It has the following deep structure:

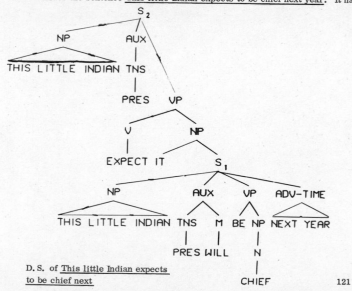

D.S. of <u>This little Indian expects to be chief next</u>

121

Q. Can anything happen on S_1?

A. No. None of our cyclic rules so far may apply on the lowest cycle. (See p. 116 .) We go to S_2.

Q. Can the first cyclic rule in our list (p. 118) apply?

A. Yes. Complementizer Placement applies on S_2. We will choose for-to complements, which will be placed in S_1.

Ordering of rules:

Complementizer Placement

Equi NP Deletion

Extraposition

It-Deletion

Preposition Deletion

After for-to Complementizer Placement has applied on the S_2 cycle.

Q. Can the next rule on our list, namely Extraposition, apply?

A. Yes, but nothing happens because the clause which would be extraposed is already at the end.

Q. Now we come to It-Deletion. Must It-Deletion apply?

A. Yes, It-Deletion must apply since an it is directly before an S (S_1) within an NP.

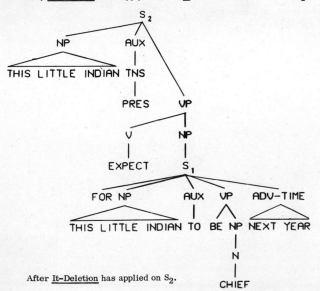

After It-Deletion has applied on S_2.

122

Q. What do we have?

A. Two possibilities: 1) With <u>Pronominalization</u> and <u>Affix Hopping</u> we have *<u>This little Indian expected for him to be chief next year</u>. (This is ungrammatical unless <u>him</u> does not refer to <u>this little Indian</u>, as is intended here.) Or 2) without <u>Pronominalization</u> but with <u>Affix Hopping</u> we have *<u>This little Indian expects for this little Indian to be chief next year</u>.

Q. What do we do?

A. There is an operation for just this situation, called <u>Equi NP Deletion</u>. But let us start with the structure derived after <u>Complementizer Placement</u> has applied (as on p. 122).

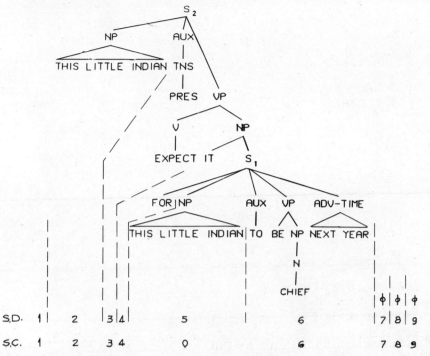

Analysis of tree for <u>Equi NP Deletion</u> after <u>for-to</u> <u>Complementizer Placement</u> has applied on the S_2 cycle.

Q. After <u>Complementizer Placement</u>, what must now happen to obtain <u>This little Indian expects to be chief next year</u>?

A. We must apply <u>Equi NP Deletion</u>. The tree has been so analyzed and the following shows the effects of its application to the above tree.

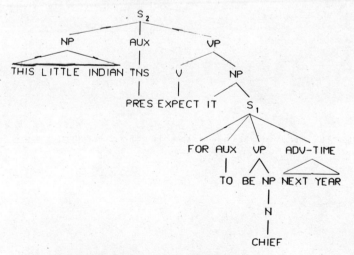

After <u>Equi NP Deletion</u> has applied on the S_2 cycle.

Q. What part of the rule applied to this structure?

A. In our case, NP2 = NP5, and 7, 8, and 9 were null. Later we will give an example in which we analyze a structure so that 5 = 8, and <u>Equi NP Deletion</u> will apply then, also.

Q. Can <u>Equi NP Deletion</u> apply any time there are two identical NP's in two adjacent sentences?

A. No. Note that <u>Equi NP Deletion</u> applies only with <u>for-to</u> and <u>poss-ing</u> complementizers. For this reason, <u>Equi NP Deletion</u> must follow <u>Complementizer Placement</u> (see p. 122). If we applied <u>Equi NP Deletion</u> with a <u>that</u> complementizer, as on p. 120 , we would get the unacceptable *<u>This little Indian expects that will be chief next year</u>.

123

Q. However, we are not yet finished. What S will we have should nothing else apply?
A. If nothing else happens except <u>Affix Hopping</u>, we will have <u>*This little Indian expects it for to be chief next year</u>.
Q. What should we do?
A. We must continue down our list (p. 122). Next is <u>Extraposition</u>.
Q. Will <u>Extraposition</u> apply?
A. Yes, but nothing will happen because S_1 is already at the end of the structure. We now come to <u>It-Deletion</u>.
Q. Must <u>It-Deletion</u> apply?
A. Yes, because an <u>it</u> directly precedes an S (S_1).

<u>Complementizer Deletion</u>

$$\text{S.D.} \quad X - [\ \begin{Bmatrix} \text{for} \\ \text{poss} \end{Bmatrix}_S \ -\!- \ \begin{Bmatrix} \text{to} \\ \text{ing} \end{Bmatrix} \ Y]_S - Z$$

$$\qquad\qquad 1 \qquad\quad 2 \qquad\qquad 3 \qquad\quad 4 \qquad \Longrightarrow$$

$$\text{S.C.} \quad 1 \qquad\quad 0 \qquad\qquad 3 \qquad\quad 4$$

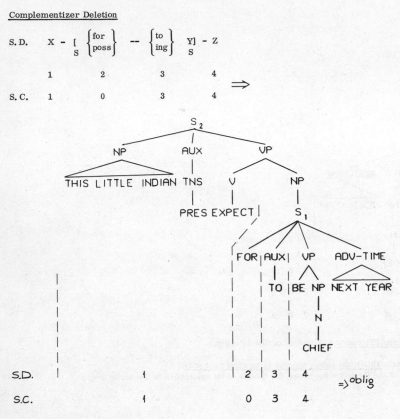

After <u>It-Deletion</u> has applied on S_2.

We now come to <u>Preposition Deletion</u>.

Q. Can it apply?
A. No. There is no preposition before any S to delete.
Q. What S do we have now?
A. <u>*This little Indian expects for to be chief next year</u>.
Q. What must we do?
A. We must apply <u>Complementizer Deletion</u> now, after having gone through the cyclic rules so far. The tree has been analyzed to undergo <u>Complementizer Deletion</u>.

Ordering of rules:

   <u>Complementizer Placement</u>

   <u>Equi NP Deletion</u>

   <u>Extraposition</u>

   <u>It-Deletion</u>

   <u>Preposition Deletion</u>

   <u>Complementizer Deletion</u>

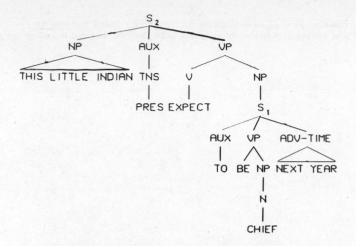

After <u>Complementizer Deletion</u> has applied on the S$_2$ cycle.

Q. What do we have now?

A. After <u>Affix Hopping</u>, we have the desired sentence <u>This little Indian expects to be chief next year</u>.

Further Application of <u>Equi NP Deletion</u>

The next sentence we will consider is <u>To learn this was hell for me</u>. It has the following deep structure:

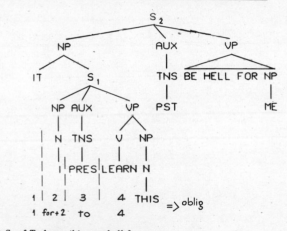

S.D.   1 | 2 | 3 | 4 THIS
S.C.   1 for+2 to   4   => oblig

D. S. of <u>To learn this was hell for me</u>.

Q. Can any of our cyclic rules so far discussed apply on S$_1$?

A. No. All the cyclic rules we have so far apply only when there are at least two sentences, i.e., all of their S. D.'s require at least two sentences.

Q. What must happen first on S$_2$?

A. <u>Complementizer Placement</u> must apply first. We will choose <u>for-to</u>. (The tree has been analyzed to undergo <u>Complementizer Placement</u>.)

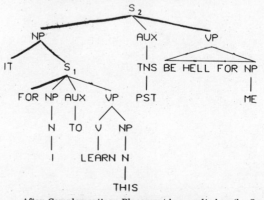

After <u>Complementizer Placement</u> has applied on the S$_2$ cycle.

125

Q. We now come to <u>Equi NP Deletion</u>. Must it apply on S_2?

A. Yes, because there are two identical NP's, one in S_1 (<u>I</u>) and one in S_2 (<u>me</u>). (Consider <u>I</u> and <u>me</u> as identical for the time being.) Notice that <u>Equi NP Deletion</u> could not have applied on S_1 because there were no two identical NP's at that point. Consider the structure so far derived, analyzed to undergo this rule:

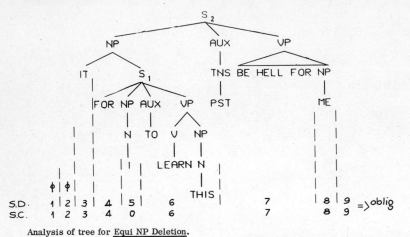

Analysis of tree for <u>Equi NP Deletion</u>.

Note that in this case, 5 = 8. Let us now apply <u>Equi NP Deletion</u>:

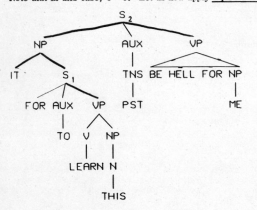

After <u>Equi NP Deletion</u> has applied on the S_2 cycle.

Q. We now continue down our list on p. 124 to <u>Extraposition</u>. Can it apply?

A. Yes, but it is optional. Suppose we don't apply it. Next is <u>It-Deletion</u>.

Q. Must <u>It-Deletion</u> apply?

A. Yes, because an <u>it</u> directly precedes an S within an NP (S_1).

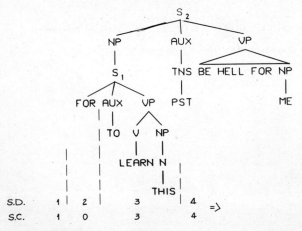

After <u>It-Deletion</u> has applied on S_2.

126

Q. We come to <u>Preposition Deletion</u>. Can it apply?

A. No. There is one preposition, <u>for</u>, in S_2, which precedes an NP, but not an S. So <u>Preposition Deletion</u> will not apply. Now we come to <u>Complementizer Deletion</u>.

Q. Must <u>Complementizer Deletion</u> apply?

A. Yes. <u>Complementizer Deletion</u> applies with <u>for-to</u> or <u>poss-ing</u> complementizers. Since we have <u>for-to</u> complements, the <u>for</u> will be deleted. (The tree has been analyzed to undergo <u>Complementizer Deletion</u>.)

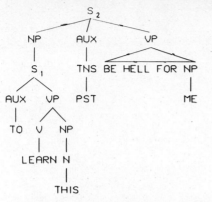

After <u>Complementizer Deletion</u> has applied on the S_2 cycle.

Q. What S do we now have?

A. After <u>Affix Hopping</u> we have <u>To learn this was hell for me</u>.

Note that if we had applied <u>Extraposition</u> to this structure after <u>Complementizer Placement</u> and <u>Equi NP Deletion</u> (p. 126) we would have had *<u>It was hell for me for to learn this</u>. To this <u>Complementizer Deletion</u> and <u>Affix Hopping</u> would have applied, giving <u>It was hell for me to learn this</u>. Consider once more the same D.S. as on p. 125.

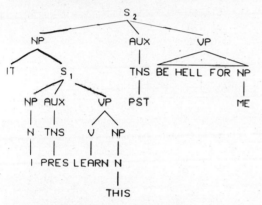

D.S. of <u>Learning this was hell for me</u>.

As usual, all of our cyclic rules so far require at least two sentences in order to apply. On the S_1 cycle, we have only one sentence. We go to S_2 and start again at the top of our list of cyclic rules on p. 124. <u>Complementizer Placement</u> is first.

Q. Must <u>Complementizer Placement</u> apply on S_2?

A. Yes. This time we will choose <u>poss-ing</u>.

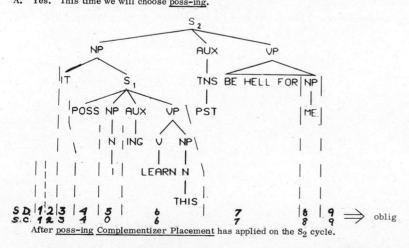

After <u>poss-ing</u> <u>Complementizer Placement</u> has applied on the S_2 cycle.

127

We now come to Equi NP Deletion. (The tree has been analyzed to undergo Equi NP Deletion.)

Q. Does Equi NP Deletion apply?
A. Yes. S₁ and S₂ contain identical NP's. (Again, assume that I = me for the time being.)

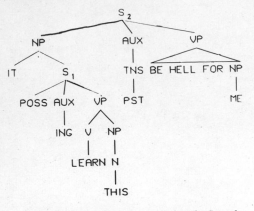

After Equi NP Deletion has applied on the S₂ cycle.

We continue down our list and come to Extraposition.

Q. Can Extraposition apply?
A. No. Extraposition can never apply when there are poss-ing complements (p. 115). We come to It-Deletion.
Q. Must It-Deletion apply?
A. Yes. There is an it directly before an S within an NP, so It-Deletion must apply.

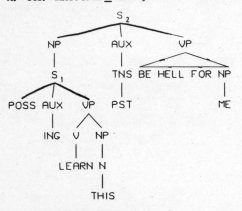

After It-Deletion has applied on S₂.

Q. We now come to Preposition Deletion. Can it apply?
A. No. As before, the only preposition we have precedes an NP (in S₂) but not an S. Therefore, Preposition Deletion does not apply. Now we come to Complementizer Deletion.
Q. Does Complementizer Deletion apply?
A. Yes. Complementizer Deletion applies with for-to or poss-ing complementizers. Since we have poss-ing complements, Complementizer Deletion will apply.

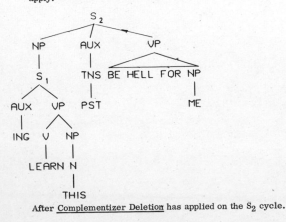

After Complementizer Deletion has applied on the S₂ cycle.
128

Q. What rule must now apply?
A. Affix Hopping will apply to give us Learning this was hell for me.

The Principle of Minimal Distance

In reference to Equi NP Deletion, there is a principle which states that the NP which causes the subject NP of an embedded clause to be deleted by Equi NP Deletion must not only be identical with the NP to be deleted, but must also be closest to it. (This term will be explained shortly.) In addition, other NP's within the S in which an NP is to be deleted are not to be considered. This means we start counting branches upwards until we find the closest NP. If it is identical to the subject NP in the lower S, the latter is deleted. This is called the Principle of Minimal Distance by Peter S. Rosenbaum.[4] In case two Np's are equally close to the subject NP of the lower S, if either is identical, deletion will take place.[5] This Principle of Minimal Distance (hereafter PMD) works as follows. Consider the sentence Jason forced the Hollanders into going. It has the following D. S.:

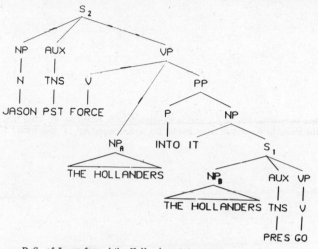

D. S. of Jason forced the Hollanders into going.

Again, no cyclic rules we have so far (p. 124) apply on the S_1 cycle. We go to S_2.

Q. What transformation must first apply on the S_2 cycle?
A. Complementizer Placement. We will choose poss-ing.

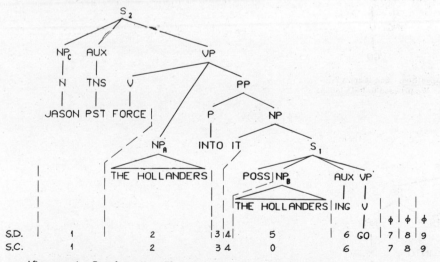

After poss-ing Complementizer Placement has applied on the S_2 cycle.

Q. Now we come to Equi NP Deletion. Does it apply?
A. Yes. We have poss-ing complementizers and there are two identical NP's within two adjacent sentences. (Note that the S. D. for Equi NP Deletion requires either for-to or poss-ing complementizers.) The tree has been analyzed to undergo Equi NP Deletion.

[4]The Grammar of English Predicate Complement Constructions (Cambridge, Mass.: M. I. T. Press, 1967).
[5]An exception to this principle is the verb, promise (Rosenbaum, Grammar). If you apply the PMD to a deep structure containing promise, it will predict the wrong results.

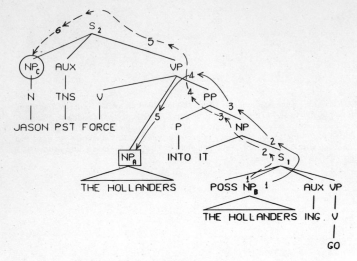

Analysis of tree for <u>Equi NP Deletion</u>.

We have numbered branches starting with term 5. The NP_a in the box is five branches away from NP_b in S_1, and is identical with it. (solid lines). The NP_c is six branches away from term 5 and is not identical with it (with NP_b). (This is illustrated by the dotted lines and by the encircling of NP_c.) The PMD states that NP_a will cause NP_b to be deleted by <u>Equi NP Deletion</u>.

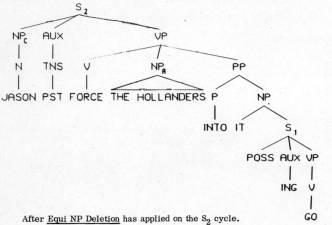

After <u>Equi NP Deletion</u> has applied on the S_2 cycle.

Q. We continue down our list (p. 124) and come to <u>Extraposition</u>. Can it apply?
A. No, not with <u>poss-ing</u> complementizers (see p. 115). We proceed to <u>It-Deletion</u>.
Q. Can <u>It-Deletion</u> apply?
A. Yes. It must apply because <u>it</u> directly precedes S_1.

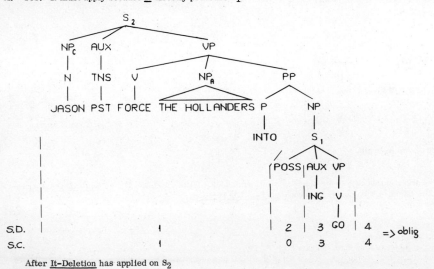

S.D.					2		3	GO		4	$\Rightarrow$ oblig
S.C.					0		3			4	

After <u>It-Deletion</u> has applied on S_2

130

Q. Next is <u>Preposition Deletion</u>. Can it apply?
A. No. <u>Preposition Deletion</u> does not apply with <u>poss-ing</u> complementizers (see p.115). We now come to <u>Complementizer Deletion</u>.
Q. Can <u>Complementizer Deletion</u> apply?
A. Yes. Since we have <u>poss-ing</u> complements, <u>Complementizer Deletion</u> must apply.

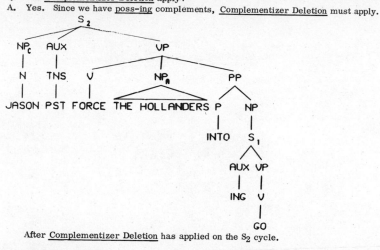

After <u>Complementizer Deletion</u> has applied on the S_2 cycle.

Q. What do we have?
A. After <u>Affix Hopping</u> we have <u>Jason forced the Hollanders into going</u>.

Another example of how the PMD works in the application of <u>Equi NP Deletion</u> can be seen in the following sentence: <u>I boil beans with Mother to make my-self rich</u>. It has the following deep structure:

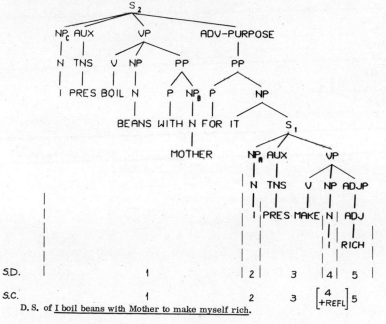

D. S. of <u>I boil beans with Mother to make myself rich</u>.

Q. Can any of the cyclic rules that we have presented so far apply on S_1?
A. None of the cyclic rules yet given can apply on S_1.
Q. But must another rule apply on S_1?
A. Yes. There are two identical NP's within S_1. Whenever two identical NP's are within the same simplex sentence, we know <u>Reflexive</u> must apply. The D. S. has been analyzed accordingly (see pp. 13-14).

Ordering of rules:

Complementizer Placement

Equi NP Deletion

Reflexive

Extraposition

It–Deletion

Preposition Deletion

Complementizer Deletion

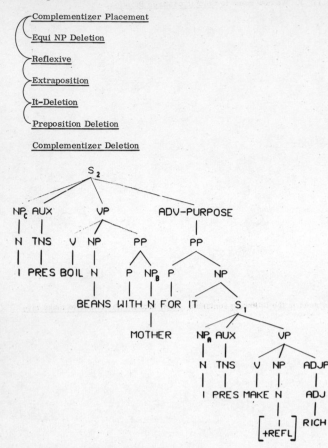

After <u>Reflexive</u> has applied on S$_1$.

We have not yet justified this, but <u>Reflexive</u> is also a cyclic rule. For the time being, we will place it just before <u>Extraposition</u>. Since none of our other cyclic rules listed can apply on the S$_1$ cycle, we go to S$_2$ and start over with our list again. First is <u>Complementizer Placement</u>.

Q. Must <u>Complementizer Placement</u> apply on S$_2$?
A. Yes. Every embedded complement sentence must have complementizers. We will choose <u>for–to</u> complementizers.

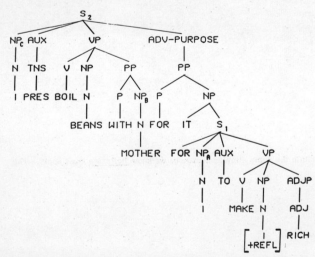

After <u>for–to</u> <u>Complementizer Placement</u> has applied on the S$_2$ cycle.

Now we come to <u>Equi NP Deletion</u>. We start from NP$_a$ in S$_1$ and count branches upward into the next sentence (S$_2$).

132

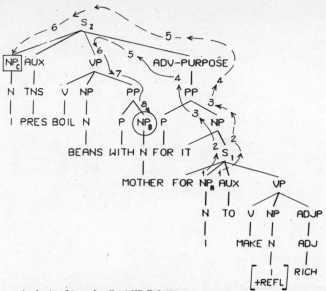

Analysis of tree for <u>Equi NP Deletion</u>.

After counting branches upward and out of S_1 (starting with the subject NP_a in S_1) we find NP_b in S_2 which is eight branches away and not identical with NP_a, so nothing will happen. (Follow solid lines. NP_b is encircled.) However, NP_c (follow dotted lines; NP_c is in the rectangle) is only six branches away from NP_a and is identical with NP_a. Therefore, according to the PMD, NP_c in S_2 will cause the identical NP_a in S_1 to be deleted by <u>Equi NP Deletion</u>.

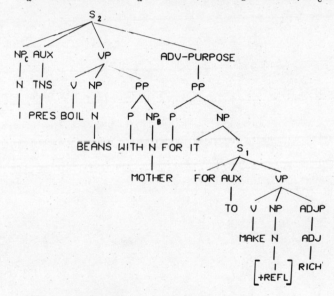

After <u>Equi NP Deletion</u> has applied on the S_2 cycle.

Continuing down the list, <u>Reflexive</u> is next.

Q. Can <u>Reflexive</u> apply on S_2?
A. No, because there are no two identical NP's within S_2. We come to <u>Extraposition</u>.
Q. Can <u>Extraposition</u> apply?
A. Yes, optionally. But since the clause to be extraposed is already at the end of the structure, nothing will happen to it. Next is <u>It-Deletion</u>.
Q. Does <u>It-Deletion</u> apply?
A. Yes. There is an <u>it</u> directly before S_1 within an NP, so <u>It-Deletion</u> will apply.

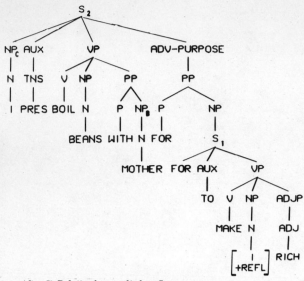

After <u>It-Deletion</u> has applied on S2

Q. <u>Preposition Deletion</u> is the next rule. Can it apply?

A. Yes, because the preposition <u>for</u> in S2 directly precedes S1.

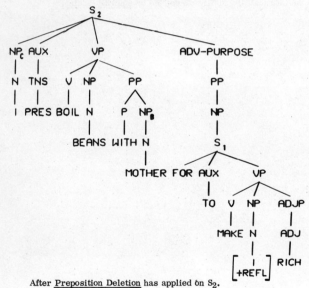

After <u>Preposition Deletion</u> has applied on S2.

Q. We now proceed to <u>Complementizer Deletion</u>. Must <u>Complementizer Deletion</u> apply on the S2 cycle?

A. Yes. <u>Complementizer Deletion</u> applies with <u>for-to</u> or <u>poss-ing</u> complementizers. Since we have for-to complementizers, <u>Complementizer Deletion</u> must apply.

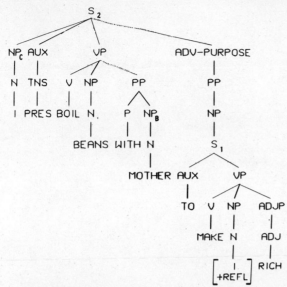

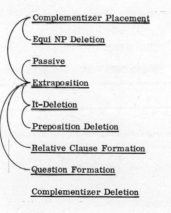

After <u>Complementizer Deletion</u> has applied on the S_2 cycle.

Q. What else must apply?

A. <u>Affix Hopping</u> must still apply, and this will give us <u>I boil beans with Mother to make myself rich</u>.

Ordering of Rules Presented in Part III

<u>Complementizer Placement</u>

<u>Equi NP Deletion</u>

<u>Passive</u>

<u>Extraposition</u>

<u>It-Deletion</u>

<u>Preposition Deletion</u>

<u>Relative Clause Formation</u>

<u>Question Formation</u>

<u>Complementizer Deletion</u>

Part IV Complex Complement Structures

New Rules to be Presented in Part IV

Intervening Rules

So far, the rules have applied in a linear order although we have encountered cases where one rule must apply more than once in a derivation. A case like this is the tree on p. 17 , where <u>Affix Hopping</u> applied to several parts of a tree simultaneously. As another example of this, consider the deep structure for <u>I am writing</u>:

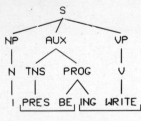

D.S. of <u>I am writing</u>.

<u>Affix Hopping</u> will apply two times to the areas marked off by the brackets:

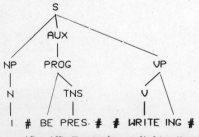

After <u>Affix Hopping</u> has applied two times in two different places.

136

In the above derivations, even though the same rule had to operate a number of times, it could be said that the rule was performing these operations all at once. However, we can show derivations where the same rule applies more than once, but where another rule must intervene between two applications of this rule. We will show this to be the case with respect to Passive and Equi NP Deletion.

To begin with, we will illustrate a case where Passive must operate before Equi NP Deletion. Then we will show a case where Passive must apply two separate times, where the first application of this rule must precede Equi NP Deletion, and where the second application must follow Equi NP Deletion. Consider first the sentence Mary forced John to be examined. It has the following deep structure.

Passive in S_1 and Equi NP Deletion in S_2

Ordering of rules:

- Complementizer Placement
- Equi NP Deletion
- Passive
- Reflexive
- Extraposition
- It-Deletion
- Preposition Deletion

Complementizer Deletion

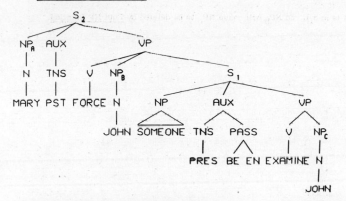

D.S. of Mary forced John to be examined.

Q. What rule must apply first on S_1?

A. Complementizer Placement cannot apply because its S.D. is not met. Equi NP Deletion cannot apply either, because its S.D. also requires two sentences to apply. However, Passive can and must apply because the constituent Passive is in the auxiliary of S_1.

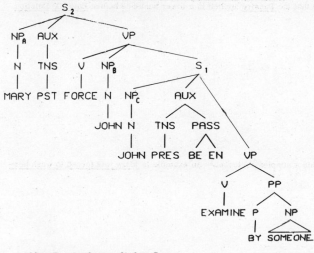

After Passive has applied on S_1.

137

No other rules will apply on S_1 We proceed to the S_2 cycle.

Q. What rule must apply first?
A. <u>Complementizer Placement</u> must apply first on the S_2 cycle. We will choose <u>for-to</u>.

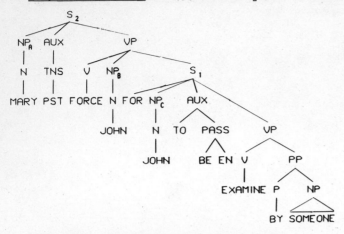

After <u>Complementizer Placement</u> has applied on the S_2 cycle.

Q. Now we come to <u>Equi NP Deletion</u>. Does it apply on S_2?
A. Yes. Note NP_b in S_2 = NP_c in S_1. NP_b is also the closest NP to NP_c (which is in S_1). So NP_b will cause NP_c to be deleted by <u>Equi NP Deletion</u>.

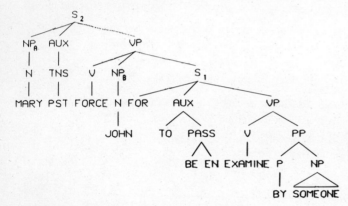

After <u>Equi NP Deletion</u> has applied on the S_2 cycle.

If we skip details, we will apply next <u>Complementizer Deletion</u> and <u>Affix Hopping</u> to produce <u>Mary forced John to be examined by someone</u>. <u>Agent Deletion</u> may optionally apply to give us <u>Mary forced John to be examined</u>. In this case we see that the <u>Passive</u> applied in a lower sentence before <u>Equi NP Deletion</u> is applied in a higher sentence. So the order of operations in this example is:

> <u>Passive</u>
> <u>Equi NP Deletion</u>.

But now we will show a case where the order must be:

> <u>Equi NP Deletion</u>
> <u>Passive</u>.

<u>Equi NP Deletion</u> and <u>Passive</u> in S_2

We will now consider a sentence in which the order is <u>Passive</u> – <u>Equi NP Deletion</u> within a simplex sentence.[1] An example is <u>Mary was forced to wash herself by Sam</u>. It has the following D.S.:

---

[1]A simplex sentence is a sentence which does not have another sentence embedded in it, or, it is a sentence being considered as if it had no embedded sentence, as the S_2 is considered in the derivation above.

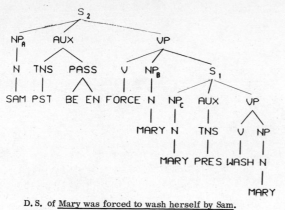

D.S. of <u>Mary was forced to wash herself by Sam.</u>

Q. What must happen on S_1?
A. <u>Reflexive</u> must apply since there are two identical NP's within S_1.

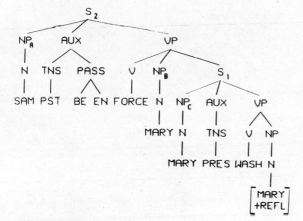

After <u>Reflexive</u> has applied on S_1.

No other rules will apply on S_1. We go to S_2.

Q. What is the first rule which must apply on S_2?
A. <u>Complementizer Placement</u>. We'll use <u>for-to</u>.

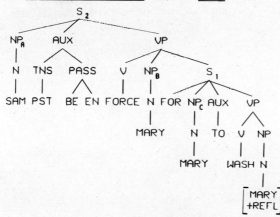

After <u>Complementizer Placement</u> has applied on the S_2 cycle.

Q. Can <u>Passive</u> and <u>Equi NP Deletion</u> both apply on the S_2 cycle?
A. Yes. Let us assume that <u>Passive</u> precedes <u>Equi NP Deletion</u>.

139

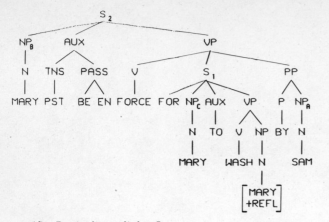

After <u>Passive</u> has applied on S_2.

Q. Can <u>Equi NP Deletion</u> now apply?

A. In this case, yes, because both NP_a and NP_b are equi-distant from NP_c, as shown on the following diagram:

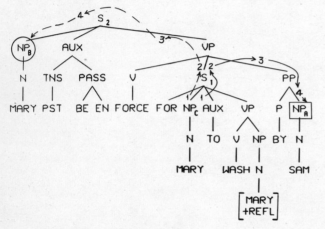

Analysis of tree for <u>Equi NP Deletion</u>.

After counting branches upward and out of S_1 (starting with NP_c) we see that NP_b (follow dotted lines; NP_b is encircled) and NP_a (follow solid lines; NP_a is in the box) are equi-distant from NP_c. According to the <u>PMD</u>, when two NP's in a higher S are equi-distant from the subject NP of the next lower S, if either is identical with the subject NP of the lower S, this subject NP will be deleted. In our case, since $NP_b = NP_c$, NP_c will be deleted by <u>Equi NP Deletion</u>.

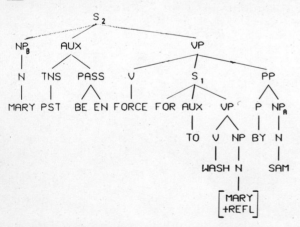

After <u>Equi NP Deletion</u> has applied on the S_2 cycle.

Skipping other details, we will end up with the sentence <u>Mary was forced by Sam to wash herself</u>. Now we have shown an instance where within one S (S_2) we obtained an accéptable sentence when <u>Passive</u> preceded <u>Equi NP Deletion</u>. However, because of other kinds of sentences (too complicated to consider

140

here) which cannot be generated if <u>Passive</u> precedes <u>Equi NP Deletion</u> in a simplex sentence, we must order the rules as follows:

<u>Equi NP Deletion</u>

<u>Passive</u>

(We still can derive <u>Mary was forced by Sam to wash herself</u> if we follow this ordering of the rules.)

<u>Passive, END Passive</u>

As we have just seen, we have a case where <u>Passive</u> precedes <u>Equi NP Deletion</u> (pp. 138-140), but we have decided that, within an S, <u>Passive</u> cannot precede <u>Equi NP Deletion</u> (p. 140 and above). Now we shall illustrate a case in which <u>Passive</u> applies twice, but with other rules intervening. Consider the sentence <u>John was compelled to be bribed by Harry</u>. It has the following deep structure:

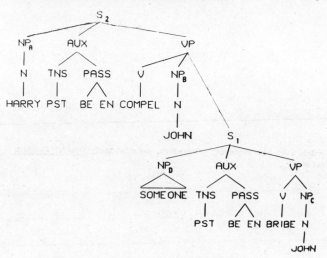

D.S. of <u>John was compelled to be bribed by Harry</u>.

Q. What must happen on S_1?
A. <u>Passive</u> must apply because the constituent Passive is in the auxiliary of S_1.

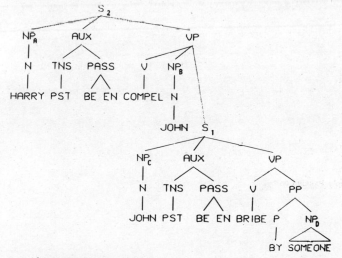

After <u>Passive</u> has applied on S_1.

Q. Do any other rules apply on S_1?
A. No. We proceed to S_2.
Q. What happens first on the S_2 cycle?
A. <u>Complementizer Placement</u> must apply first. We'll choose <u>for-to</u>.

141

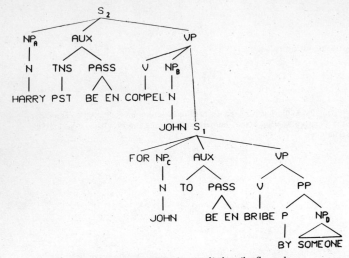

After <u>Complementizer Placement</u> has applied on the S$_2$ cycle.

Q. Can both <u>Equi NP Deletion</u> and <u>Passive</u> apply?
A. Yes. But as was decided on p. 141 , <u>Passive</u> cannot precede <u>Equi NP Deletion</u> within a simplex sentence. Therefore, we must apply <u>Equi NP Deletion</u> (hereafter <u>END</u>) first. NP$_b$ will delete NP$_c$, since NP$_b$ = NP$_c$ and NP$_b$ is closest to NP$_c$.

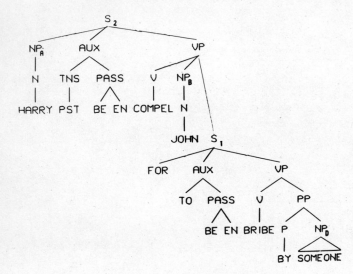

After <u>Equi NP Deletion</u> (<u>END</u>) has applied on the S$_2$ cycle.

Q. Must <u>Passive</u> now apply on S$_2$?
A. Yes, since there is a constituent <u>Passive</u> in the auxiliary of S$_2$, we must apply <u>Passive</u> on S$_2$.

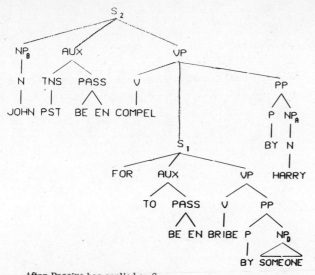

After _Passive_ has applied on S$_2$.

Q. What happens now?

A. _Complementizer Deletion_ must apply, since we have _for-to_ complementizers.

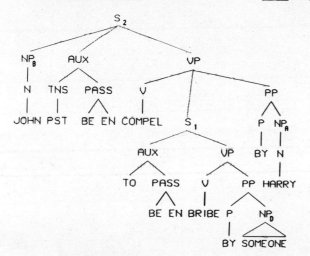

After _Complementizer Deletion_ has applied on the S$_2$ cycle.

Q. What do we have?

A. After _Affix Hopping_ and _Agent Deletion_ we will have _John was compelled to be bribed by Harry_. This illustrates the order:

  Passive (on S$_1$)

  Equi NP Deletion (on S$_2$)

  Passive (on S$_2$)

END, Passive, END

We will now give a derivation where the ordering must be:

  END

  Passive

  END

Consider the sentence _Tom resented being forced to dress by his mother_. It has the following D.S.:

143

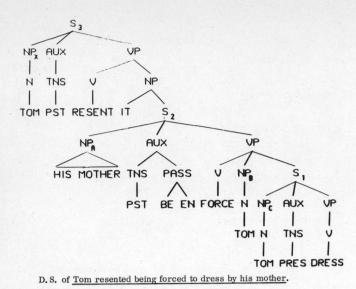

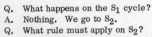

D. S. of <u>Tom resented being forced to dress by his mother</u>.

We start with the most deeply embedded S, as usual.

Q. What happens on the S_1 cycle?
A. Nothing. We go to S_2.
Q. What rule must apply on S_2?
A. <u>Complementizer Placement</u> must apply. We will choose <u>for-to</u>.

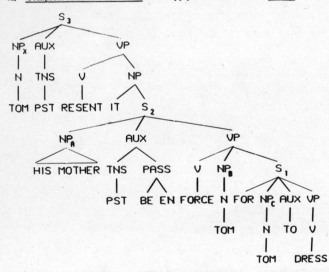

After <u>Complementizer Placement</u> has applied on the S_2 cycle.

Q. Can both <u>END</u> and <u>Passive</u> apply on the S_2 cycle?
A. Yes, but as we saw on p.141 , within a simplex sentence, <u>Passive</u> may not precede <u>END</u>. Therefore, <u>END</u> must apply first on S_2. NP_b in S_2 = NP_c in S_1, so NP_b will cause NP_c to be deleted.

144

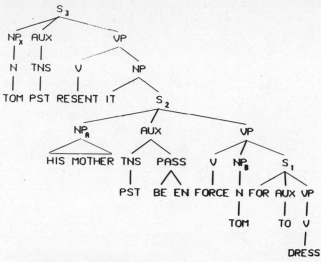

After <u>END</u> has applied on the S_2 cycle.

Q. Must <u>Passive</u> now apply on S_2?

A. Yes. The auxiliary of S_2 contains <u>Passive</u>, so we must apply <u>Passive</u> on S_2.

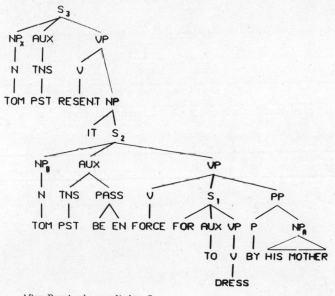

After <u>Passive</u> has applied on S_2.

No other rules will apply on the S_2 cycle. We proceed to S_3.

Q. What rule must apply first on S_3?

A. <u>Complementizer Placement</u> must apply first. This time, we'll take <u>poss-ing</u>.

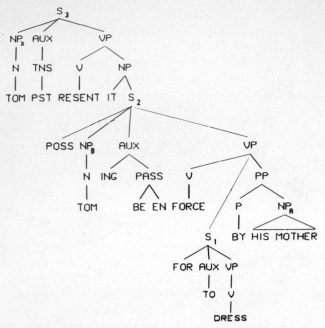

After <u>Complementizer Placement</u> has applied on the S_3 cycle in S_2.

Q. Does <u>END</u> apply?
A. Yes. NP_x in S_3 = NP_b in S_2. So NP_x will cause NP_b to be deleted by <u>END</u>.

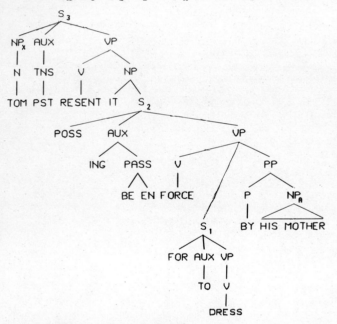

After <u>END</u> has applied on the S_3 cycle.

Q. Does <u>Passive</u> now apply on S_3?
A. No. There is no constituent <u>Passive</u> in the auxiliary of S_3.
Q. What rule must now apply on the S_3 cycle?
A. <u>Complementizer Deletion</u> must apply now.

146

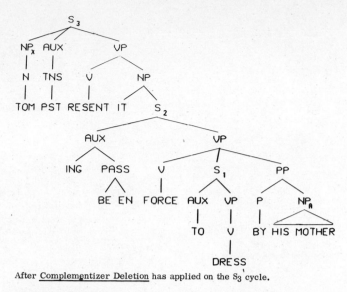

After <u>Complementizer Deletion</u> has applied on the S₃ cycle.

Q. What will this give us?

A. After <u>Affix Hopping</u> we will have <u>Tom resented being forced to dress by his mother</u>. This derivation has shown that the order of <u>Passive</u> and <u>END</u> in this case is:

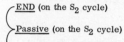

<u>END</u> (on the S₂ cycle)

<u>Passive</u> (on the S₂ cycle)

<u>END</u> (on the S₃ cycle)

Passive, END, Passive, END, Passive

So far, we have shown a case in which <u>Passive</u> in S₁ must precede <u>END</u> in S₂ (pp. 137-138), decided that <u>Passive</u> cannot precede <u>END</u> (within a simplex S, p.141), shown a case in which <u>Passive</u> has applied twice with other rules intervening between the two applications (namely <u>Complementizer Placement</u> and <u>END</u>) (pp.141-143), and a case in which <u>END</u> has applied twice with another rule intervening between the two applications (pp.143-147). Now, we can easily complicate these last two cases to show three applications of the same rule, in which another rule intervenes between the first and second application and between the second and third application of the rule. First, we will show a derivation in which the rules apply in the order:

<u>Passive</u>

<u>END</u>

<u>Passive</u>

<u>END</u>

<u>Passive</u>

Then we will show a derivation in which they must apply in such an order that <u>Passive</u> intervenes between each pair of applications of <u>END</u>, i.e.

<u>END</u>

<u>Passive</u>

<u>END</u>

<u>Passive</u>

<u>END</u>

Consider the following sentence: <u>Tiny Tim was persuaded to be bribed to be searched</u>, which has the following deep structure:

147

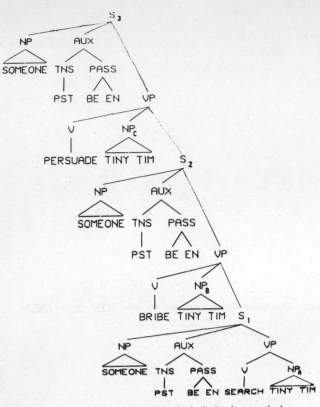

D. S. of <u>Tiny Tim was persuaded to be bribed to be searched</u>.

Q. What can happen on S_1?
A. Only <u>Passive</u> can apply on S_1. NP_a will be moved to the front of S_1.

Rules which have applied:

<u>Passive</u> (on S_1)

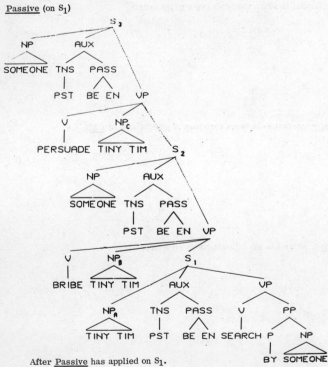

After <u>Passive</u> has applied on S_1.

Since nothing else happens on S_1, we go to S_2.

Q. What rule must apply first on the S_2 cycle?

A. <u>Complementizer Placement</u>. We will choose <u>for-to</u>.

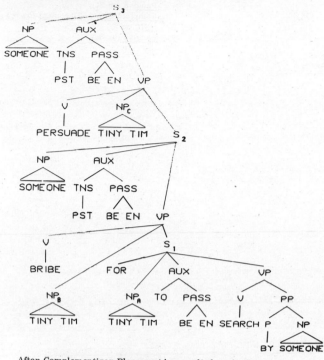

After <u>Complementizer Placement</u> has applied on the S_2 cycle.

Q. Can both <u>END</u> and <u>Passive</u> apply on the S_2 cycle?

A. Yes. But as was decided on p. 141 , <u>Passive</u> cannot precede <u>END</u> within a simplex sentence. Therefore, since both these rules are applicable on S_2, we must apply END first. Since NP_b = NP_a and since NP_b is the closest to NP_a, NP_a will be deleted.

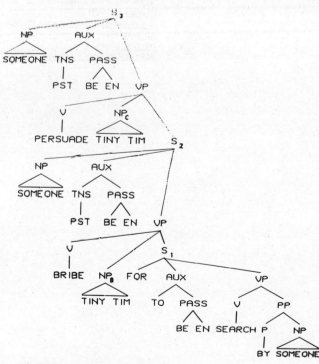

After <u>END</u> has applied on the S_2 cycle.

Q. Must <u>Passive</u> now apply on the S_2 cycle?

A. Yes, because the auxiliary of S_2 has a <u>Passive</u> constituent in it, <u>Passive</u> must apply, i.e., NP_b will move to the front of S_2.

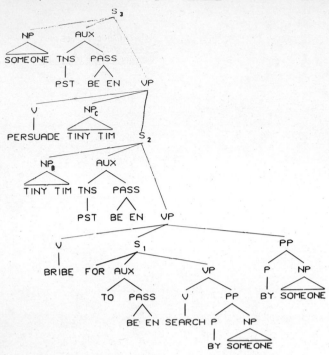

After <u>Passive</u> has applied on S_2.

Nothing else happens on the S_2 cycle. (The order of the two rules of <u>END</u> and <u>Passive</u> so far is given above, to the right of the tree.) We proceed to S_3.

Q. What happens first?

A. We place complementizers first. They will again be <u>for-to</u>.

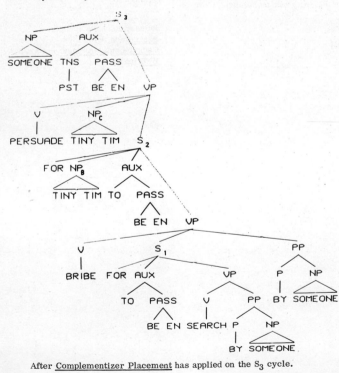

After <u>Complementizer Placement</u> has applied on the S_3 cycle.

Q. Can both <u>END</u> and <u>Passive</u> apply?

150

A. Yes, but as was decided on p.141 , within a simplex sentence, <u>Passive</u> cannot precede <u>END</u>. Therefore, on the S_3 cycle, <u>END</u> must apply first. Since NP_c in S_3 is the closest NP to NP_b (in S_2), and $NP_c = NP_b$, NP_b will be deleted by <u>END</u>.

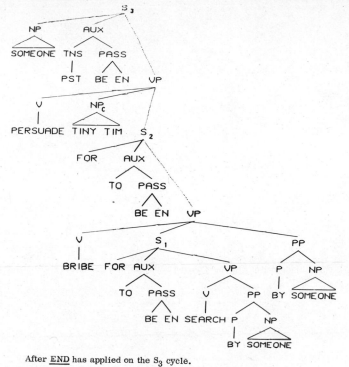

Rules which have applied:
<u>Passive</u> (on S_1)
<u>Complementizer Placement</u> (on S_2)
<u>END</u> (on S_2)
<u>Passive</u> (on S_2)
<u>Complementizer Placement</u> (on S_3)
<u>END</u> (on S_3)

After <u>END</u> has applied on the S_3 cycle.

Q. Must <u>Passive</u> now apply on S_3?
A. Yes. There is a <u>Passive</u> auxiliary in S_3, so <u>Passive</u> must apply, that is, NP_c will be moved to the front of S_3.

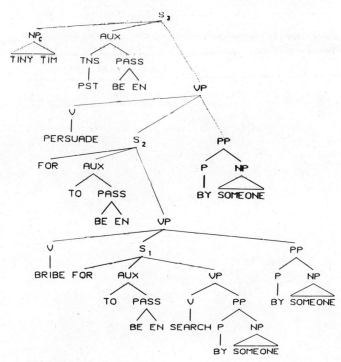

Rules which have applied:
<u>Passive</u> (on S_1)
<u>Complementizer Placement</u> (on S_2)
<u>END</u> (on S_2)
<u>Passive</u> (on S_2)
<u>Complementizer Placement</u> (on S_3)
<u>END</u> (on S_3)
<u>Passive</u> (on S_3)

After <u>Passive</u> has applied on S_3.

Q. What must happen now?
A. <u>Complementizer Deletion</u> must apply, and <u>Agent Deletion</u> may. We will apply both.

151

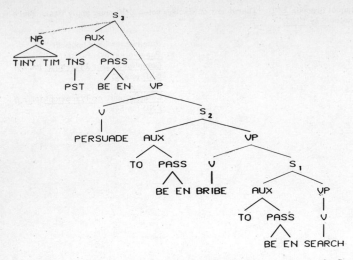

After <u>Complementizer Deletion</u> and <u>Agent Deletion</u> have applies on the S$_3$ cycle.

Q. What do we have?
A. After <u>Affix Hopping</u> we have <u>Tiny Tim was persuaded to be bribed to be searched</u>. The order of <u>END</u> and <u>Passive</u> in this example, as given above, is:

<u>Passive</u>

<u>END</u>

<u>Passive</u>

<u>END</u>

<u>Passive</u>

END, Passive, END, Passive, END

We also can show a case where <u>END</u> must apply at three different times, with two applications of <u>Passive</u> sandwiched in between. Consider this sentence:
<u>Pete imagined being bribed to be persuaded to kiss Liberace</u>, which has the following deep structure:

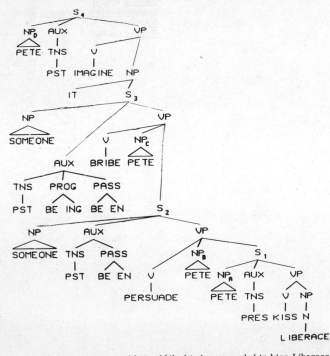

D. S. of <u>Peter imagined being bribed to be persuaded to kiss Liberace</u>.

Q. What can happen on S_1?

A. Nothing. Complementizer Placement and END both require two sentences, and Passive cannot apply because there is no Passive auxiliary in S_1. We proceed to S_2.

Q. What must apply first on S_2?

A. Complementizer Placement. We will choose for-to.

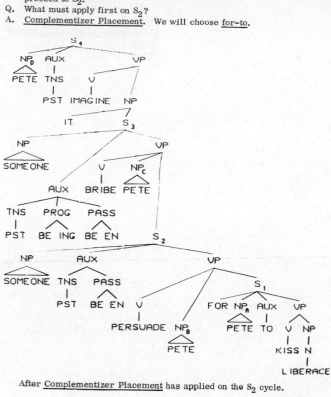

After Complementizer Placement has applied on the S_2 cycle.

As in the previous example, the rules will be listed to the right of the tree in their order of application, as we apply them.

Q. Must END apply on S_2?

A. Yes. Note NP_b in S_2 = NP_a in S_1, and that NP_b is the NP closest to NP_a, so NP_b will cause NP_a to be deleted by END.

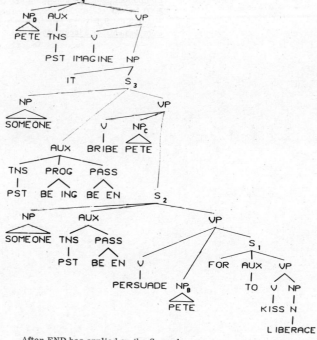

After END has applied on the S_2 cycle.

Q. Must <u>Passive</u> apply on S_2?

A. Yes, since the constituent <u>Passive</u> is in the auxiliary of S_2. NP_b will move to the front of S_2, and the subject NP <u>someone</u> of S_2 will be prefixed by the preposition <u>by</u> and daughter-adjoined[2] to the right of the verb in S_2.

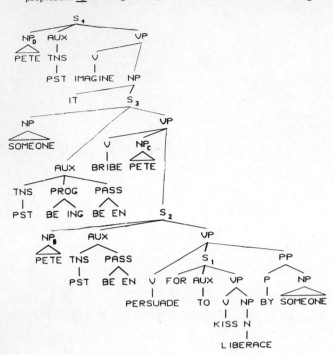

Rules which have applied:
Complementizer Placement (on S_2)
<u>END</u> (on S_2)
<u>Passive</u> (on S_2)

After <u>Passive</u> has applied on S_2.

Q. Does anything else happen on S_2?

A. No. We go to S_3. Going through out list of cyclic rules again (on p. 137), we first come to <u>Complementizer Placement</u>.

Q. Must <u>Complementizer Placement</u> apply on the S_3 cycle?

A. Yes. We will take <u>for-to</u> again.

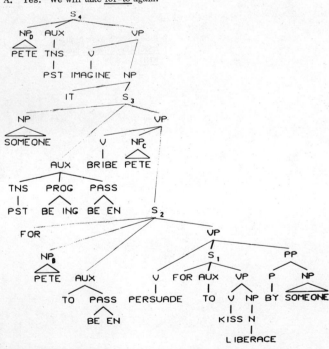

Rules which have applied:
Complementizer Placement (on S_2)
<u>END</u> (on S_2)
<u>Passive</u> (on S_2)
Complementizer Placement (on S_3)

After <u>Complementizer Placement</u> has applied on the S_3 cycle.

[2]When an element is "daughter-adjoined" it will be "immediately dominated" by the same node to which it is daughter-adjoined.

164

Q. Must END apply on S₃?

A. Yes. NP_c in S_3 = NP_b in S_2, and NP_c is the closest NP to NP_b. In END, NP_b will be deleted by NP_c.

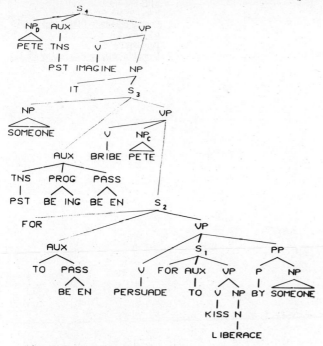

Rules which have applied:
Complementizer Placement (on S_2)
END (on S_2)
Passive (on S_2)
Complementizer Placement (on S_3)
END (on S_3)

After END has applied on the S₃ cycle.

Q. Must Passive apply on the S₃ cycle?

A. Yes. There is a Passive auxiliary in S_3, so Passive must apply. NP_c in S_3 will move to the front of S_3, and the subject NP someone in S_3 will be prefixed by the preposition by and attached to the verb of S_3.

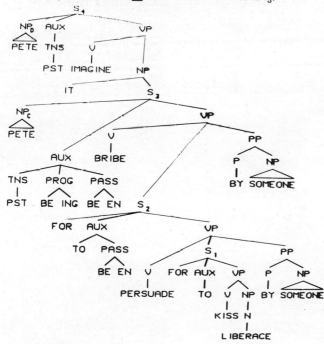

Rules which have applied:
Complementizer Placement (on S_2)
END (on S_2)
Passive (on S_2)
Complementizer Placement (on S_3)
END (on S_3)
Passive (on S_3)

After Passive has applied on S₃.

Nothing else will happen on the S₃ cycle. We proceed to S₄, and the top of our list of cyclic rules (p. 137).

Q. Must Complementizer Placement apply on the S₄ cycle?

A. Yes. And once more, we will have for-to.

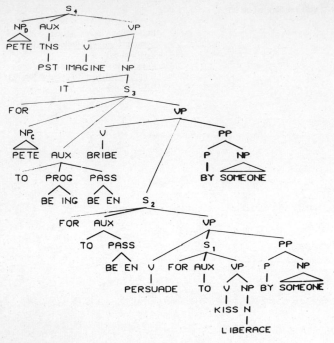

Rules which have applied:
Complementizer Placement (on S_2)
END (on S_2)
Passive (on S_2)
Complementizer Placement (on S_3)
END (on S_3)
Passive (on S_3)
Complementizer Placement (on S_4)

After for-to complements have been placed on the S_4 cycle.

Q. We now come to END. Must it apply on S_4?

A. Yes. Note NP_d of S_4 = NP_c of S_3, and NP_d is the NP closest to NP_c, so NP_d in S_4 will delete NP_c in S_3 when END applies on S_4.

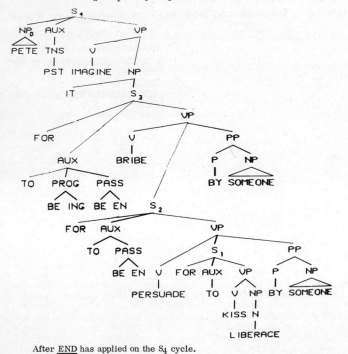

Rules which have applied:
Complementizer Placement (on S_2)
END (on S_2)
Passive (on S_2)
Complementizer Placement (on S_3)
END (on S_3)
Passive (on S_3)
Complementizer Placement (on S_4)
END (on S_4)

After END has applied on the S_4 cycle.

Q. We now come to Passive. Must Passive apply on the S_4 cycle?

A. No. There is no constituent Passive in the auxiliary of S_4, so Passive cannot apply there.

Q. What other rule must apply on S_4?

A. It-Deletion must apply because an it directly precedes an S (S_3) within an NP.

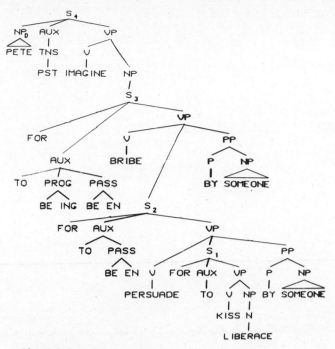

After It-Deletion has applied on S_4.

Q. What sentence do we have?
A. After Complementizer Deletion, Agent Deletion, and Affix Hopping we have Pete imagined being bribed to be persuaded to kiss Liberace.

The Cycle Principle

Ignoring irrelevant rules(such as It-Deletion and Preposition Deletion), we have just shown (pp. 152 –156) the ordering of END and Passive to be:

Complementizer Placement (S_2)
END (S_2)
Passive (S_2)
Complementizer Placement (S_3)
END (S_3)
Passive (S_3)
Complementizer Placement (S_4)
END (S_4)

On pp. 147-152, we had an example illustrating the other ordering, in which Passive sandwiched END:

Passive (S_1)
Complementizer Placement (S_2)
END (S_2)
Passive (S_2)
Complementizer Placement (S_3)
END (S_3)
Passive (S_3)

Clearly, this process can be extended indefinitely. Thus, if we assume a theory which allows only a linear ordering of rules, we must have an infinite number of Passive rules and an infinite number of END and Complementizer Placement rules. In other words, assuming only the existence of linearly ordered rules, we could never bring our list to an end, so we could not state the number of possible applications of these rules. This would seem to contradict what proponents of linearly ordered rules consider fundamental, namely, that grammars are finite. Clearly, if one cannot list the number of possible applications of linearly ordered rules (since, as we have just illustrated, certain rules may reapply indefinitely), the grammar is not finite, after all. It is therefore impossible to maintain any position which allows only for rules to be linearly ordered. Because it was senseless to maintain this contradictory position, it was necessary to find another solution for the problem of infinite reapplication of certain rules. This solution is the "cycle." The cycle is a finite list of rules which reapplies indefinitely to a tree. This is exactly what happened from pp. 147-152 and pp. 152 –156. We will use these illustrations again to explain what we mean by "cycle."

First, we will go through the derivation presented from pp. 147-152. We had the following deep structure (ignoring irrelevant details) on p. 148:

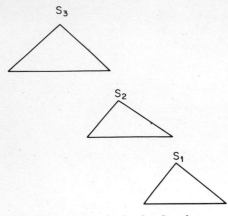

and the following list of ordered cyclic rules:

    <u>Complementizer Placement</u>

    <u>END</u>

    <u>Passive</u>

    <u>Reflexive</u>

    <u>Extraposition</u>

    <u>It-Deletion</u>

    <u>Preposition Deletion</u>

    <u>Complementizer Deletion</u>

We started with the most deeply embedded S (the one which has no others embedded in it, S_1). Of our list of ordered cyclic rules given, only <u>Passive</u> was applicable, so we had to apply it (p. 148):[3]

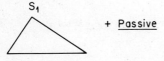

+ Passive

Since no other rules in the list were applicable, we went to the second most deeply embedded S (S_2). We then started at the top of our list of rules again. The first rule we came to that had to apply on S_2 was <u>Complementizer Placement</u> (p. 149).

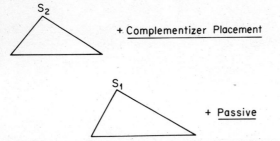

+ Complementizer Placement

+ Passive

Next, we came to <u>END</u>, which was applicable, and therefore had to apply (p. 149):

[3]Since we have already gone through the cycle (the ordered list of rules above) on S_1 and since no more cyclic rules will apply to it, we will list the names of the rules that applied on the cycle in question to the right of the tree (and other finished S's later) to show how the cycle progresses from the most deeply embedded S (S_1) upward.

158

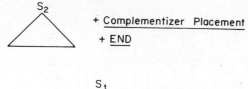

+ <u>Complementizer Placement</u>
+ <u>END</u>

+ <u>Passive</u>

We then came to <u>Passive</u>, which was also applicable and had to apply to S₂ (p. 150):

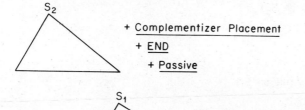

+ <u>Complementizer Placement</u>
+ <u>END</u>
+ <u>Passive</u>

+ <u>Passive</u>

None of the other rules on our list were applicable to S₂, so we continued to S₃. Starting with our list again, the first rule to apply was <u>Complementizer Placement</u> (p. 150):

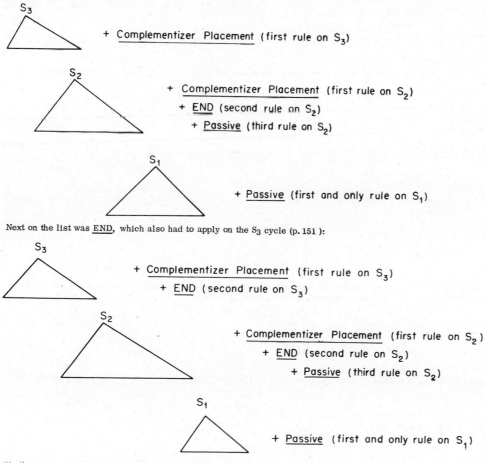

+ <u>Complementizer Placement</u> (first rule on S₃)

+ <u>Complementizer Placement</u> (first rule on S₂)
+ <u>END</u> (second rule on S₂)
+ <u>Passive</u> (third rule on S₂)

+ <u>Passive</u> (first and only rule on S₁)

Next on the list was <u>END</u>, which also had to apply on the S₃ cycle (p. 151):

+ <u>Complementizer Placement</u> (first rule on S₃)
+ <u>END</u> (second rule on S₃)

+ <u>Complementizer Placement</u> (first rule on S₂)
+ <u>END</u> (second rule on S₂)
+ <u>Passive</u> (third rule on S₂)

+ <u>Passive</u> (first and only rule on S₁)

We then came to <u>Passive</u>, which also had to apply on S₃ (p. 151):

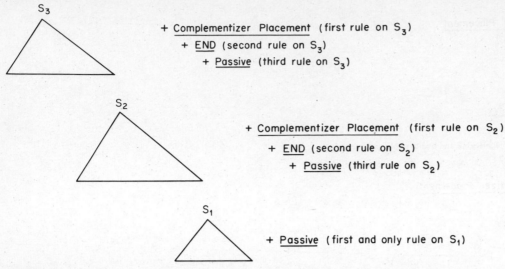

+ Complementizer Placement (first rule on S_3)

   + <u>END</u> (second rule on S_3)

      + <u>Passive</u> (third rule on S_3)

+ <u>Complementizer Placement</u> (first rule on S_2)

   + <u>END</u> (second rule on S_2)

      + <u>Passive</u> (third rule on S_2)

+ <u>Passive</u> (first and only rule on S_1)

Other rules which applied are not relevant to our present discussion.

What we see now is that the same ordered block of eight rules (we will add a few more later) has applied to each sentence. The finite group of rules reapplying in this fashion, from the most deeply embedded S upward, comprises the cycle. In this derivation, the order of <u>END</u> and <u>Passive</u> (which are a part of the cycle), was as follows:

<u>Passive</u> (S_1)
<u>Complementizer Placement</u> (S_2)
<u>END</u> (S_2)
<u>Passive</u> (S_2)
<u>Complementizer Placement</u> (S_3)
<u>END</u> (S_3)
<u>Passive</u> (S_3)

We will now briefly illustrate the ordering of rules within the cycle as it was discussed in the derivation on pp. $\overline{152\text{-}156}$. We started with the following structure (irrelevant details aside) on p. 152:

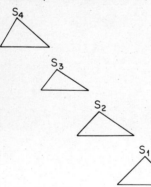

and the list of ordered rules which were given on p. 158. Again, we started with the most deeply embedded S (S_1). We began at the top of the list of rules (p. 158), and found that none of these rules were applicable to S_1. So nothing happened on the S_1 cycle (p. 153).

      − (= nothing)

We then proceeded to S_2 and began again at the top of our list of ordered rules. The first rule to apply was <u>Complementizer Placement</u>, which we applied (p. 153):

S_2

    + <u>Complementizer Placement</u> (first rule on S_2)

    − (= nothing)

Next on our list was <u>END</u>, which also had to apply to S_2 (p. 153):

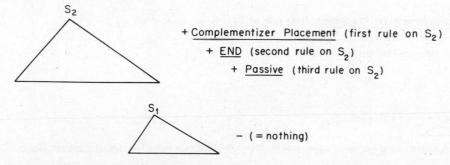

+ <u>Complementizer Placement</u> (first rule on S_2)

  + <u>END</u> (second rule on S_2)

     − (=nothing)

<u>Passive</u> was next on the list, and it also had to apply on S_2 (p. 154):

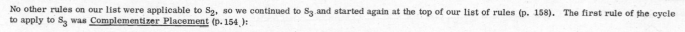

+ <u>Complementizer Placement</u> (first rule on S_2)

  + <u>END</u> (second rule on S_2)

    + <u>Passive</u> (third rule on S_2)

     − (= nothing)

No other rules on our list were applicable to S_2, so we continued to S_3 and started again at the top of our list of rules (p. 158). The first rule of the cycle to apply to S_3 was <u>Complementizer Placement</u> (p. 154):

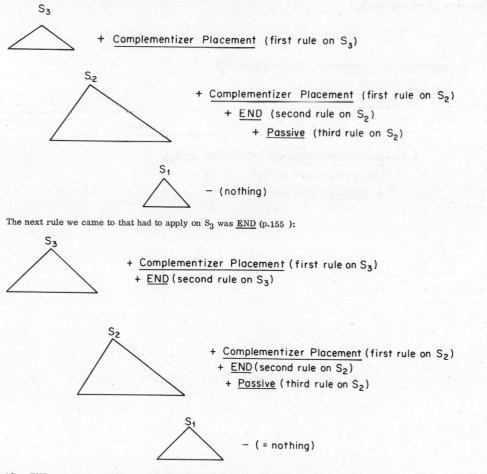

+ <u>Complementizer Placement</u> (first rule on S_3)

+ <u>Complementizer Placement</u> (first rule on S_2)

  + <u>END</u> (second rule on S_2)

    + <u>Passive</u> (third rule on S_2)

     − (nothing)

The next rule we came to that had to apply on S_3 was <u>END</u> (p. 155):

+ <u>Complementizer Placement</u> (first rule on S_3)

 + <u>END</u> (second rule on S_3)

+ <u>Complementizer Placement</u> (first rule on S_2)

 + <u>END</u> (second rule on S_2)

  + <u>Passive</u> (third rule on S_2)

   − (= nothing)

After <u>END</u>, we came to <u>Passive</u>, which also had to apply on the S_3 cycle (p. 155):

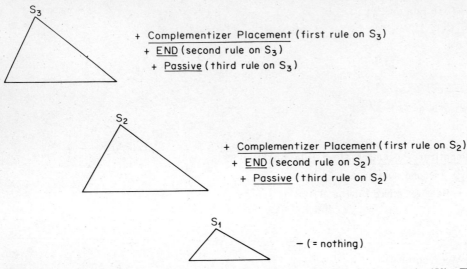

S_3

+ Complementizer Placement (first rule on S_3)
 + <u>END</u> (second rule on S_3)
  + <u>Passive</u> (third rule on S_3)

S_2

+ <u>Complementizer Placement</u> (first rule on S_2)
 + <u>END</u> (second rule on S_2)
  + <u>Passive</u> (third rule on S_2)

S_1

− (= nothing)

No further rules applied on the S_3 cycle, so we sent to S_4 and the top of our list of rules again (p. 158). The first rule on the list, <u>Complementizer Place-</u><u>ment</u>, applied on S_4 (p. 156):

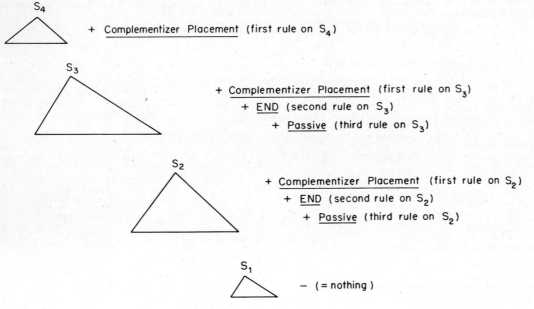

S_4

+ <u>Complementizer Placement</u> (first rule on S_4)

S_3

+ <u>Complementizer Placement</u> (first rule on S_3)
 + <u>END</u> (second rule on S_3)
  + <u>Passive</u> (third rule on S_3)

S_2

+ <u>Complementizer Placement</u> (first rule on S_2)
 + <u>END</u> (second rule on S_2)
  + <u>Passive</u> (third rule on S_2)

S_1

− (= nothing)

The next applicable rule on our list was <u>END</u> (p. 156):

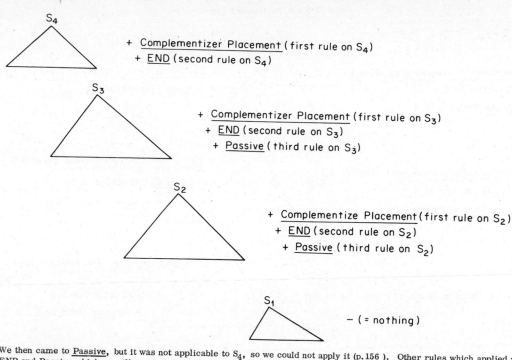

S_4

+ <u>Complementizer Placement</u> (first rule on S_4)
  + <u>END</u> (second rule on S_4)

S_3

+ <u>Complementizer Placement</u> (first rule on S_3)
  + <u>END</u> (second rule on S_3)
   + <u>Passive</u> (third rule on S_3)

S_2

+ <u>Complementize Placement</u> (first rule on S_2)
  + <u>END</u> (second rule on S_2)
   + <u>Passive</u> (third rule on S_2)

S_1

− (= nothing)

We then came to <u>Passive</u>, but it was not applicable to S_4, so we could not apply it (p. 156). Other rules which applied are irrelevant now. The order of <u>END</u> and <u>Passive</u> which was illustrated in the derivation of pp. 152-156 and repeated here is as follows:

_ _ (S_1)
<u>Complementizer Placement</u> (S_2)
<u>END</u> (S_2)
<u>Passive</u> (S_2)
<u>Complementizer Placement</u> (S_3)
<u>END</u> (S_3)
<u>Passive</u> (S_3)
<u>Complementizer Placement</u> (S_4)
<u>END</u> (S_4)

Again, the cycle (i.e., the ordered block of eight rules which includes <u>Complementizer Placement</u>, <u>END</u>, and <u>Passive</u>) has applied on each S, starting with the most deeply embedded S and working upward. Now, what can we say about the ordering of <u>END</u> and <u>Passive</u> with respect to each other in these derivations? From pp. 147-152 we showed that <u>Passive</u> applied before <u>END</u>, and from pp. 152-156 we showed <u>END</u> precedes <u>Passive</u>. Let us compare the two structures we have completed:

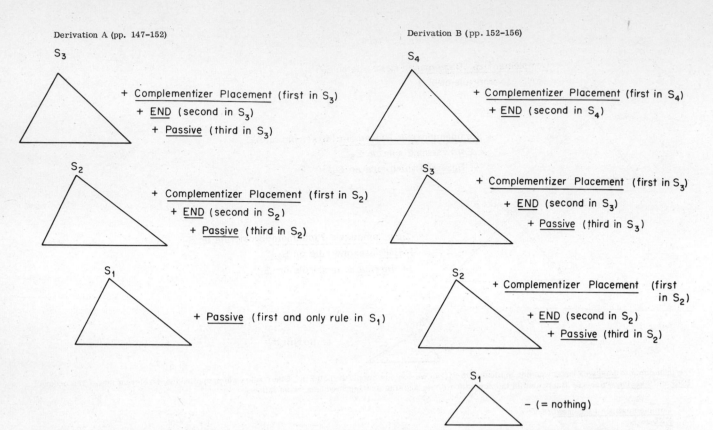

To determine the ordering of any number of cyclic rules, we must first find a "simplex" sentence where all the rules (whose order we are trying to establish) apply. In our case, the three rules whose order we are trying to establish all appear in S_2, and also in S_3, of Derivation A, and all three also apply on S_2, and again on S_3, in Derivation B. As soon as we find a "simplex" sentence (in Derivations A and B, S_1, S_2, S_3, and S_4 are each simplex sentences) in which all cyclic rules (whose order we wish to determine) apply, we look to see what the order of these rules is within that simplex sentence.

Q. In Derivation A, is the simplex S_1 a candidate for trying to establish the order of our three rules, Complementizer Placement, END, and Passive?
A. No.
Q. Why not?
A. Because only one rule, Passive, applies in S_1. To determine the ordering of our three cyclic rules within a simplex sentence, all three rules must apply. Since only one rule applies on S_1 in Derivation A, S_1 cannot help us determine the order of three rules.
Q. Again, in Derivation A, can S_2 help us determine the order of our three rules?
A. Yes.
Q. Why?
A. Because all three rules apply on S_2.
Q. What is the order of the three rules within the simplex S_2?
A. As on pp. 149-150 , the order is:

S_2

Complementizer Placement

END

Passive

Q. Can S_3 of Derivation A help us determine the order of the three rules?
A. Yes.
Q. Why?
A. For the same reasons as given for S_2 of Derivation A. Namely, three rules apply on the simplex S_3, and they are just the rules whose ordering is at stake.
Q. How are these three rules ordered within S_3?
A. Just as they were ordered in S_2 in Derivation A:

Complementizer Placement

END

Passive

Now let us look at Derivation B.

Q. Can S_1 in Derivation B help us determine the order of our rules?

164

A. No. Since nothing happens on S_1, it is difficult for S_1 to have much to say in the way of ordering rules.

Q. How about S_2 in Derivation B?

A. Yes. Here three rules apply, and they happen to be the rules with whose ordering we are concerned.

Q. What is the ordering within the simplex S_2 of Derivation B?

A. Just as in S_2 and S_3 of Derivation A, the ordering within S_2 of Derivation B is:

Complementizer Placement

END

Passive

Q. What about S_3 in Derivation B?

A. All three rules again apply within S_3.

Q. What is their order?

A. Their order is:

Complementizer Placement

END

Passive

Q. What about S_4 in Derivation B?

A. The first two rules apply, but since we are trying to establish the order of three rules, two are not enough. Therefore, S_4 in Derivation B is disqualified.

We see in every case where all three rules apply within a simplex S (S_2 and S_3 in Derivation A, and S_2 and S_3 in Derivation B) that their order is always:

Complementizer Placement

END

Passive

Therefore, this is the order of these three rules within the cycle (the ordered list of cyclic rules which reapply to a tree), starting with the most deeply embedded S and working upward through the entire tree, until there are no more sentences to be processed.

It-Replacement

The next rule we will present is It-Replacement. First, let us look at the deep structure of the sentence It is likely that John will blab.

Ordering of rules:

Complementizer Placement

END

Passive

Reflexive

Extraposition

It-Deletion

Preposition Deletion

Complementizer Deletion

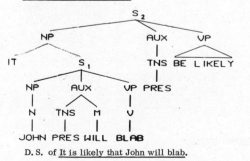

D.S. of It is likely that John will blab.

Q. What are the possible sentences we can derive from this structure with the cyclic rules (list at top) we know so far?

A. We will try some of the possibilities.

Q. What happens on the S_1 cycle?

A. No rules in our list can apply on S_1. We go to S_2.
Q. What rule applies first?
A. The first one on the list, <u>Complementizer Placement</u>, applies. We will choose a <u>that</u> complementizer.

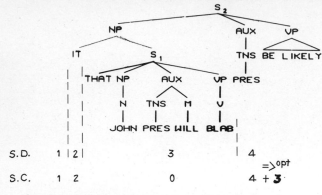

S.D.   1 |2| 3 | 4
$$\Longrightarrow \text{opt}$$
S.C.   1 2   0   4 + **3**

After <u>Complementizer Placement</u> has applied on the S_2 cycle.

Q. We continue down the list to <u>END</u>. Can it apply?
A. No. There are no two identical NP's between S_2 and S_1.
Q. Can <u>Passive</u> apply?
A. No. There is no <u>Passive</u> constituent anywhere.
Q. Can <u>Reflexive</u> apply?
A. No. There are no two identical NP's within the S.
Q. Can <u>Extraposition</u> apply?
A. Yes, optionally. Let us apply this rule. (The tree has been analyzed to undergo <u>Extraposition</u>.)

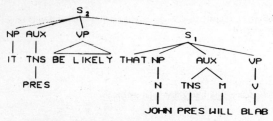

After <u>Extraposition</u> has applied on the S_2 cycle.

Q. Can <u>It-Deletion</u> apply?
A. No. The <u>it</u> in S_2 is no longer before an S (since S_1 has been moved away by <u>Extraposition</u>), so <u>It-Deletion</u> can't apply.
Q. Will any other rules apply?
A. Only <u>Affix Hopping</u>.
Q. What S do we have, then?
A. <u>It is likely that John will blab</u>.
Q. What would we have had without <u>Extraposition</u>, but with <u>It-Deletion</u>?
A. <u>That John will blab is likely</u>. Consider again the same D.S. as on p. 165 again:

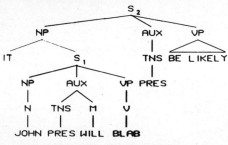

D.S. of <u>It is likely that John will blab</u>.

Q. Which rules (of our list on p. 165) will apply to S_1?
A. Just as before, none. We go to S_2 and the top of our list of rules again.
Q. What must apply first on S_2?
A. <u>Complementizer Placement</u>. This time we will choose <u>for-to</u>. (Note that the to replaces both <u>Tns</u> and <u>Modal</u>.)

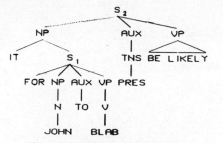

After <u>Complementizer Placement</u> has applied on the S$_2$ cycle.

As before, <u>END</u>, <u>Passive</u>, and <u>Reflexive</u> are not applicable on S$_2$.

Q.   Can <u>Extraposition</u> apply?
A.   Yes, optionally. We will apply it.

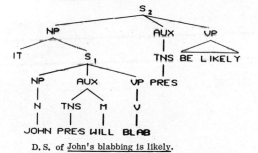

After <u>Extraposition</u> has applied on the S$_2$ cycle.

No other rules will apply except <u>Affix Hopping</u>.

Q.   What S do we have?
A.   <u>It is likely for John to blab</u>.
Q.   If we had not applied <u>Extraposition</u> and had applied <u>It–Deletion</u>, what S would we have?
A.   After <u>Affix Hopping</u> we would have <u>For John to blab is likely</u>. Once more, consider the deep structure of p. 165.

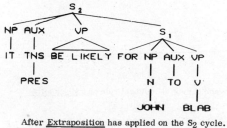

D. S. of <u>John's blabbing is likely</u>.

As before, no rules apply on the S$_1$ cycle. We go to S$_2$.

Q.   Must the first rule on our list (p. 165), <u>Complementizer Placement</u>, apply?
A.   Yes. This time, we will have <u>poss-ing</u>.

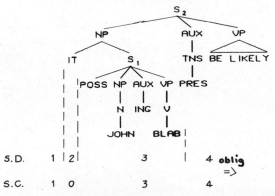

S.D.	1	2		3		4 oblig
						=>
S.C.	1	0		3		4

After <u>Complementizer Placement</u> has applied on the S$_2$ cycle.

END, Passive, and Reflexive do not apply for the reasons given on p. 166.   Next is Extraposition.

Q.   Can Extraposition apply?
A.   No.   Never with poss-ing complementizers.   If we applied Extraposition, we would get *It is likely John's blabbing (with no pause between likely and John's).
Q.   Next is It-Deletion.   Must it apply?
A.   Yes, because an it directly precedes an S (S$_2$) within an NP.   (The tree has been analyzed to undergo It-Deletion.)

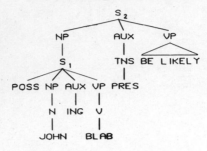

          After It-Deletion has applied on S$_2$.

No other rules except Affix Hopping will apply.

Q.   What S do we have?
A.   We have John's blabbing is likely, which, though not the best, is not the worst, either.

From one D.S. then (p. 165), we have been able to derive at least five sentences by changing complements and having the optional rule of Extraposition apply or not apply.   They are:

    It is likely that John will blab (+ that complementizer, + Extraposition, – It-Deletion)
    That John will blab is likely (+ that complementizer, – Extraposition, + It-Deletion)
    For John to blab is likely (+ for-to complementizers, + It-Deletion, – Extraposition)
    It is likely for John to blab (+ for-to complementizers, + Extraposition, – It-Deletion)
    ?John's blabbing is likely (+ poss-ing complementizers, – Extraposition, + It-Deletion)

(Again, a "+" means the rule applied, and a "–" means the rule did not apply.)
Now, how can we get the obviously related sentence John is certain to blab?   Let's start off with the same deep structure as on p. 165.

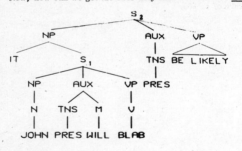

          D.S. of John is likely to blab.

On S$_1$, no rules apply.   We go to S$_2$.

Q.   What happens on S$_2$?
A.   First Complementizer Placement must apply.   We'll use for-to.

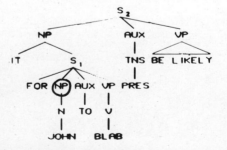

          After Complementizer Placement has applied on the S$_2$ cycle.

Q.   What now?
A.   As before, END, Passive, and Reflexive are not applicable.   However, if we go on to Extraposition, we will get only the sentences above.

Q. How can we get the S <u>John is likely to blab</u>?

A. There is an operation called <u>It-Replacement</u>,[4] which does the following for a certain class of verbs: The subject NP of our S_1 (circled) will move up to replace the subject NP it in S_2, and the remainder of S_1 will be daughter-adjoined to the VP of S_2. This works as follows:

Ordering of rules:

<u>Complementizer Placement</u>

<u>END</u>

<u>It-Replacement</u>

<u>Passive</u>

<u>Reflexive</u>

<u>Extraposition</u>

<u>It-Deletion</u>[5]

<u>Preposition Deletion</u>

<u>Complementizer Deletion</u>

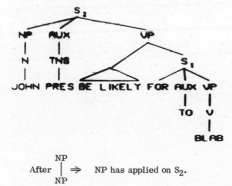

After It-Replacement has applied on the S_2 cycle.

Note first that we have two identical nodes over each other (they are circled). Whenever we have a double node like this, one will be wiped out by a convention in the grammar. The results of this convention are shown below.

After $\begin{array}{c} NP \\ | \\ NP \end{array} \Rightarrow$ NP has applied on S_2.

In the remaining examples of the rule <u>It-Replacement</u>, we will assume that this convention has already applied. We will not state the S. D. for <u>It-Replace</u>ment because it is complicated, and it is much simpler merely to illustrate what happens to a structure when <u>It-Replacement</u> applies to it, as we have done. One fact about this operation is clear, however. Since <u>It-Replacement</u> is concerned with the subject NP of the lower S, and since parts of that lower S are attached to the next higher S, we must have at least one embedded sentence present if we wish to apply this rule. This means, then, that like <u>Complementizer Placement</u> and <u>END</u>, <u>It-Replacement</u> can never apply on the most deeply embedded sentence.

Q. What are some other verbs that undergo <u>It-Replacement</u>?

A. A special group of intransitive verbs and adjectives.

[4]Rosenbaum (<u>Grammar</u>) proposes a rule with a similar operation, which he calls <u>Pronoun Replacement</u>.
[5]We have placed <u>It-Replacement</u> between <u>END</u> and <u>Passive</u>, a decision we will justify later.

Be likely, be certain, happen, turn out, appear, and seem are among the adjectives and verbs which undergo It-Replacement. We will illustrate some of these. Consider a sentence like John is certain to find out, which has the following D.S.:

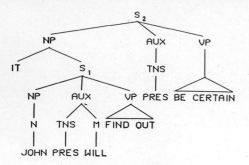

D. S. of John is certain to find out.

Q. Do any rules apply on S_1?
A. No. We go to S_2.
Q. What rule applies first on S_2?
A. Complementizer Placement. Suppose we choose a that complementizer.

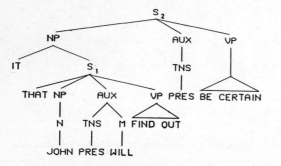

After Complementizer Placement has applied on the S_2 cycle.

Q. Can It-Replacement now apply?
A. Let's try it.

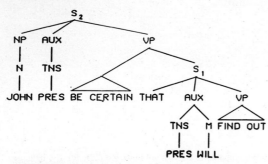

After It-Replacement has applied on the S_2 cycle.

Q. What S do we have?
A. After Affix Hopping, we have the unacceptable *John is certain that will find out. Or, if we deleted the complementizer that, we would have *John is certain that will find out. The unacceptability of these sentences brings out a restriction placed on It-Replacement. Namely, It-Replacement cannot apply with a that complementizer. Clearly then, It-Replacement must follow Complementizer Placement. Let us now reconsider the deep structure given on top of this page.

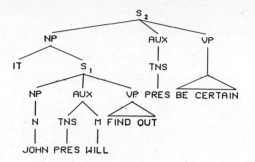

D. S. of <u>John is certain to find out</u>.

Again, on S$_1$, no rules apply. We go to S$_2$.

Q. What happens first on S$_2$?
A. <u>Complementizer Placement</u>. We will use <u>for-to</u> this time.

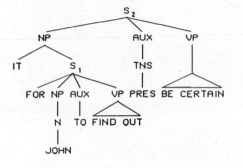

After <u>for-to</u> <u>Complementizer Placement</u> has applied on the S$_2$ cycle.

Q. What rule must we now apply to obtain <u>John is certain to find out</u>?
A. We can apply <u>It-Replacement</u> on the S$_2$ cycle.

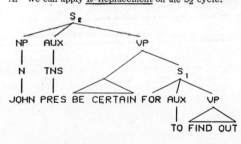

After <u>It-Replacement</u> has applied on the S$_2$ cycle.

Q. Must any other rules apply to this structure?
A. Yes. Since we have <u>for-to</u> complementizers, <u>Complementizer Deletion</u> must apply.

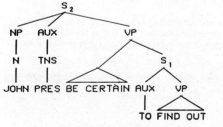

After <u>Complementizer Deletion</u> has applied on the S$_2$ cycle.

Q. What S do we have?
A. After <u>Affix Hopping</u> we have <u>John is certain to find out</u>. Note that if we had bypassed <u>It-Replacement</u> and gone to <u>Extraposition</u> and <u>It-Deletion</u>, all those possibilities given on p. 168 would have been realizable for this structure, also. We will now provide yet another application of <u>It-Replacement</u> in which the clause which undergoes the process of <u>It-Replacement</u> is in the subject position of the higher S.

171

Consider the sentence <u>It seems that John has arisen</u>. It has the following deep structure:

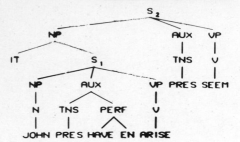

D. S. of <u>It seems that John has arisen</u>.

Q. Do any of our rules (listed to the right of the tree) apply on S_1?
A. No. We go to S_2.
Q. What rule must apply first on the S_2 cycle?
A. The first rule on our list (p. 165), <u>Complementizer Placement</u>. We will choose a <u>that</u> complementizer.

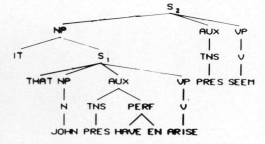

After <u>Complementizer Placement</u> has applied on S_2.

Q. Can <u>It-Replacement</u> apply?
A. No, not with a <u>that</u> complementizer, as was illustrated on p. 170. The next rule on our list that can apply is <u>Extraposition</u>.
Q. We have said before that <u>Extraposition</u> is optional. What happens if we choose not to apply it here with the verb <u>seem</u>?
A. We would eventually have the unacceptable *<u>That John has arisen seems</u>.
Q. What does this mean?
A. With the verb <u>seem</u>, <u>Extraposition</u> is obligatory. There are also some other restrictions on the verb <u>seem</u>, which we will come to shortly. We now apply <u>Extraposition</u>.

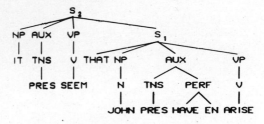

After <u>Extraposition</u> (obligatory with the verb <u>seem</u>) has applied on the S_2 cycle.

Q. What S do we have?
A. After <u>Affix Hopping</u> we have <u>It seems that John has arisen</u>. Note that with <u>Extraposition</u>, the lower S_1 is sister-adjoined[6] to the VP of S_2. (They [the VP of S_2, and S_1] are dominated by the same node, S_2.) With <u>It-Replacement</u>, however, the lower S becomes daughter-adjoined to the VP of the next higher S, as was illustrated on p. 169. Because of the ungrammaticality of the S above, the verb <u>seem</u> will be marked [+ <u>Extraposition</u>] when it has a that complementizer.
Q. What are some other restrictions on the verb <u>seem</u>?
A. The verb <u>seem</u> is restricted in that it cannot take <u>poss-ing</u> complementizers, e.g., *<u>John's having arisen seems</u>. Another restriction is that with <u>for-to</u> complementizers, <u>Extraposition</u> does not apply with <u>seem</u>, e.g., *<u>It seems for John to arise</u>.
Q. What rule must apply, then, when we have <u>for-to</u> complementizers?
A. With <u>for-to</u> complementizers, <u>It-Replacement</u> must apply. Consider the D.S. on p. 172 again:

---

[6]An element is "sister-adjoined" so that it is immediately dominated by the same node which immediately dominates the node to which the element is to be sister-adjoined.

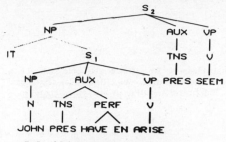

D. S. of <u>John seems to have arisen</u>.

Q. Do any rules apply on S_1?
A. None of the rules we have listed (p. 165) apply. We go to S_2 and the top of our list again.
Q. Must <u>Complementizer Placement</u> apply?
A. Yes. This time we will use <u>for-to</u>.

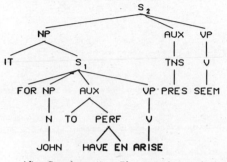

After <u>Complementizer Placement</u> has applied on the S_2 cycle.

Q. Can <u>END</u> apply?
A. No, because there are no two identical NP's between S_2 and S_1. We now come to <u>It-Replacement</u>.
Q. Does <u>It-Replacement</u> apply?
A. Yes. As was just noted, with <u>for-to</u> complementizers <u>It-Replacement</u> will apply.

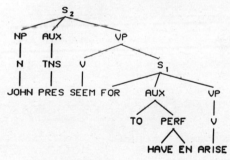

After <u>It-Replacement</u> has applied on the S_2 cycle.

Q. What other rule on our list must apply?
A. <u>Complementizer Deletion</u> must apply, because we have <u>for-to</u> complementizers.

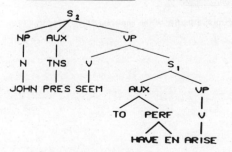

After <u>Complementizer Deletion</u> has applied on the S_2 cycle.

Q. What S do we have?

A. After <u>Affix Hopping</u> we have <u>John seems to have arisen</u>. The grammaticality of this S and the ungrammaticality of the one given on p. 172 show that with <u>for-to</u> complementizers, <u>It-Replacement</u>, and not <u>Extraposition</u>, must apply.

<u>It-Replacement</u> in Object Position and <u>Know</u>

So far, we have considered how <u>It-Replacement</u> operates with verbs and adjectives whose subject NP's contain clauses. We will now give some examples to show how <u>It-Replacement</u> works with transitive verbs when the clauses to which <u>It-Replacement</u> applies are in object position. We will consider sentences containing transitive verbs such as <u>know</u>, <u>want</u>, <u>believe</u>, and <u>expect</u>, all of which undergo <u>It-Replacement</u>. The first S we will derive is <u>I know this to be false</u>, which has the following deep structure:

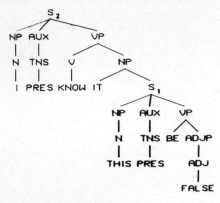

 D. S. of <u>I know this to be false</u>.

Q. Do any rules apply on S_1?
A. No. We go to S_2.
Q. First on our list is <u>Complementizer Placement</u>. Must it apply?
A. Yes. We will use <u>for-to</u>.

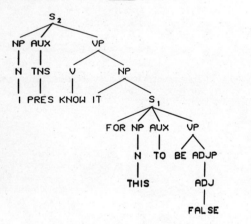

After <u>Complementizer Placement</u> has applied on the S_2 cycle.

Q. Going through our list, can <u>END</u> apply?
A. No. As there are no two identical NP's between S_2 and S_1, <u>END</u> cannot apply. We now come to <u>It-Replacement</u>.
Q. Does <u>It-Replacement</u> apply?
A. Yes, because the verb <u>know</u> belongs to the class of verbs undergoing <u>It-Replacement</u>. In fact, the ungrammaticality of the sentence *<u>I know for this to be false</u> shows that with <u>for-to</u> complementizers, <u>know</u> (like <u>seem</u>) <u>must</u> undergo <u>It-Replacement</u>.

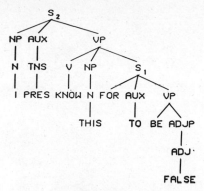

After <u>It-Replacement</u> has applied on the S$_2$ cycle.

Q. What other rule in our list must apply here?
A. <u>Complementizer Deletion</u> must apply.

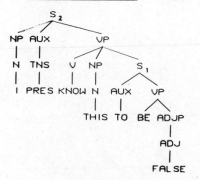

After <u>Complementizer Deletion</u> has applied on the S$_2$ cycle.

Q. What do we get?
A. After <u>Affix Hopping</u> we have <u>I know this to be false</u>.

We will next consider the sentence <u>This is known to be false</u>, which has the following D. S.:

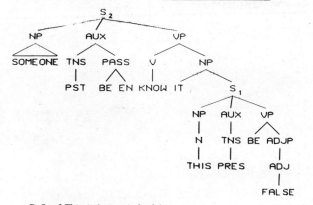

D. S. of <u>This is known to be false</u>.

Q. Do any rules apply on the S$_1$ cycle?
A. No. We go to S$_2$.
Q. Starting at the top of our list (p. 169) again, what rule must apply first on the S$_2$ cycle?
A. <u>Complementizer Placement</u>. We'll choose <u>for-to</u>.

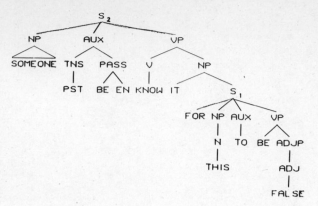

After <u>Complementizer Placement</u> has applied on the S$_2$ cycle.

Q. Can <u>END</u> apply on the S$_2$ cycle?
A. No, because there are no two identical NP's in the S.
Q. Next is <u>It-Replacement</u>. Does it apply?
A. Yes. <u>Know</u> is one of the verbs which obligatorily undergoes <u>It-Replacement</u>.

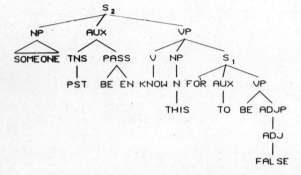

After <u>It-Replacement</u> has applied on the S$_2$ cycle.

Q. The next rule is <u>Passive</u>. Does it apply on the S$_2$ cycle?
A. Yes. The auxiliary of S$_2$ contains the constituent <u>Passive</u>, so the rule must apply. The object NP of S$_2$, <u>this</u>, will be moved to the front of S$_2$. Since S$_1$ has been moved out of the object NP by <u>It-Replacement</u>, it is not included in the operation of <u>Passive</u>.

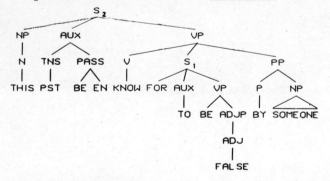

After <u>Passive</u> has applied on S$_2$.

Notice that the NP <u>this</u>, which started out in the subject position of S$_1$, was first moved into the object position of S$_2$ by <u>It-Replacement</u>, and then moved to the front of S$_2$ by <u>Passive</u>.

Q. What other rule in our list must now apply?
A. <u>Complementizer Deletion</u>.

176

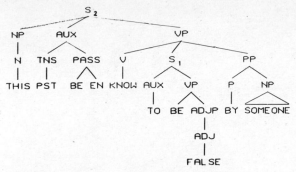

After <u>Complementizer Deletion</u> has applied on the S₂ cycle.

Q. What other rules must apply?
A. <u>Affix Hopping</u> must, and <u>Agent Deletion</u> may apply. They will give us <u>This is known to be false</u>.

<u>It-Replacement</u> in Object Position and <u>Believe</u>

Let us now consider a sentence which is related to the last one, but a little more complicated: <u>It is believed to be obvious that the Russians are crazy</u>. It has the following deep structure:

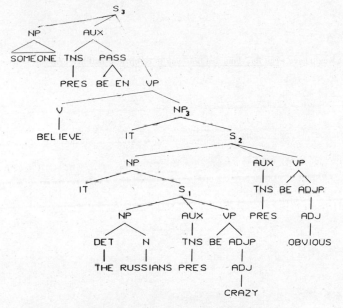

D.S. of <u>It is believed to be obvious that the Russians are crazy</u>.

As usual, we start with the most deeply embedded sentence, S₁.

Q. Do any of our listed cyclic rules apply on the S₁ cycle?
A. No. We go to S₂.
Q. What is the first rule that must apply on S₂?
A. <u>Complementizer Placement</u>. We will place a <u>that</u> complementizer.

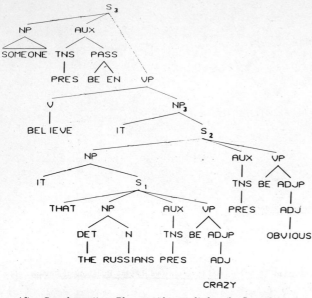

After _Complementizer Placement_ has applied on the S$_2$ cycle.

Q. Can _END_ apply (see p. 169)?
A. No, not with a _that_ complementizer.
Q. Does _It-Replacement_ apply?
A. No. _It-Replacement_ cannot apply with a that complementizer. (If it did, we would have *_The Russians are believed to be obvious that are crazy._)
Q. Can _Passive_ apply on S$_2$?
A. No, because there is no _Passive_ auxiliary in S$_2$
Q. _Reflexive_?
A. No, because there are no two identical NP's within S$_2$.
Q. Can _Extraposition_ apply?
A. Yes, optionally. Let us apply this rule.

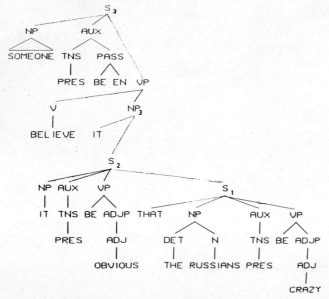

After _Extraposition_ has applied on the S$_2$ cycle.

If we disregard S$_3$, so far we have _It is obvious that the Russians are crazy_ (with just S$_1$ and S$_2$).

Q. Does _It-Deletion_, the next rule on our list, apply?
A. No, because the _it_ in S$_2$ no longer precedes S$_1$ within an NP, since S$_1$ has been extraposed. No other rules on our list will apply on the S$_2$ cycle. We now proceed to S$_3$ and the top of our list of rules again.
Q. What is the first rule to apply on S$_3$?
A. _Complementizer Placement_. Let us use _for-to_ complementizers.

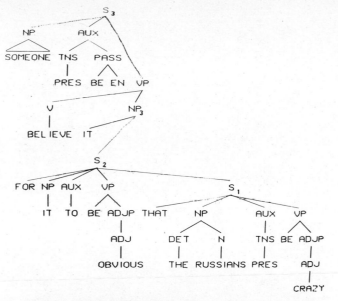

After *for-to* Complementizer Placement has applied on the S$_3$ cycle.

We now come to It-Replacement (see p. 169).

Q. Does It-Replacement apply?

A. Yes. Believe is one of the verbs which undergoes It-Replacement. Note that the subject NP it of S$_2$, will be moved up into the object NP position of S$_3$, replacing the it that is now immediately dominated by NP$_3$. The rest of S$_2$ (its complementizer for, its auxiliary, and VP, as well as S$_1$ which has been extraposed to its end) will be daughter-adjoined to the VP of S$_3$:

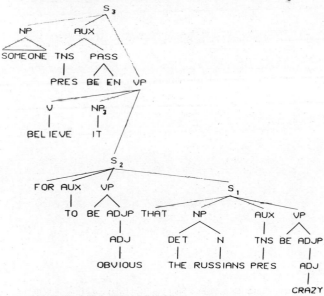

After It-Replacement has applied on the S$_3$ cycle.

Next we come to Passive.

Q. Does Passive apply on S$_3$?

A. Yes. The auxiliary of S$_3$ contains the constituent Passive, so it must apply. Notice that all that remains in the object NP position of S$_3$ is the it, since S$_2$ has been moved away by It-Replacement.

179

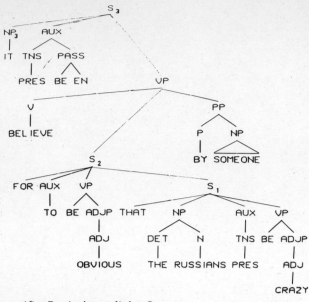

After <u>Passive</u> has applied on S$_3$

Q. What rules still apply on the S$_3$ cycle?
A. <u>Complementizer Deletion</u> must apply, and <u>Agent Deletion</u> may.

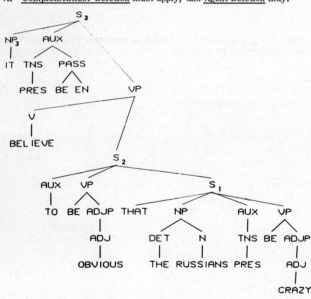

After <u>Complementizer Deletion</u> and <u>Agent Deletion</u> have applied on the S$_3$ cycle.

Q. What S do we have?
A. After <u>Affix Hopping</u> we have <u>It is believed to be obvious that the Russians are crazy</u>.

We will now briefly consider one more related sentence, whose details will be reviewed later. Take the sentence <u>That the Russians are crazy is believed to be obvious</u>, which has the same deep structure as the previous sentence (p. 177).

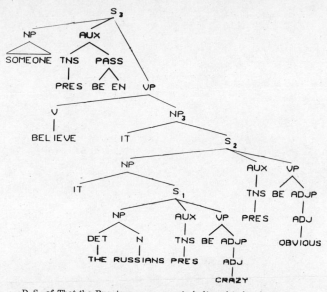

D.S. of <u>That the Russians are crazy is believed to be obvious</u>.

Q. Do any rules on our list (p. 169) apply on the S_1 cycle?
A. No. We continue to S_2.
Q. What rule must apply first on S_2?
A. <u>Complementizer Placement</u>. We will use a <u>that</u> complementizer.

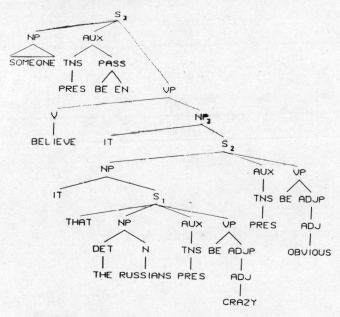

After <u>Complementizer Placement</u> has applied on the S_2 cycle.

Q. Can <u>END</u> apply on S_2?
A. No. <u>END</u> applies only with <u>for-to</u> or <u>poss-ing</u> complementizers.
Q. Can <u>It-Replacement</u> apply?
A. No, not with a <u>that</u> complementizer (see p. 170).
Q. Can <u>Passive</u> apply on S_2?
A. No, there is no <u>Passive</u> in the auxiliary of S_2.
Q. Can <u>Reflexive</u> apply?
A. No, because there are no two identical NP's within S_2.
Q. Can <u>Extraposition</u> apply on S_2?
A. Yes, optionally. We will choose not to apply it this time.
Q. Must <u>It-Deletion</u> apply?
A. Yes, the <u>it</u> in S_2 directly precedes an S within an NP.

181

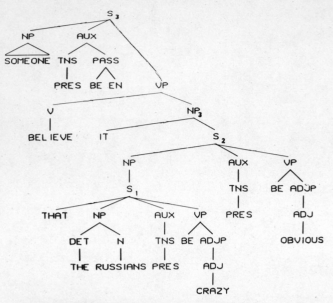

After <u>It-Deletion</u> has applied on S_2.

No other rules in our list (p. 169) apply on S_2. We proceed to S_3 and the top of our list of rules again.

Q. What rule must apply first on S_3?
A. <u>Complementizer Placement</u>. We will place <u>for-to</u> complementizers .

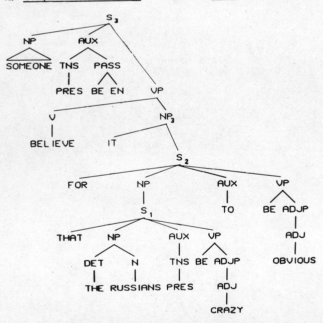

After <u>Complementizer Placement</u> has applied on the S_3 cycle.

Q. Does <u>END</u> apply on S_3?
A. No, there are no two identical NP's between S_3 and S_2.
Q. Does <u>It-Replacement</u> apply?
A. Yes. Notice that the subject NP of S_2, which is about to undergo <u>It-Replacement</u>, contains the entire S_1 in it. Therefore, this entire subject NP of S_2, including the clause, will move up into the object NP position of S_3, which is presently occupied by NP_3, <u>it</u>, as is seen in the above tree. As usual, the rest of S_2(i.e., the complementizer <u>for</u>, the auxiliary, and VP) will be daughter-adjoined to the VP of S_3.

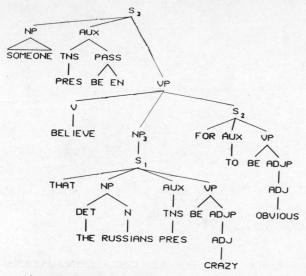

After <u>It-Replacement</u> has applied on the S₃ cycle.

Q. Does our next rule, <u>Passive</u>, now apply?

A. Yes. <u>Passive</u> must apply on S₃, since the constituent <u>Passive</u> is in the auxiliary of S₃. We know <u>Passive</u> moves the object NP to the front of the S. Now, however, the object NP of S₃ is the entire S₁, which was placed in that position by <u>It-Replacement</u> earlier.

Q. Does <u>Passive</u> move to the front object NP's which contain full sentences?

A. Yes.

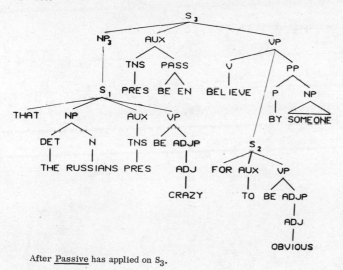

After <u>Passive</u> has applied on S₃.

Q. What applies next?

A. <u>Complementizer Deletion</u> must apply, and <u>Agent Deletion</u> may apply.

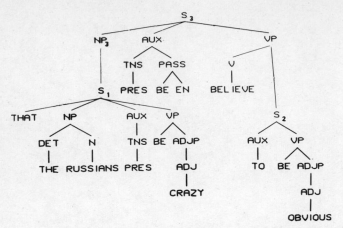

After application of Complementizer Deletion and Agent Deletion on the S$_3$ cycle.

Q. What S do we have?
A. After Agent Deletion, Complementizer Deletion, and Affix Hopping (which is not shown), we have That the Russians are crazy is believed to be obvious.

In this derivation, we have illustrated that subject NP's (of embedded sentences) containing full sentences may be It-Replaced (p. 182), and that full object NP's (of a main sentence) containing a clause must be Passivized (p. 183) if they are in the object NP position of an S (as in our S$_3$, p. 183) which contains a Passive auxiliary.

END and Believe

Now consider a sentence of the form John believes himself to be cool, which has the following deep structure:

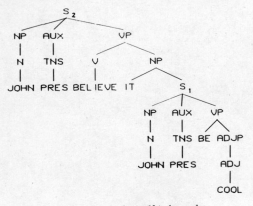

D. S. of John believes himself to be cool.

Q. Starting with S$_1$, can we apply any of our listed cyclic rules (p. 169)?
A. No. Complementizer Placement, END, and It-Replacement all require at least one embedded S. Passive cannot apply on S$_1$ because there is no Passive constituent in the auxiliary of S$_1$.
Q. Can Reflexive apply on S$_1$?
A. No, because there are no two identical NP's within S$_1$. The last four rules on our list also require at least one embedded S, which we do not have when we are working only with S$_1$. We go to S$_2$.
Q. What rule applies first on S$_2$?
A. Complementizer Placement. We'll choose for-to.

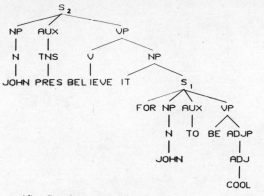

After <u>Complementizer Placement</u> has applied on the S₂ cycle.

Q. Can <u>END</u> apply to this structure?
A. The S.D. for <u>END</u> is met, for there are two identical NP's between S_2 and S_1 (<u>John</u>). Let us apply this rule and see what happens.

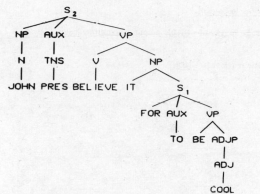

After <u>END</u> has applied on the S_2 cycle.

Q. Now we come to <u>It-Replacement</u>. Can it apply?
A. No, because there is no subject NP in S_1 to <u>It-Replace</u> into S_2. The subject NP, <u>John</u>, in S_1, has just been eliminated by <u>END</u>, so there's nothing to <u>It-Replace</u>. Next is <u>Passive</u>.
Q. Can <u>Passive</u> apply?
A. No, there is no <u>Passive</u> auxiliary in S_2. On to <u>Reflexive</u>.
Q. Can <u>Reflexive</u> apply on S_2?
A. No, there are no two identical NP's within S_2. Next is <u>Extraposition</u>.
Q. Can <u>Extraposition</u> apply?
A. It could, but nothing happens because the clause is already at the end of the structure (see p. 96). Next is <u>It-Deletion</u>.
Q. Must <u>It-Deletion</u> apply?
A. Yes. An <u>it</u> directly precedes an S within an NP.

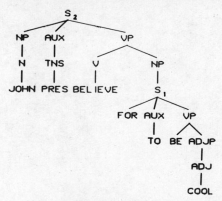

After <u>It-Deletion</u> has applied on S_2.

Q. We come to <u>Preposition Deletion</u>. Can it apply?
A. No, because there is no preposition preceding an S anywhere.

185

Q. Must <u>Complementizer Deletion</u> apply?
A. Yes, because we have <u>for-to</u> complementizers.

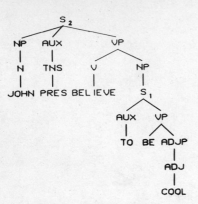

After <u>Complementizer Deletion</u> has applied on the S_2 cycle.

Q. What S do we have?
A. After <u>Affix Hopping</u> and all the above applications, we come out with a bad sentence *<u>John believes to be cool</u>.
Q. Where did we go wrong?
A. With <u>END</u>. It was a mistake to apply <u>END</u> when the verb was <u>believe</u>. Therefore, <u>believe</u> must be marked [- <u>END</u>], as our ungrammatical sentence shows. Let's try again, starting with the same D.S. as on p. 184.

The D.S. of <u>John believes himself to be cool</u> is the same as that on p. 184, except that <u>believe</u> is now marked [- <u>END</u>].

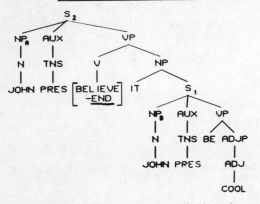

Revised D.S. of <u>John believes himself to be cool</u>.

Q. What rules apply on S_1?
A. Just as before (p. 184), none. We go to S_2.
Q. What rule must apply first on S_2?
A. <u>Complementizer Placement</u>. We will use <u>for-to</u>.

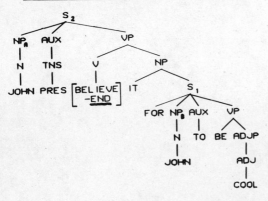

After <u>Complementizer Placement</u> has applied on the S_2 cycle.

Q. Next is <u>END</u>. Can it apply?
A. No. <u>Believe</u> is marked [- <u>END</u>]. We come to <u>It-Replacement</u>.

186

Q. Must It-Replacement apply?

A. Yes. Believe is one of the verbs which must undergo It-Replacement with for-to complementizers.

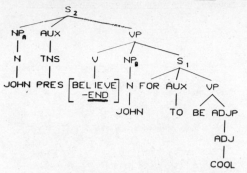

After It-Replacement has applied on the S$_2$ cycle.

Q. Continuing down our list, we come to Passive. Does it apply on the S$_2$ cycle?

A. No, because there is no constituent Passive in auxiliary of S$_2$. Next is Reflexive.

Q. Does Reflexive apply?

A. Yes. Notice that after It-Replacement has applied on S$_2$, the subject NP$_b$, John, of S$_1$ has been moved into S$_2$, which has NP$_a$, John, in its own subject position. Before It-Replacement had applied on S$_2$, we could not apply Reflexive on S$_2$ because NP$_a$ and NP$_b$ were not in the same simplex S. After It-Replacement has applied on S$_2$, we must also apply Reflexive on S$_2$ in our example.

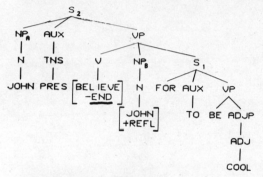

After Reflexive has applied on S$_2$

As was discussed above (pp. 157-165), when trying to establish the order of any number of cyclic rules, we must see what their order is within one simplex S. Within our simplex S$_2$, It-Replacement had to apply first to set up the environment for Reflexive in S$_2$. Therefore, their order within the cycle (the ordered list of cyclic rules) is:

It-Replacement

Reflexive

Of the remaining cyclic rules, only Complementizer Deletion is applicable. (Note that It-Deletion can no longer apply after It-Replacement, since that it has been replaced by the subject NP, John, of the next lower S.

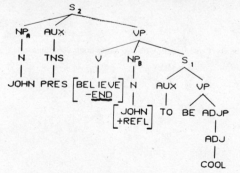

After Complementizer Deletion has applied on the S$_2$ cycle.

After Affix Hopping we have John believes himself to be cool. As our derivation has shown, to get himself (in our example) in the object NP position of S$_2$, we must first apply It-Replacement on S$_2$ so that there will be two identical NP's within S$_2$, to which Reflexive must apply to give us the correct sentence.

Passive and There-Insertion

We will now give some examples illustrating the order of Passive and There-Insertion. Consider this sentence There was a bike being ridden by a cow, which has the following deep structure:

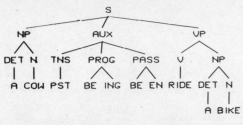

D. S. of There was a bike being ridden by a cow.

Q. What rules can apply to this deep structure?
A. Since there is only one S, Complementizer Placement, END, and It-Replacement are excluded, for they all require at least one embedded S.
Q. Must Passive apply?
A. Yes, but There-Insertion may also apply. To show that Passive precedes There-Insertion, let us apply There-Insertion first. (This derivation is presented for review. A similar derivation was presented earlier [pp. 41-42].)

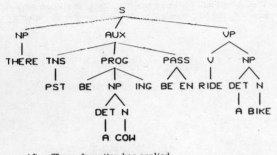

After There-Insertion has applied.

Q. Must Passive now apply?
A. Yes. Let's see what it produces.

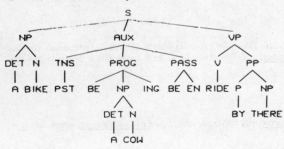

After Passive has applied.

Q. What S do we have?
A. After Affix Hopping we have the rather odd sentence *A bike was a cow being ridden by there. Let's start over again with the same deep structure as that at the top of this page.

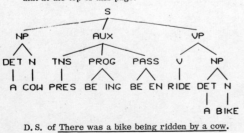

D. S. of There was a bike being ridden by a cow.

This time we will apply Passive first.

188

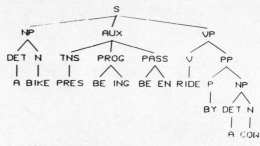

After <u>Passive</u> has applied.

Q. May we now apply <u>There-Insertion</u>?
A. Yes. (<u>Reflexive</u> cannot apply here.)

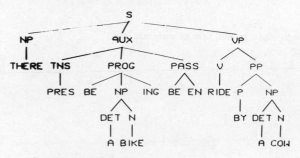

After <u>There-Insertion</u> has applied.

Q. What do we have?
A. After <u>Affix Hopping</u> we have <u>There was a bike being ridden by a cow</u>. The ungrammaticality of the S on p. 188 and the grammaticality of the one just derived show that the order of <u>Passive</u> and <u>There-Insertion</u> within one simplex S, and therefore, the order in the cycle, must be <u>Passive</u> first, then <u>There-Insertion</u>.

Note that although in the list we have the order:

> <u>Passive</u>
>
> <u>Reflexive</u>
>
> <u>There-Insertion</u>

it happens that <u>Passive</u> and <u>Reflexive</u> never apply within the same simplex S, i.e., *<u>Mary was understood by herself</u> or *<u>John was kissed by himself</u>. We will discuss later two other rules which do not apply within the same simplex S. But now we will show how <u>There-Insertion</u> is a cyclic rule.

<u>There-Insertion</u> as a Cyclic Rule

Let us first consider the sentence <u>Henry believed there to have been a bean in his bed</u>. It has the following deep structure:

Ordering of rules:

> <u>Complementizer Placement</u>
>
> <u>END</u>
>
> <u>It-Replacement</u>
>
> <u>Passive</u>
>
> <u>Reflexive</u>
>
> <u>There-Insertion</u>
>
> <u>Extraposition</u>
>
> <u>It-Deletion</u>
>
> <u>Preposition Deletion</u>
>
> <u>Complementizer Deletion</u>

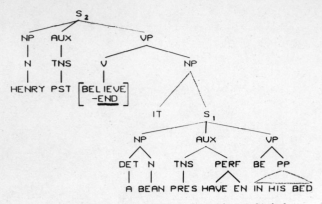

D.S. of <u>Henry believed there to have been a bean in his bed</u>.

Q. Are any of our listed cyclic rules (p. 189) applicable on the S_1 cycle?
A. Only <u>There-Insertion</u>, which may optionally apply because S_1 has an indefinite subject NP and a <u>be</u> in it. Let us apply this rule.

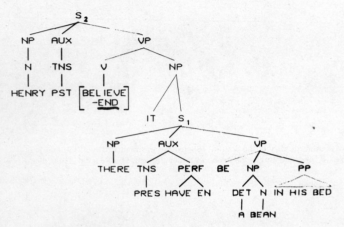

After <u>There-Insertion</u> has applied on S_1.

No other rules on our list apply on S_1.

Q. On S_2, which is the first rule to apply?
A. <u>Complementizer Placement</u> must apply. We will choose <u>for-to</u>.

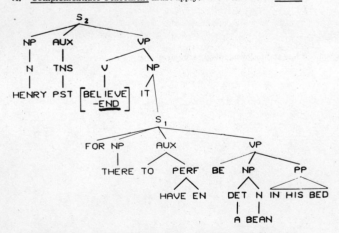

After <u>Complementizer Placement</u> has applied on the S_2 cycle.

Q. Can <u>END</u> apply?
A. No. <u>Believe</u> is marked [- <u>END</u>].
Q. Does <u>It-Replacement</u> now apply?
A. Yes. <u>Believe</u> must undergo <u>It-Replacement</u> when the next lower S (S_1) has <u>for-to</u> complementizers.

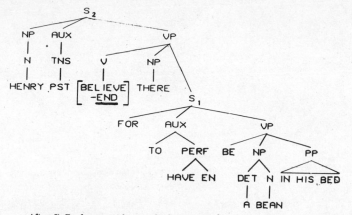

After <u>It-Replacement</u> has applied on the S_2 cycle.

Now notice that <u>there</u> of S_1 has moved up into the object NP position (formerly occupied by <u>it</u>) of S_2. Although we have not shown the ordering of <u>There-Insertion</u> and <u>It-Replacement</u> within one simplex S (<u>There-Insertion</u> applied on the S_1 cycle, and <u>It-Replacement</u> applied on the S_2 cycle), if we want the <u>there</u> to be in the object NP position of S_2, <u>There-Insertion</u> must already have applied on S_1. If we had not applied <u>There-Insertion</u> on S_1, we could not have applied it on the S_2 cycle, for there is no indefinite subject NP or <u>be</u> in S_2. So for sentences of the kind we are now illustrating, <u>There-Insertion</u> must have applied on S_1, so that <u>there</u> can be moved up into S_2 when we apply <u>It-Replacement</u> on S_2. The last rule on our list to apply is <u>Complementizer Deletion</u>.

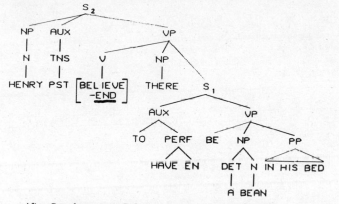

After <u>Complementizer Deletion</u> has applied on the S_2 cycle.

Q. What S do we have?

A. After <u>Affix Hopping</u> we have <u>Henry believed there to have been a bean in his bed</u>. This derivation has illustrated that if we want <u>there</u> to appear in the object NP position of the next higher S (in this case, S_2), <u>There-Insertion</u> must have applied on the S_1 cycle, so that it will be moved up into the next higher S by <u>It-Replacement</u>. Thus, <u>There-Insertion</u> must be a cyclic rule.

<u>It-Replacement</u> and <u>Passive</u>

Let us consider another sentence which is closely related to the last one: <u>There was believed by Henry to have been a bean in his bed</u>. It has the following D.S.:

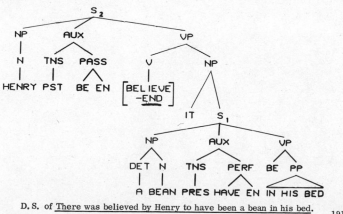

D.S. of <u>There was believed by Henry to have been a bean in his bed</u>.

191

Q. Of our list of cyclic rules (p. 189), can any apply on S$_1$?
A. Yes. There-Insertion may optionally apply.

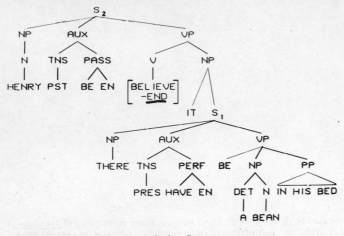

After There-Insertion has applied on S$_1$.

No other rules apply on S$_1$. We go to S$_2$.

Q. What rule must apply first on S$_2$?
A. Complementizer Placement. We'll use for-to again.

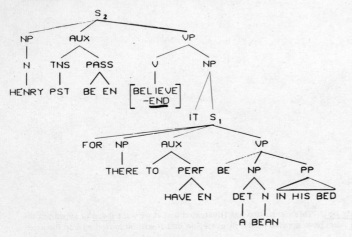

After Complementizer Placement has applied on the S$_2$ cycle.

As before (p. 190), END cannot apply here.

Q. Does It-Replacement apply?
A. Yes. It must apply with the verb believe when we have for-to complementizers.

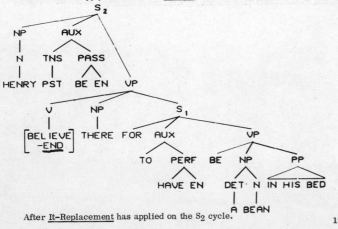

After It-Replacement has applied on the S$_2$ cycle.   192

Q. Next is <u>Passive</u>. Does it apply on S_2?
A. Yes, it must apply because S_2 has a <u>passive</u> auxiliary.

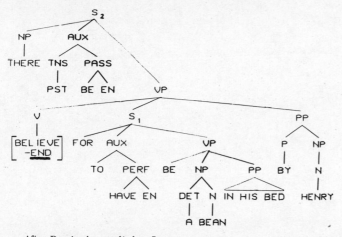

After <u>Passive</u> has applied on S_2.

Q. What other rule on our list must still apply?
A. <u>Complementizer Deletion</u> must apply.

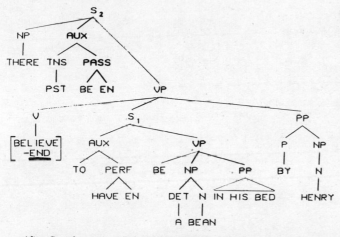

After <u>Complementizer Deletion</u> has applied on the S_2 cycle.

Q. What do we have?
A. After <u>Affix Hopping</u> we have <u>There was believed by Henry to have been a bean in his bed</u>. Note the progress of <u>there</u>. It started in S_1 (by <u>There-Insertion</u>), was moved up into object NP position of S_2 by <u>It-Replacement</u> on that cycle, and was finally moved to the front of S_2 by <u>Passive</u>. In this sentence, then, <u>There-Insertion</u> had to apply on S_1 so that it could come to the subject NP position of S_2 by the operations performed in this derivation. Notice also that within a simplex S (S_2), <u>It-Replacement</u> had to apply before <u>Passive</u>, or else <u>there</u> would never have been included in the <u>Passive</u> operation of S_2. The ordering of <u>It-Replacement</u> and <u>Passive</u>, as we have just shown, is therefore:

> It-Replacement
>
> Passive

We will now consider other examples illustrating the above ordering of <u>It-Replacement</u> and <u>Passive</u>. First, we shall derive a sentence which has <u>Passive</u> auxiliaries in both S_1 and S_2: <u>Some ants were believed by Mary to have been eaten by John</u>. It has the following D.S.:

193

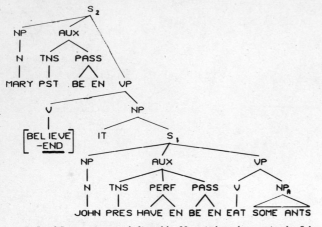

D. S. of <u>Some ants were believed by Mary to have been eaten by John</u>.

Q. What rules on our list (p. 189) apply on S$_1$?
A. Only <u>Passive</u> must apply on the S$_1$ cycle.

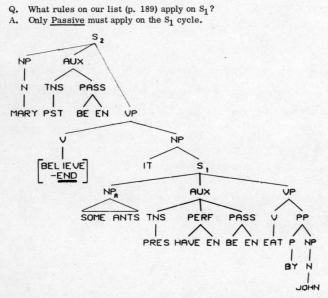

After <u>Passive</u> has applied on S$_1$.

Q. No other rules apply on S$_1$. What rule must apply first on the S$_2$ cycle?
A. As usual, <u>Complementizer Placement</u> is first. We'll choose <u>for-to</u>.

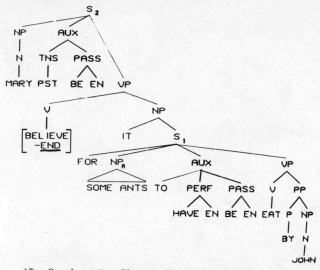

After <u>Complementizer Placement</u> has applied on the S$_2$ cycle.

Q. Can <u>END</u> apply?
A. No. As was shown before (pp. 185–186), <u>believe</u> must be marked [- <u>END</u>].   Next is <u>It–Replacement</u>.
Q. Must <u>It–Replacement</u> apply?
A. Yes. <u>Believe</u> is a verb which must undergo <u>It–Replacement</u>.

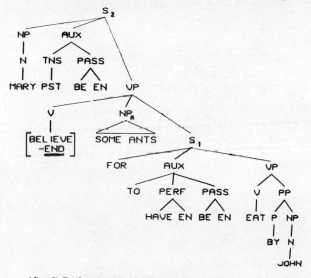

After <u>It–Replacement</u> has applied on the S$_2$ cycle.

Note that NP$_a$, which was originally in S$_1$, has now risen into S$_2$ by <u>It–Replacement</u> on that cycle.   Next, we come to <u>Passive</u> (see list, p. 189).

Q. Does <u>Passive</u> apply on S$_2$?
A. Yes. There is a <u>Passive</u> auxiliary in S$_2$, so <u>Passive</u> must apply.

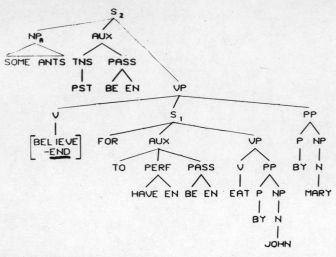

After <u>Passive</u> has applied on S_2.

Note that NP_a has gone to the front of S_2, though it originally started out in the object NP position of S_1 (p. 194).

Q. What other rule must apply?
A. <u>Complementizer Deletion</u> must apply.

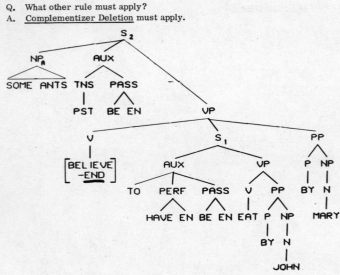

After <u>Complementizer Deletion</u> has applied on the S_2 cycle.

Q. What S do we have?
A. After <u>Affix Hopping</u> we have <u>Some ants were believed by Mary to have been eaten by John</u>. There are other possibilities for this deep structure.
Q. For instance, what would we have if <u>Passive</u> had applied on S_2, but not on S_1?
A. Let us see.

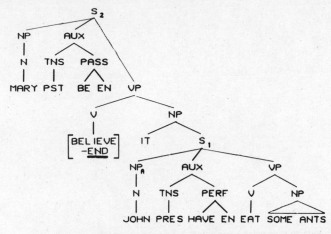

D. S. of <u>John was believed by Mary to have eaten some ants</u>.

No rules will apply on S_1. (Since there is no <u>Passive</u> auxiliary in S_1, <u>Passive</u> cannot apply.) We go to S_2 and the top of our list of rules again.

Q.   What rule applies first?
A.   <u>Complementizer Placement</u>. We will use <u>for-to</u>.

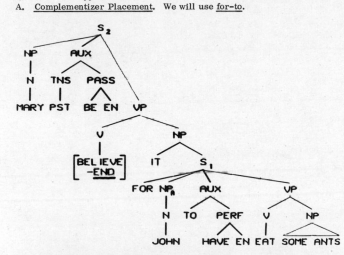

After <u>Complementizer Placement</u> has applied on the S_2 cycle.

Q.   What rule must apply next on the S_2 cycle?
A.   As we have said before, <u>believe</u> cannot undergo <u>END</u>, instead it must undergo <u>It-Replacement</u>. Now NP_a of S_1 will be moved up into S_2 by this rule.

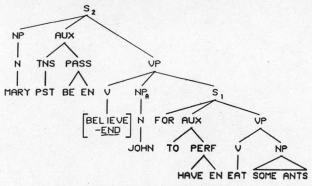

After <u>It-Replacement</u> has applied on the S_2 cycle.

Q.   Must <u>Passive</u> now apply on S_2?
A.   Yes. NP_a will now be moved to the front of S_2.

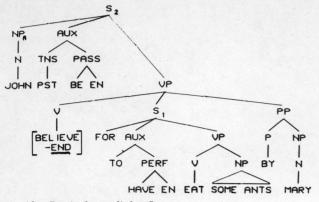

After <u>Passive</u> has applied on S_2.

Q. What S do we have?
A. After <u>Affix Hopping</u> and <u>Complementizer Deletion</u> we have <u>John was believed by Mary to have eaten some ants</u>.
Q. What S would we have if there were a <u>Passive</u> in the auxiliary of S_1, but not in S_2?
A. Let us derive that sentence:

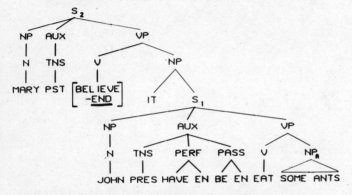

D. S. of <u>Mary believed some ants to have been eaten by John</u>.

Q. What rule must apply on S_1?
A. <u>Passive</u>, because S_1 has the constituent <u>Passive</u> in its auxiliary.

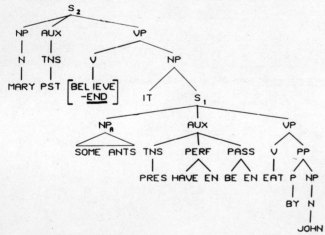

After <u>Passive</u> has applied on S_1.

No other rules apply on the S_1 cycle. We go to S_2.

Q. What rule must apply first on the S_2 cycle?
A. <u>Complementizer Placement</u>. Again, we will use <u>for-to</u>.

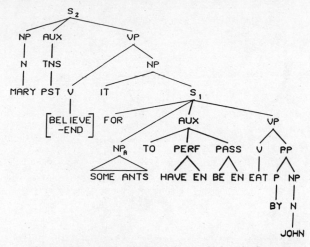

After <u>Complementizer Placement</u> has applied on the S$_2$ cycle.

Q. Can <u>END</u> apply now?

A. No. <u>Believe</u> may not undergo <u>END</u>, as was shown before (pp. 185–186), but must instead undergo <u>It–Replacement</u>. NP$_a$ in S$_1$ (which was placed in the subject NP position in S$_1$ by the application of <u>Passive</u> on that cycle) will now move up into S$_2$.

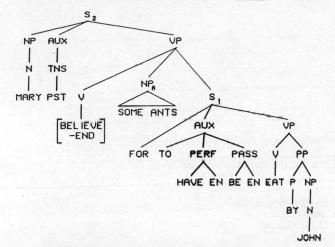

After <u>It–Replacement</u> has applied on the S$_2$ cycle.

Q. Does <u>Passive</u> apply on S$_2$?

A. No, because there is no <u>Passive</u> in the auxiliary of S$_2$.

Q. What S do we have?

A. After <u>Affix Hopping</u> and <u>Complementizer Deletion</u> we have <u>Mary believed some ants to have been eaten by John</u>.

Q. What sentence would we get if there were no <u>Passive</u> in either S$_1$ or S$_2$?

A. We will derive this possibility, also.

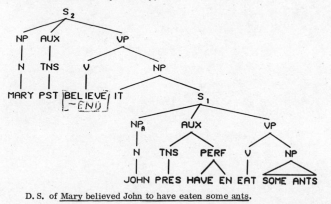

D. S. of <u>Mary believed John to have eaten some ants</u>.

199

Q. What rules apply on the S_1 cycle?
A. None. We go to S_2.
Q. What rule must apply first on the S_2 cycle?
A. <u>Complementizer Placement</u>. We will use <u>for-to</u> again.

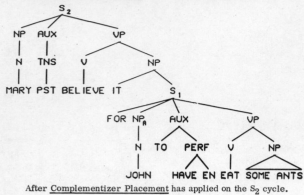

After <u>Complementizer Placement</u> has applied on the S_2 cycle.

Q. What rule must apply now?
A. <u>It-Replacement</u> must apply. NP_a in S_1 will move into the object NP position of S_2.

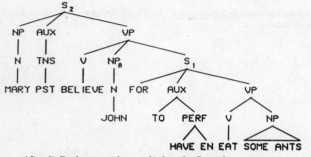

After <u>It-Replacement</u> has applied on the S_2 cycle.

Q. Will any other rules apply to this structure?
A. Only <u>Affix Hopping</u> and <u>Complementizer Deletion</u>. Then we will have <u>Mary believed John to have eaten some ants</u>.

From one deep structure, then, we have derived four possible sentences:

> <u>Passive</u> on both S_1 and S_2 (pp. 194-196): <u>Some ants were believed by Mary to have been eaten by John</u>.
> <u>Passive</u> on S_2 but not on S_1 (pp. 197-198): <u>John was believed by Mary to have eaten some ants</u>.
> <u>Passive</u> on S_1, but not on S_2 (pp. 197-198): <u>Mary believed some ants to have been eaten by John</u>.
> No <u>Passive</u> on S_1 or S_2 (pp. 199-200): <u>Mary believed John to have eaten some ants</u>.

The structure of p. 194 can easily be complicated by embedding it once more, as in the following sentence: <u>Some ants were known to be believed by Mary to have been eaten by John</u>. It is certainly not an ordinary sentence, but probably acceptable. This derivation will again illustrate that the order of <u>It-Replacement</u> and <u>Passive</u> within a simplex S (and therefore in the cycle) must be

> It-Replacement
>
> Passive

The above sentence has the following deep structure:

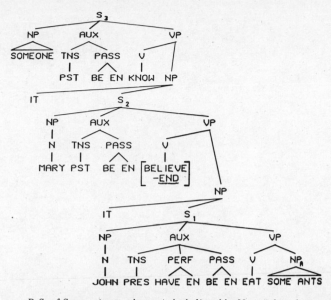

D.S. of <u>Some ants were known to be believed by Mary to have been eaten by John.</u>

Q. What must happen on S₁?
A. <u>Passive</u> must apply on S₁ because the auxiliary of S₁ contains the constituent <u>Passive</u>. NP_a will move to the front of S₁.

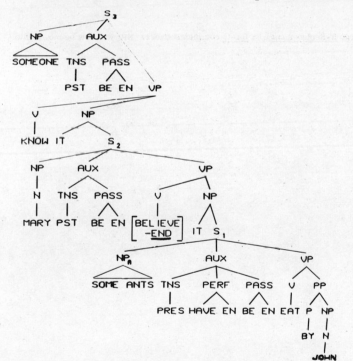

After <u>Passive</u> has applied on S₁.

No other rules apply on S₁. We move to S₂.

Q. What rule must first apply on S₂?
A. <u>Complementizer Placement</u> is first on the list (p. 189). We will choose <u>for-to</u>.

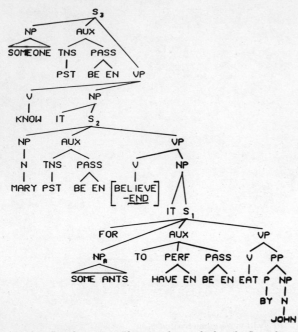

After <u>Complementizer Placement</u> has applied on the S_2 cycle.

Q. Can <u>END</u> apply?

A. No. <u>Believe</u> cannot undergo <u>END</u> (see pp. 185–186) but must instead undergo <u>It-Replacement</u> with <u>for-to</u> complementizers. NP_a will now be moved into the object NP position of S_2.

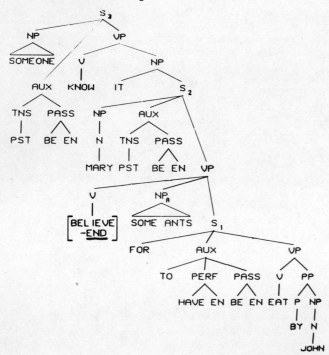

After <u>It-Replacement</u> has applied on the S_2 cycle.

NP_a is now in the object NP position of S_2. The next rule is <u>Passive</u>.

Q. Must <u>Passive</u> apply on S_2?

A. Yes, because the auxiliary in S_2 contains the constituent <u>Passive</u>. NP_a will now move into the subject position of S_2.

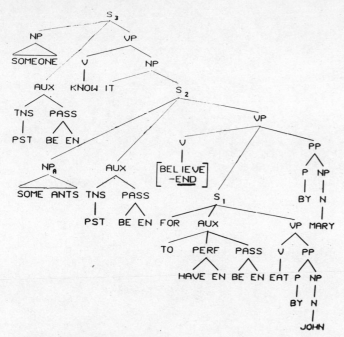

After <u>Passive</u> has applied on S_2.

Now NP_a is in the subject NP position of S_2. No other rules apply on the S_2 cycle. We move on to S_3.

Q. What rule must apply first on the S_3 cycle?
A. <u>Complementizer Placement</u>. We will use <u>for-to</u>.

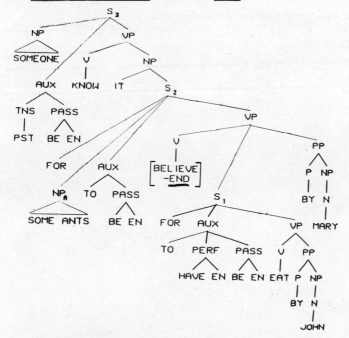

After <u>Complementizer Placement</u> has applied on the S_3 cycle.

Q. Can <u>END</u> apply on the S_3 cycle?
A. No, because there are no two identical NP's between S_3 and S_2.
Q. Does <u>It-Replacement</u> apply?
A. Yes, because <u>know</u> is a verb undergoing <u>It-Replacement</u>.

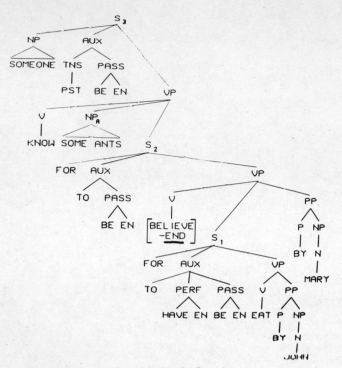

After **It-Replacement** has applied on the S₃ cycle.

Now NP_a has moved up into object position in S₃, and the remainder of S₂, which includes S₁ in its VP, has been daughter-adjoined to the VP of S₃.

Q. Must <u>Passive</u> now apply on S₃?
A. Yes. The auxiliary of S₃ contains the constituent <u>Passive</u>, so the rule must apply. NP_a will be moved to the front of S₃.

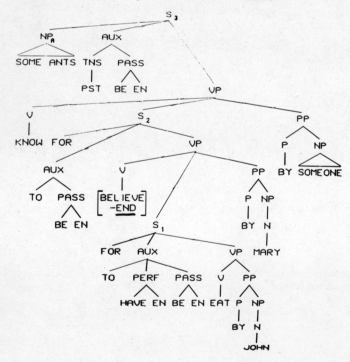

After **Passive** has applied on S₃.

NP_a, which started in the object NP position of S₁, has traveled to the front of S₃ by the operations of <u>It-Replacement</u> and <u>Passive</u>.

Q. What other rules may apply?
A. <u>Agent Deletion</u> may apply, and <u>Complementizer Deletion</u> must apply.

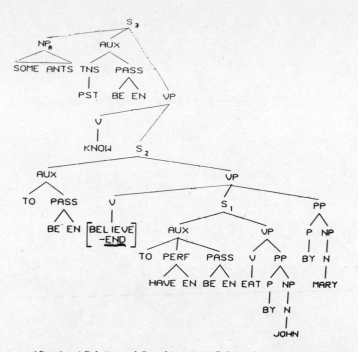

After <u>Agent Deletion</u> and <u>Complementizer Deletion</u> have applied on the S₃ cycle.

Q. What S do we have?

A. After <u>Affix Hopping</u> we have the questionable <u>Some ants were known to be believed by Mary to have been eaten by John</u>. As this derivation has illustrated, no matter how many embedded sentences we have, <u>It-Replacement</u> must always be applied before <u>Passive</u> within a simplex S (as within S₂ and within S₃).

If <u>Passive</u> had not applied on all 3 S's in the structure on p. 201, that structure would have given us other sentences. (We will list only the possibilities here, because they are derived in the same manner as the four sentences derived from the deep structure on p. 194).

If <u>Passive</u> had applied on S₁ and S₂, but not on S₃:
    <u>Someone knew some ants to be believed by Mary to have been eaten by John.</u>
If <u>Passive</u> had applied on S₁, but not on S₂ or on S₃:
    <u>Someone knew Mary to believe some ants to have been eaten by John.</u>
If <u>Passive</u> had applied on S₁ and S₃, but not on S₂:
    <u>Mary was known to believe some ants to have been eaten by John.</u>
If <u>Passive</u> had applied on S₂, but not on S₃ or on S₁:
    <u>Someone knew John to be believed by Mary to have eaten some ants.</u>
If <u>Passive</u> had applied on S₃, but not on S₂ or on S₁:
    <u>Mary was known to believe John to have eaten some ants.</u>
If <u>Passive</u> had applied on S₂ and on S₃, but not on S₁:
    <u>John was known to be believed by Mary to have eaten some ants.</u>
If <u>Passive</u> had applied on all three S's (as in our derivation just given):
    <u>Some ants were known to be believed by Mary to have been eaten by John.</u>
If <u>Passive</u> had applied nowhere:
    <u>Someone knew Mary to believe John to have eaten some ants.</u>

The above sentences vary in acceptability from person to person, but all can be derived from the D.S. given on p. 194.

<u>It-Replacement</u> and <u>END</u>

Some time back (p. 189), we stated that two cyclic rules, <u>Passive</u> and <u>Reflexive</u>, do not both apply within a single clause. Two other rules which are mutually exclusive in this way (i.e., they do not both apply within one clause) are <u>It-Replacement</u> and <u>END</u>. To illustrate this, consider the sentence <u>Henry tried to duck out</u>, which has the following D.S.:

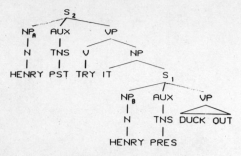

D. S. of <u>Henry tried to duck out</u>.

On S_1, none of our listed cyclic rules (p. 189) apply. We go to S_2.

Q.   What rule must apply first on the S_2 cycle?
A.   <u>Complementizer Placement</u>. We will choose <u>for-to</u>.

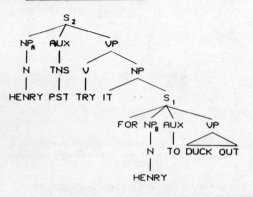

After <u>Complementizer Placement</u> has applied on the S_2 cycle.

Q.   Now we come to <u>END</u>. Must it apply?
A.   Yes. NP_a is the NP which is closest to NP_b, and NP_a in S_2 = NP_b in S_1, so NP_b will be deleted by NP_a.

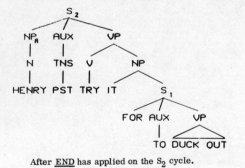

After <u>END</u> has applied on the S_2 cycle.

Q.   Can <u>It-Replacement</u> now apply?
A.   No. The subject NP of S_1 cannot be <u>It-Replaced</u> since it has just been deleted by <u>END</u>. Let us consider the same D. S. again, this time applying <u>It-Re-placement</u> first.

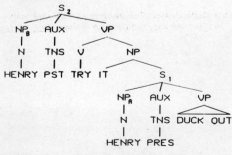

D. S. of <u>Henry tried to duck out</u>.

On S_1, nothing happens. We continue to S_2.

Q. What rule must apply first on S_2?

A. __Complementizer Placement__. We will use __for-to__.

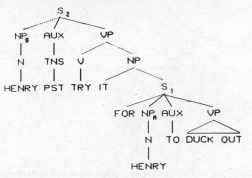

After __Complementizer Placement__ has applied on the S_2 cycle.

Q. Now what will we apply?

A. We will apply __It-Replacement__. NP_a of S_1 will be moved up into S_2.

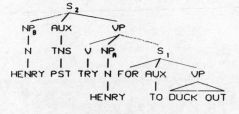

After __It-Replacement__ has applied on the S_2 cycle.

Q. Can __END__ now apply?

A. No, because there is now no subject NP in S_1 which equals NP_b in S_2, and __END__ can delete only subjects of embedded clauses. We see, then, that in theory, either __END__ or __It-Replacement__ may apply on one simplex S, but not both together.

__Number Agreement__[7]

S.D. (PreS) - $\begin{Bmatrix} NP \\ + Sing \\ - Sing \end{Bmatrix}$ - Tns - X

$\qquad\qquad\quad 1\quad 1$

$\qquad\qquad 1 \qquad\qquad 2 \qquad\qquad 3 \qquad 4$

$\qquad\qquad\qquad\qquad\qquad\qquad\qquad\qquad\qquad\Longrightarrow$ oblig

S.C. $\quad 1 \qquad\qquad 2 \qquad \begin{bmatrix} 3 \\ \begin{Bmatrix} + Sing \\ - Sing \\ 1\quad 1 \end{Bmatrix} \end{bmatrix}\quad 4$

The last cyclic rule we shall consider in this section is __Number Agreement__. This rule is placed between Passive and Reflexive. This rule changes structures of the Form A into the form B:

---

[7] A + indicates that the feature is present, e.g., __buffalo__ + Sing will be written out by later rules as __buffalo__. A − indicates that the feature in question is absent, e.g., __buffalo__ − Sing will be written out by later rules as __buffaloes__, since if a noun is not singular, it is plural.

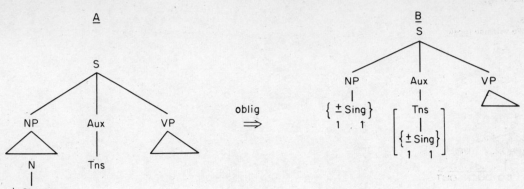

If the subject NP = [+ sing], then the <u>Tns</u> is also marked [+ sing].   If the subject NP = [- sing], then the <u>Tns</u> is also marked [- sing].   Let us now consider an example.   Consider the sentence <u>Buffaloes are in the air</u>, which has the following D. S. :

Ordering of rules:

- Complementizer Placement
- END
- It-Replacement
- Passive
- Number Agreement
- Reflexive
- There-Insertion
- Extraposition
- It-Deletion
- Preposition Deletion

Complementizer Deletion

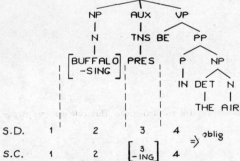

| S.D. | 1 | 2 | 3 | 4 | $\Rightarrow$ oblig |
| S.C. | 1 | 2 | $\begin{bmatrix} 3 \\ -ING \end{bmatrix}$ | 4 | |

   D. S. of <u>Buffaloes are in the air</u>.

Q.   Must <u>Number Agreement</u> apply to this structure?
A.   Yes.   <u>Number Agreement</u> is an obligatory rule.   The tree has been analyzed to undergo the rule.

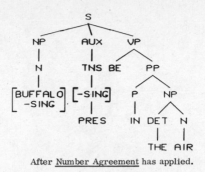

After <u>Number Agreement</u> has applied.

Q. What S do we have?

A. After <u>Affix Hopping</u> we have <u>Buffaloes are in the air</u>. We will now order <u>Number Agreement</u> and <u>Passive</u>.

<u>Passive</u> and <u>Number Agreement</u>

Consider the sentence: <u>The buffaloes were put into the air by a snowstorm</u>, which has the following D.S.:

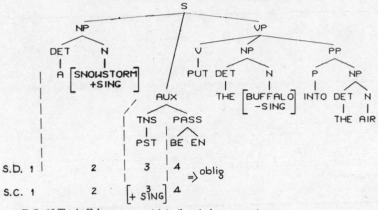

D.S. of <u>The buffaloes were put into the air by a snowstorm</u>.

Q. Must both <u>Passive</u> and <u>Number Agreement</u> apply to this D.S.?

A. Yes. Let us assume that <u>Number Agreement</u> applies before <u>Passive</u>. Since the subject NP, <u>snowstorm</u>, is [+ Sing], <u>Number Agreement</u> will attach [+ Sing] to the <u>Tns</u>, also.

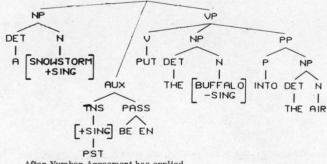

After <u>Number Agreement</u> has applied.

Q. Must <u>Passive</u> now apply?

A. Yes, because the constituent <u>Passive</u> is in the auxiliary of the S.

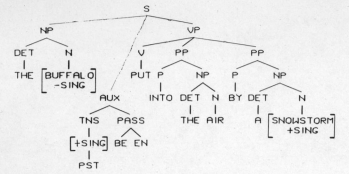

After <u>Passive</u> had applied.

Q. What do we have?

A. After <u>Affix Hopping</u> we have the sentence *<u>The buffaloes is put into the air by a snowstorm</u>. Since we get an ungrammatical sentence with the order:

<u>Number Agreement</u>

<u>Passive</u>

we must order <u>Passive</u> before <u>Number Agreement</u> so that the number will agree with the <u>derived</u> subject after <u>Passive</u> has applied. Let's start again, with the same D.S. as on p. 209.

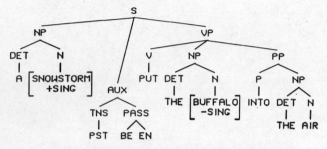

D.S. of <u>The buffaloes were put into the air by a snowstorm</u>.

Q. Must both <u>Passive</u> and <u>Number Agreement</u> apply to the above deep structure?

A. Yes. This time we will apply <u>Passive</u> first.

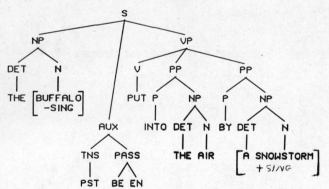

After <u>Passive</u> has applied.

The tree has now been analyzed to meet the S.D. for <u>Number Agreement</u>: The subject NP after <u>Passive</u> is now [- Sing], and when <u>Number Agreement</u> applies, the <u>Tns</u> will also be marked [- Sing].

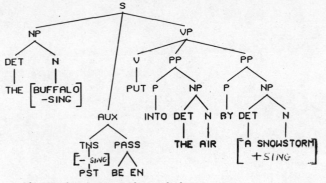

After <u>Number Agreement</u> has applied.

Q. What S do we have?

A. After <u>Affix Hopping</u> we have <u>The buffaloes were put into the air by a snowstorm</u>. This S and the ungrammaticality of the S on p. 210 show that the order of <u>Passive</u> and <u>Number Agreement</u> must be:

<u>Passive</u>

<u>Number Agreement</u>

<u>Passive</u>, <u>Number Agreement</u> and <u>There-Insertion</u>

Consider now the following sentence: <u>There were many protests being investigated</u>. It has the following D.S.:

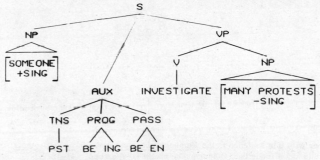

D.S. of <u>There were many protests being investigated</u>.

Q. What rules apply to this deep structure?

A. <u>Passive</u> and <u>Number Agreement</u> must apply, and <u>There-Insertion</u> may apply. Let us assume that the order of these three rules is:

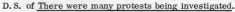
<u>There-Insertion</u>

<u>Number Agreement</u>

<u>Passive</u>

<u>There-Insertion</u> will apply first. The NP <u>there</u> will pick up the number of the NP it is replacing, which is [+ Sing] in our example.

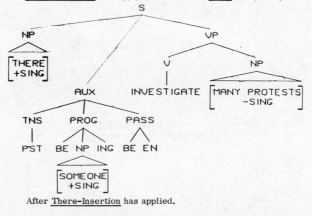

After <u>There-Insertion</u> has applied.

211

We will now apply <u>Number Agreement</u>.   Since the NP <u>there</u> is marked [+ Sing],   the <u>Tns</u> will also be marked [+ Sing] by <u>Number Agreement</u>.

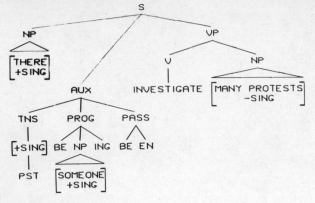

After <u>Number Agreement</u> has applied.

Q.   What do we apply now?
A.   <u>Passive</u>.

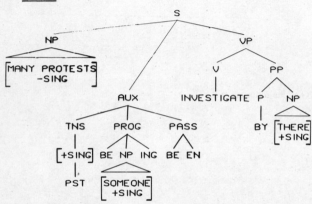

After <u>Passive</u> has applied.

Q.   What S do we have?
A.   *<u>Many protests was someone being investigated by there</u>.   Among the things wrong with this sentence is the <u>Number Agreement</u> between <u>many protests</u> and <u>is</u>.   The ordering of <u>Passive</u> after <u>There-Insertion</u> was also a mistake, but this has already been discussed on pp.188-189, and pp. 41-42.
Q.   How can we get the sentence <u>There were many protests being investigated</u>?   (We have already shown how to prevent sentences like *<u>Great protests is being investigated</u> on pp. 209-211.)
A.   Let us start again with the same D. S. as on p. 211:

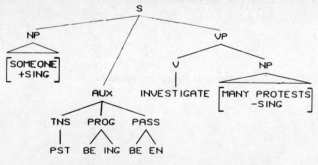

D. S. of <u>There were many protests being investigated</u>.

Q.   Do all three rules apply to this structure?
A.   Yes.   <u>Passive</u> and <u>Number Agreement</u> must apply, and <u>There-Insertion</u> may apply.   As was just shown, we must first apply <u>Passive</u>.

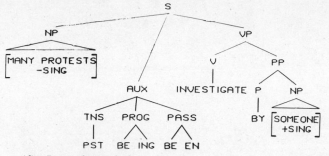

After <u>Passive</u> has applied.

Q. What rule must apply now?

A. Either <u>Number Agreement</u> or <u>There-Insertion</u> may apply, since either order is possible within a simplex sentence. Let us apply <u>Number Agreement</u> first.

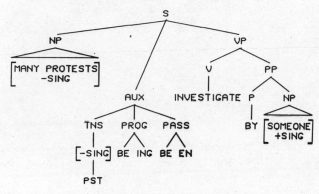

After <u>Number Agreement</u> has applied.

Now <u>There-Insertion</u> may apply. <u>There</u> will pick up the number of the NP $\begin{bmatrix} \text{many protests} \\ -\text{Sing} \end{bmatrix}$ which it is replacing.

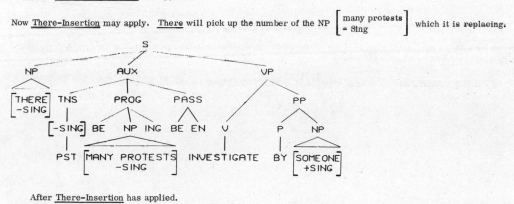

After <u>There-Insertion</u> has applied.

Q. What S do we have?

A. After <u>Affix Hopping</u> we have <u>There were many protests being investigated by someone</u>. And after <u>Agent Deletion</u> we will have <u>There were many protests being investigated</u>. Let us now reconsider the structure derived after <u>Passive</u> has applied (at top of page).

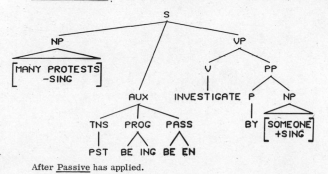

After <u>Passive</u> has applied.

This time, we will apply <u>There-Insertion</u> first. The NP <u>there</u> will pick up the number [- Sing] of the subject NP, <u>many protests</u>, which the <u>there</u> is replacing.

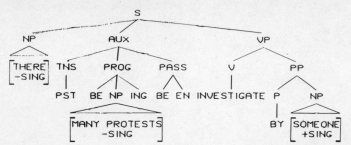

After <u>There-Insertion</u> has applied.

Q. May we now apply <u>Number Agreement</u>?
A. Yes, we must. Now the <u>Tns</u> will be marked [- Sing] because the subject NP, <u>there</u>, is marked [- Sing]. <u>There</u> picked up [- Sing] from the NP $\begin{bmatrix} \text{many protests} \\ \text{- Sing} \end{bmatrix}$, which <u>there</u> replaced when we applied <u>There-Insertion</u>.

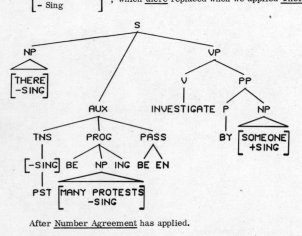

After <u>Number Agreement</u> has applied.

Q. What S do we have?
A. After <u>Affix Hopping</u> and <u>Agent Deletion</u> we have <u>There were many protests being investigated</u>. Thus, this example has shown that <u>Number Agreement</u> and <u>There-Insertion</u> are not ordered with respect to each other within a simplex S.

We will consider one more sentence illustrating <u>Number Agreement</u>: <u>There are believed to be evil ones lurking around Haj's office</u>, which has the following deep structure:

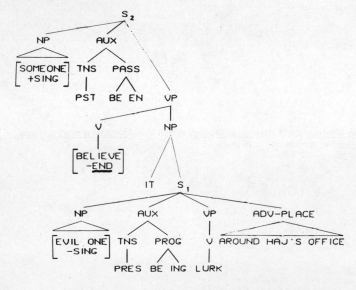

D. S. of <u>There are believed to be evil ones lurking around Haj's office</u>.

214

Q. What rules can apply on the S₁ cycle?

A. <u>There-Insertion</u> may apply, and <u>Number Agreement</u> must apply. As we have seen, these two rules are not ordered with respect to each other within a simplex sentence (pp. 211-214). Let us apply <u>Number Agreement</u> first.

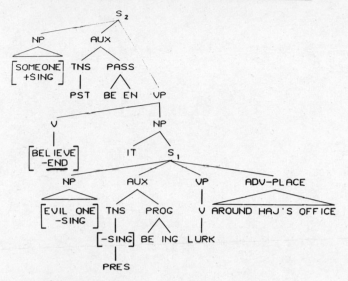

After <u>Number Agreement</u> has applied on S₁.

Q. Can <u>There-Insertion</u> now apply on S₁?

A. Yes, optionally.

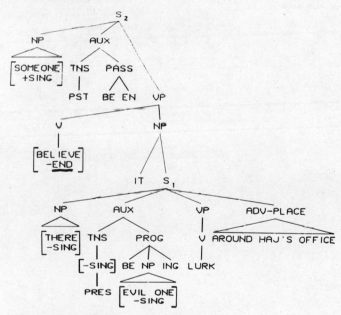

After <u>There-Insertion</u> has applied on S₁.

No other rules will apply on S₁. We go to S₂.

Q. What rule must apply first on our list (p. 208)?

A. <u>Complementizer Placement</u>. We will choose <u>for-to</u>.

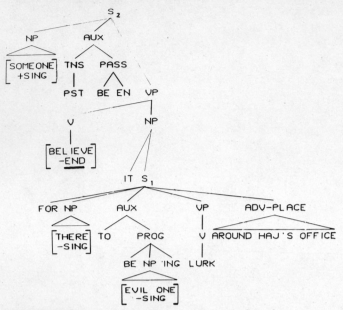

After <u>Complementizer Placement</u> has applied on the S$_2$ cycle.

Q. Next on our list (p. 208), is <u>END</u>. Can it apply?
A. No. <u>Believe</u> is marked [- <u>END</u>], and must undergo <u>It-Replacement</u> instead (pp. 185-186).

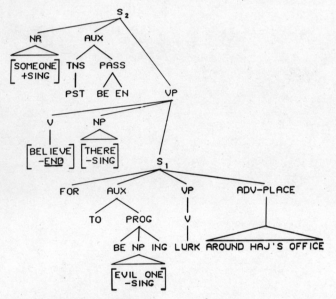

After <u>It-Replacement</u> has applied on the S$_2$ cycle.

Notice that the <u>there</u> which was moved up into S$_2$ still contains the marking [- Sing], which it received from the NP, <u>evil ones</u>, which <u>there</u> replaced in S$_1$.

Q. Can both <u>Passive</u> and <u>Number Agreement</u> apply on the S$_2$ cycle?
A. Yes, both must apply. But as we have seen on pp. 209-211, <u>Passive</u> must apply before <u>Number Agreement</u> within a simplex S (i.e., within S$_2$). Therefore, we now apply <u>Passive</u>.

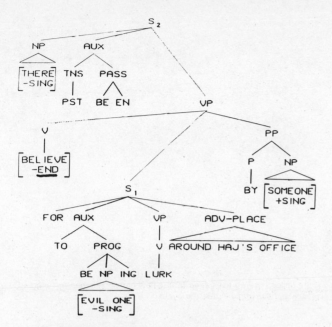

After <u>Passive</u> has applied on S_2.

Q. What rule must now apply?

A. On S_2, <u>Number Agreement</u> must again apply (as it applied on S_1), the way any other cyclic rule does. Note that since <u>there</u> still retains the mark [- Sing], the <u>Tns</u> of S_2 will likewise be marked [- Sing], by <u>Number Agreement</u>.

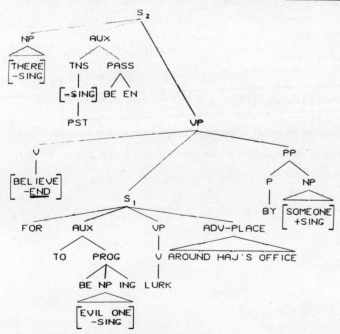

After <u>Number Agreement</u> has applied on S_2.

Notice that within S_2, <u>Number Agreement</u> had to follow <u>Passive</u>, just as was shown on pp. 209-211. If <u>Number Agreement</u> had applied before <u>Passive</u> on the S_2 cycle, we would have had *<u>There is believed to have been evil ones lurking around Haj's office</u> because the <u>Tns</u> in S_2 would have had to agree with the subject NP, someone. After <u>Passive</u>, however, $\begin{bmatrix} \text{there} \\ \text{- Sing} \end{bmatrix}$ is in subject position, and everything works out.

Q. What rules still must apply to the above structure?

A. <u>Complementizer Deletion</u> must apply, and <u>Agent Deletion</u> may apply.

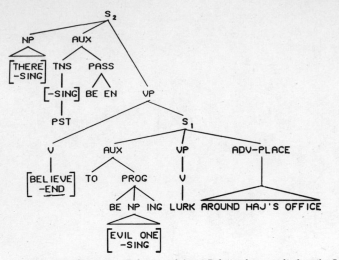

After <u>Complementizer Deletion</u> and <u>Agent Deletion</u> have applied on the S_2 cycle.

Q. What S do we have?

A. After <u>Affix Hopping</u> we derive <u>There were believed to be evil ones lurking around Haj's office</u>. As we have seen in this derivation, <u>Number Agreement</u> is a cyclic rule which must follow <u>It-Replacement</u> and <u>Passive</u> within a simplex sentence and therefore within the cycle.

<u>It-Replacement</u> vs. <u>END</u>
(Active and Passive)

We have given many examples involving verbs and adjectives which undergo <u>It-Replacement</u> and those which undergo <u>END</u>. The next pages will illustrate several important differences between the processes related to these words. The first of these differences is brought out in pairs of sentences like the following:

(1) <u>The MD is likely to examine John.</u>
(2) <u>John is likely to be examined by the MD.</u>

Here the active S, (1), is semantically equivalent to its passive S, (2). Now consider this pair:

(3) <u>The MD is eager to examine John.</u>
(4) <u>John is eager to be examined by the MD.</u>

Here, in the active S, (3), the doctor is the eager one. In the passive S, (4), John is the one who is eager. S (3) and S (4), then, are not semantically equivalent.

Q. Is this semantic difference between pair (1) and (2), which are synonymous, and pair (3) and (4), which are not, apparent in the deep structure of these sentences?

A. Yes. We will first derive (1) and (2), and then (3) and (4), so that we can see their deep structures and the rules that apply to each of them. The D. S. for (1) and (2) is as follows:

(1)

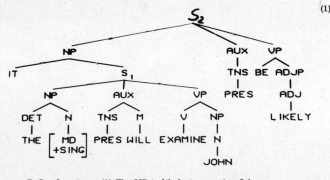

D.S. of sentence (1) <u>The MD is likely to examine John</u>.

Q. Can any rules on our list (p. 208) apply on S_1?

A. Yes. <u>Number Agreement</u> must apply.

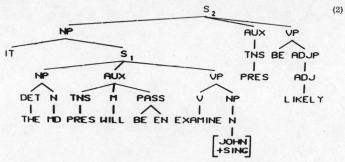

(2)

D. S. of sentence (2) <u>John is likely to be examined by the MD.</u>

Q. Do any rules on our list apply on S_1?
A. Yes. <u>Passive</u> and <u>Number Agreement</u> must apply. We must first apply <u>Passive</u> (pp. 209-211).

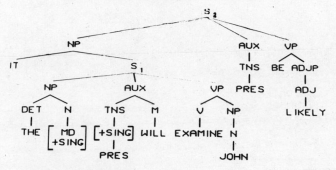

(1)

After <u>Number Agreement</u> has applied on S_1.

No other rules apply on S_1. We go to S_2.

Q. What rule on our list must apply first?
A. <u>Complementizer Placement</u>. We will use <u>for-to</u>. We will apply this rule after the next three trees (on p. 220).

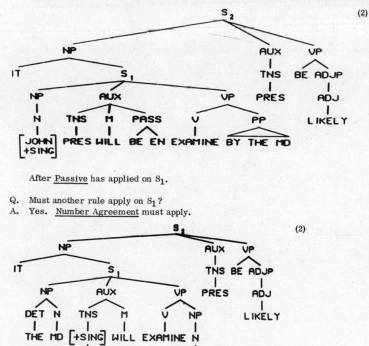

(2)

After <u>Passive</u> has applied on S_1.

Q. Must another rule apply on S_1?
A. Yes. <u>Number Agreement</u> must apply.

(2)

After <u>Number Agreement</u> has applied on S_1.

We will now place <u>for-to</u> complementizers on the S₂ cycle.

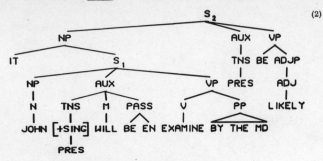

(2)

After <u>Number Agreement</u> has applied on S₁.

No other rules apply on S₁. We go to S₂.

Q. What rule must apply first on S₂?
A. <u>Complementizer Placement</u>. We will choose <u>for-to</u>.

(1)

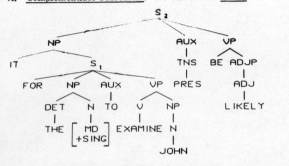

After <u>Complementizer Placement</u> has applied on the S₂ cycle.

Q. We next come to <u>END</u>. Can it apply?
A. No, because there are no two identical NP's between S₂ and S₁.
Q. Does <u>It-Replacement</u> apply?
A. Yes. <u>Likely</u> is one of the intransitive adjectives which undergoes <u>It-Replacement</u>.

(2)

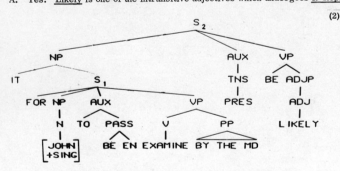

After <u>Complementizer Placement</u> has applied on the S₂ cycle.

Q. Next comes <u>END</u>. Can it apply?
A. No, because there are no two identical NP's between S₂ and S₁.
Q. Does <u>It-Replacement</u> apply on S₂?
A. Yes. <u>Likely</u> is one of the intransitive adjectives which undergoes <u>It-Replacement</u>.

(1)

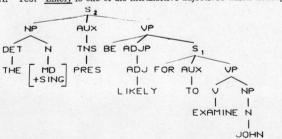

After <u>It-Replacement</u> has applied on the S₂ cycle.

Note the MD has moved up.

Q. What rules must now apply?
A. Complementizer Deletion and Number Agreement.

(2)

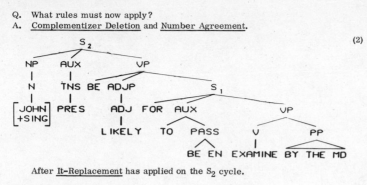

After It-Replacement has applied on the S₂ cycle.

Note that John has moved up.

Q. What rules must now apply?
A. Complementizer Deletion and Number Agreement.

(1)

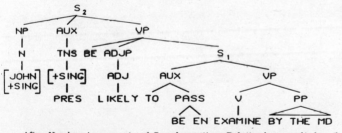

After Number Agreement and Complementizer Deletion have applied on the S₂ cycle.

This, after Affix Hopping, will give us The MD is likely to examine John. Because Passive did not apply on S₁, the MD remained in subject NP position in S₁ and was moved up into S₂ by It-Replacement.

(2)

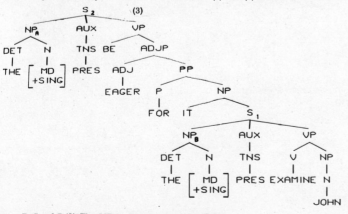

After Number Agreement and Complementizer Deletion have applied on the S₂ cycle.

After Affix Hopping we will have John is likely to be examined by the MD. Because Passive applied in S₁, the MD was no longer the subject NP of S₁. Instead, John became the subject of S₁. Therefore, when It-Replacement applied on S₂, the derived subject NP of S₁, John, was moved up into S₂.

Now compare the deep structures for sentences (3) and (4) to each other and to sentences (1) and (2) on p. 219.

S₂ (3)

D.S. of S (3) The MD is eager to examine John.

221

Q. Do any rules apply on S_1?
A. Yes. <u>Number Agreement</u> must apply.

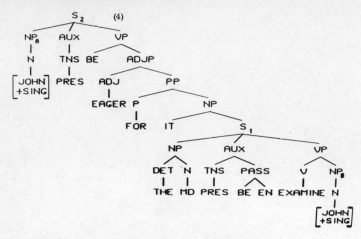

       D. S. of S (4) <u>John is eager to be examined by the MD</u>.

Q. Do any rules apply on the S_1 cycle?
A. Yes. First <u>Passive</u> must apply, and then <u>Number Agreement</u>.

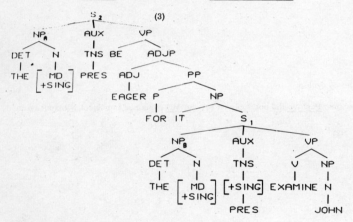

       After <u>Number Agreement</u> has applied on S_1.

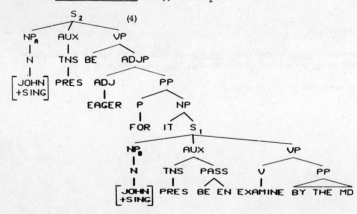

       After <u>Passive</u> has applied on S_1

Now we must apply <u>Number Agreement</u> on S_1.

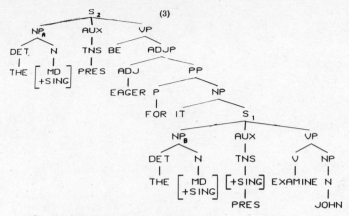

After <u>Number Agreement</u> has applied on S_1 (same as p. 222).

No other rules apply on S_1. We go to S_2.

Q. What rule must apply first on S_2?
A. <u>Complementizer Placement</u>. We will use <u>for-to</u>.

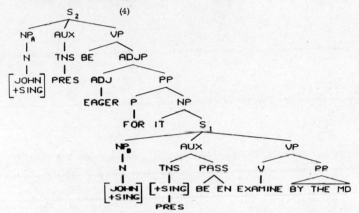

After <u>Number Agreement</u> has applied on S_1.

No other rules apply on S_1. We go to S_2.

Q. What rule must apply first on S_2?
A. <u>Complementizer Placement</u>. We will use <u>for-to</u>.

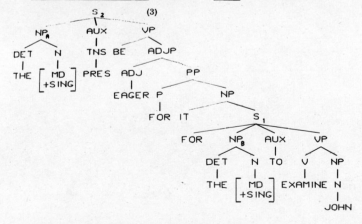

After <u>for-to</u> complements have been placed on the S_2 cycle.

Q. We now come to <u>END</u>. Does it apply on S_2?

223

A. Yes. Note that NP_a in S_2 = NP_b in S_1, and that NP_a is the closest NP to NP_b. So NP_a will delete NP_b by END.

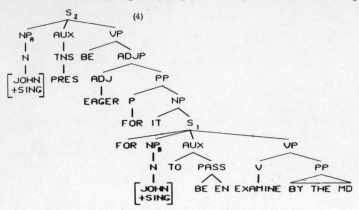

(4)

After for-to Complementizer Placement has applied on the S_2 cycle.

Q. We now come to END. Does it apply on S_2?
A. Yes. NP_a in S_2 = NP_b in S_1, and NP_a is also the NP closest to NP_b. Therefore, NP_a will delete NP_b by END.

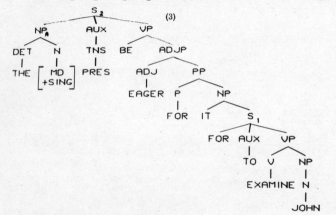

(3)

After END has applied on the S_2 cycle.

Note that NP_b, the MD, has been deleted.

Q. Can It-Replacement apply?
A. No, because there is no longer a subject NP in S_1 which can be It-Replaced.
Q. What rule on our list must apply now?
A. Number Agreement must apply.

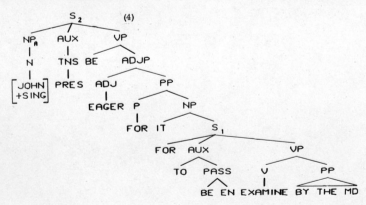

(4)

After END has applied on the S_2 cycle.

Note that NP_b, John, has been deleted.

Q. Can It-Replacement apply?
A. No, because there is no longer a subject NP in S_1 which can be It-Replaced.
Q. What rule in our list must apply now?
A. Number Agreement must apply.

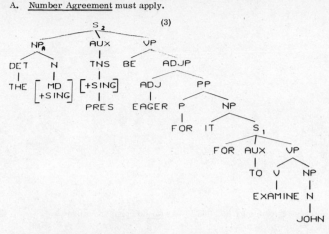

After Number Agreement has applied on S_2.

Q. What is the next rule?
A. The next rule on our list (p. 208) which must apply is It-Deletion because it in S_2 directly preces an S (S_1) within an NP.

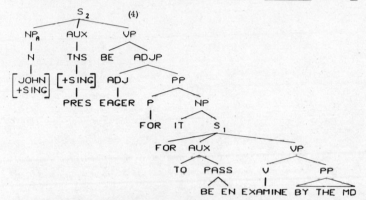

After Number Agreement has applied on S_2.

Q. What rule on our list must apply now?
A. It-Deletion must apply because the it in S_2 directly precedes an S (S_1) within an NP.

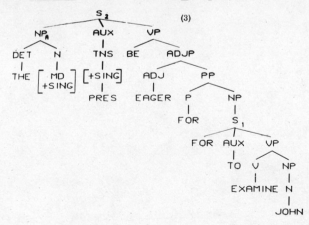

After It-Deletion has applied on S_2.

Q. What rule must apply next?
A. Preposition Deletion must apply because the preposition for in S_2 directly precedes S_1 within the same NP, and S_1 has for-to complementizers.

225

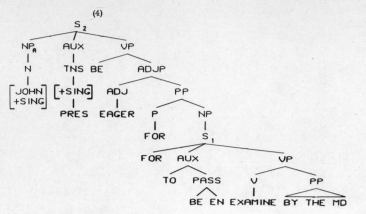

After <u>It-Deletion</u> has applied on S_2.

Q. What rule must apply now?

A. <u>Preposition Deletion</u> must apply because the preposition <u>for</u> in S_2 now directly precedes S_1 within an NP, and S_1 has <u>for-to</u> complementizers.

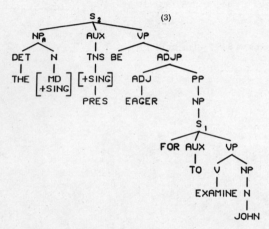

After <u>Preposition Deletion</u> has applied on S_2.

Q. What rule must apply now?

A. The last one, <u>Complementizer Deletion</u> because we have <u>for-to</u> complementizers.

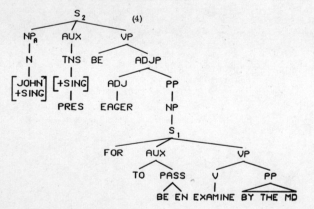

After <u>Preposition Deletion</u> has applied on S_2.

Q. What rule must still apply?

A. <u>Complementizer Deletion</u> because we have <u>for-to</u> complementizers.

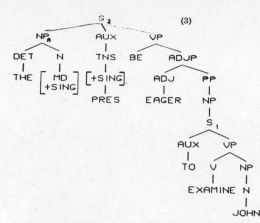

(3)

After <u>Complementizer Deletion</u> has applied on the S_2 cycle.

Q. What S do we have?
A. After <u>Affix Hopping</u> we have <u>The MD is eager to examine John</u>.

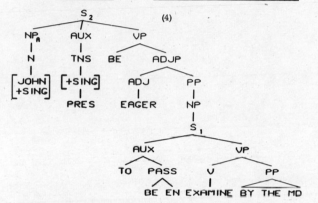

(4)

After <u>Complementizer Deletion</u> has applied on the S_2 cycle.

Q. What S do we have?
A. After <u>Affix Hopping</u> we have <u>John is eager to be examined by the MD</u>.

We have illustrated in these last pages that one difference between S's whose verbs undergo <u>It-Replacement</u> and those which undergo <u>END</u> is the synonymy between the active and passive pairs. In sentences whose verbs undergo <u>It-Replacement</u> (s (1) and S (2)), the synonymy is a result of identical deep structures (pp. 218-219). However, the nonsynonymy of active and passive pairs in sentences whose verbs undergo <u>END</u> instead of <u>It-Replacement</u> is explained by their different deep structures (pp. 221-222).

<u>It-Replacement</u> vs. <u>END</u>
(Passive Sentential Subject)

To illustrate a second difference between verbs undergoing <u>It-Replacement</u> and those undergoing <u>END</u>, we must first compare the difference between:

    (1) <u>I bribed Tom to be a teacher</u>.
    (2) <u>I believed Tom to be a teacher</u>.

There are no special difficulties with these derivations, but the difference in structure will explain some problems which will arise shortly with similar structures.

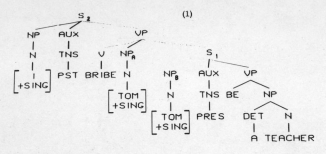

(1)

D. S. of <u>I bribed Tom to be a teacher</u>.

Q. Do any rules apply on S_1?
A. Yes. <u>Number Agreement</u> must apply.

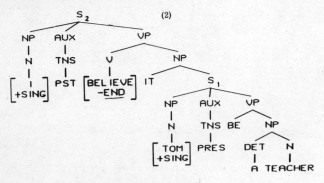

(2)

D. S. of <u>I believed Tom to be a teacher</u>.

Q. What rule must apply on S_1?
A. <u>Number Agreement</u> must apply.

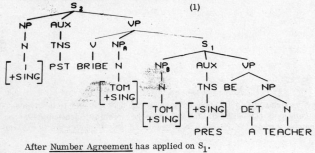

(1)

After <u>Number Agreement</u> has applied on S_1.

No other rules apply on S_1. We go to S_2.

Q. What rule must apply first on S_2?
A. <u>Complementizer Placement</u>. We will choose <u>for-to</u>.

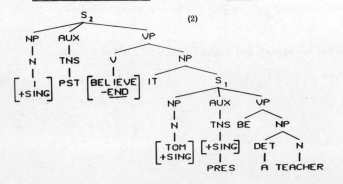

(2)

After <u>Number Agreement</u> has applied on S_1.

228

No other rules will apply on this cycle. We go to S_2.

Q.   What rule must apply first on S_2?
A.   <u>Complementizer Placement</u>. We will choose <u>for-to</u>.

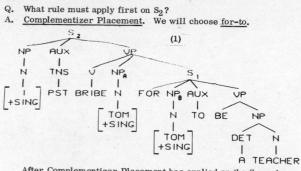

After <u>Complementizer Placement</u> has applied on the S_2 cycle.

Q.   Does <u>END</u> apply now on S_2?
A.   Yes. NP_a, <u>Tom</u>, in $S_2 = NP_b$, and NP_a is the closest NP to NP_b. By <u>END</u>, NP_a will delete NP_b.

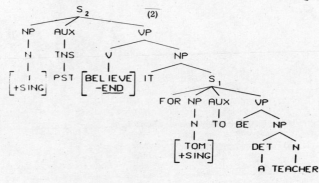

After <u>Complementizer Placement</u> has applied on the S_2 cycle.

Q.   Can <u>END</u> apply on S_2?
A.   No. There are no two identical NP's between S_2 and S_1, so <u>END</u> cannot apply. Also, <u>believe</u> is marked [- <u>END</u>] in the lexicon.

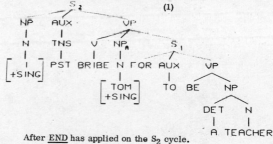

After <u>END</u> has applied on the S_2 cycle.

Q.   Can <u>It-Replacement</u> now apply?
A.   No. The subject NP of S_1 has been deleted by <u>END</u>, so there is no subject NP in S_1 to be <u>It-Replaced</u>.

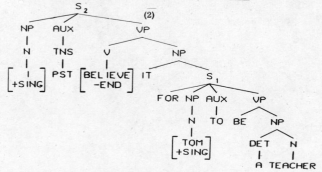

<u>END</u> could not apply on the S_2 cycle.

Q. Can It-Replacement now apply?
A. Yes, it must. Believe is a verb which undergoes It-Replacement.

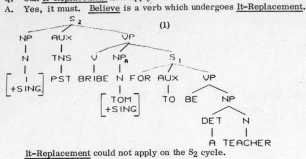

(1)

It-Replacement could not apply on the S₂ cycle.

Q. What other rules on our list must still apply on the S₂ cycle?
A. Number Agreement and Complementizer Deletion must apply.

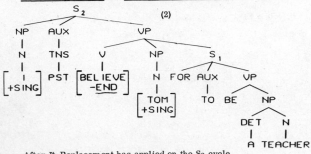

(2)

After It-Replacement has applied on the S₂ cycle.

Q. What rules now apply on S₂?
A. Number Agreement and Complementizer Deletion must now apply.

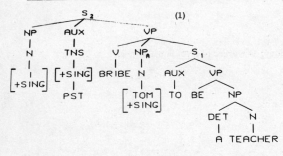

(1)

After Number Agreement and Complementizer Deletion have applied on the S₂ cycle.

Q. What do we have?
A. After Affix Hopping, we have I bribed John to be a teacher.

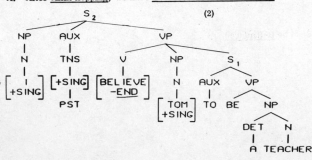

(2)

After Complementizer Deletion and Number Agreement have applied on the S₂ cycle.

Q. What do we have?
A. I believed Tom to be a teacher (after Affix Hopping).

How will the differences in structure and derivation in S (1) and S (2) explain the grammatical difference between the following two sentences?

(3) That Henry had stolen the wig was believed by everyone.

(4) *That Henry had stolen the wig was bribed by everyone (which cannot be derived).

As we proceed through these derivations, it will become clear why we can generate S (3), and why we cannot generate the unacceptable S (4).

(3)

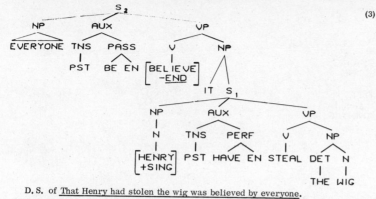

D.S. of That Henry had stolen the wig was believed by everyone.

Q. Do any rules on our list apply on S_1?

A. Yes. Number Agreement must apply.

(4)

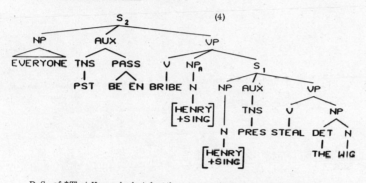

D.S. of *That Henry had stolen the wig was bribed by everyone.

Q. What rule must apply on S_1?

A. Number Agreement must apply.

(3)

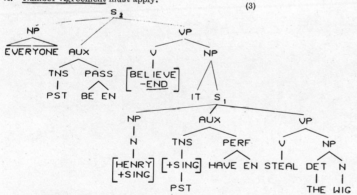

After Number Agreement has applied on S_1

No other rules apply on S_1. We proceed to S_2.

Q. What rule must apply first on the S_2 cycle?

A. Complementizer Placement. We'll use a that complementizer.

231

(4)

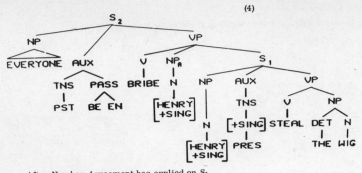

After <u>Number Agreement</u> has applied on S_1.

No further rules apply on the first cycle. Let us go on to S_2.

Q. What rule must apply first on S_2?
A. <u>Complementizer Placement</u>. We will use <u>for-to</u>. Note that we could not place a <u>that</u> complementizer with <u>bribe</u> (i.e., *<u>Henry was bribed that will go</u>
or *<u>Henry was induced that will go</u>).   (3)

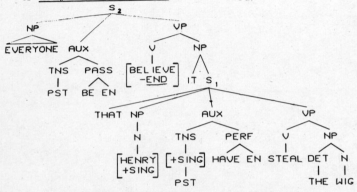

After <u>that</u> <u>Complementizer Placement</u> has applied on the S_2 cycle.

Q. Can <u>END</u> apply on S_2?
A. No. First, <u>END</u> applies only with <u>for-to</u> or <u>poss-ing</u> complementizers (p. 123). Second, there are no two identical NP's between S_2 and S_1. Third, the verb <u>believe</u> is marked [- <u>END</u>] (see pp. 185-186).   (4)

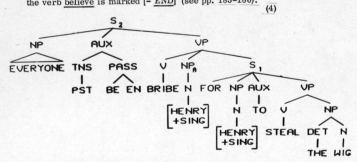

After <u>for-to</u> complements have been placed on the S_2 cycle.

Q. Does <u>END</u> apply on S_2?
A. Yes. NP_a in S_2 = NP_b in S_1, and NP_a is the closest NP to NP_b, so NP_a will delete NP_b by <u>END</u>.

232

(3)

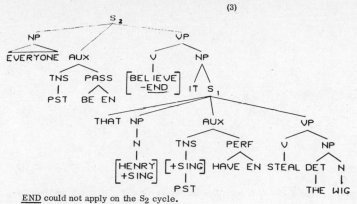

END could not apply on the S$_2$ cycle.

Q.   Can It-Replacement apply?
A.   No, It-Replacement can apply only with for-to or poss-ing complementizers (see pp. 172-174). (If we did apply It-Replacement now, we would have *Henry was believed by everyone that has stolen the wig.)
Q.   Must Passive apply on S$_2$ now?
A.   Yes. The entire object NP of S$_2$, which includes S$_1$, will be moved into the subject NP position of S$_2$.

(4)

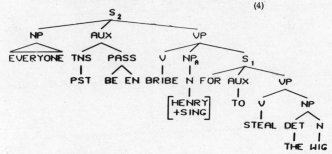

After END has applied on the S$_2$ cycle.

Q.   Can It-Replacement apply now?
A.   No, since the subject NP of S$_1$ has been deleted by END on the S$_2$ cycle.
Q.   Must Passive now apply on S$_2$?
A.   Yes. The auxiliary of S$_2$ contains the Passive constituent. The NP$_a$, Henry, in object NP position, will move to the front, as is usual with Passive, and the subject NP will be prefixed by the preposition by and daughter-adjoined to the VP of S$_2$.

(3)

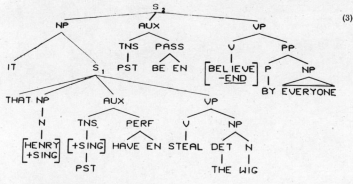

After Passive has applied on S$_2$.

As we have said, the entire object NP of S$_2$, which includes S$_1$, has been moved to the front of the sentence.

Q.   What rule must apply now?
A.   Number Agreement must now apply on S$_2$.

(4)

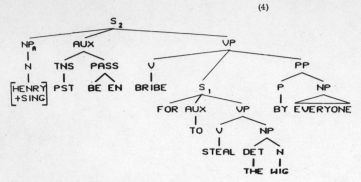

After <u>Passive</u> has applied on S_2.

The object NP of S_2, which included only the NP, <u>Henry</u>, was affected by <u>Passive</u>. The clause S_1 is not within the object NP of S_2, so it will (and has) remain(ed) untouched.

Q. What rule must now apply?
A. <u>Number Agreement</u>.

(3)

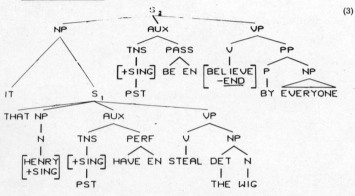

After <u>Number Agreement</u> has applied on S_2.

The next rule on our list which may apply is <u>Extraposition</u>. Since it is optional, we will choose not to apply it. (If we did we would have <u>It was believed by everyone that Henry had stolen the wig</u>.)

Q. Must <u>It-Deletion</u> apply?
A. Yes. <u>It</u> directly precedes S_1, which is within the same NP.

(4)

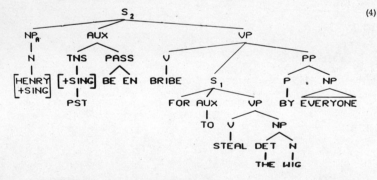

After <u>Number Agreement</u> has applied on S_2.

Q. May <u>Extraposition</u> apply here?
A. No, because there is no <u>it-S</u> in this structure. Of course, <u>It-Deletion</u> cannot apply either, since there is no <u>it</u> to delete. Nothing will apply to this structure now, except <u>Complementizer Deletion</u>.

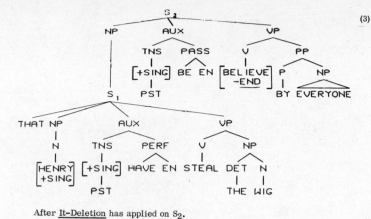

(3)

After <u>It-Deletion</u> has applied on S₂.

Q. Does <u>Complementizer Deletion</u> apply?
A. No. The S. D. for <u>Complementizer Deletion</u> is not met (<u>that</u> does not precede a VP here).
Q. What S do we have?
A. After <u>Affix Hopping</u> we have <u>That Henry had stolen the wig was believed by everyone</u>.

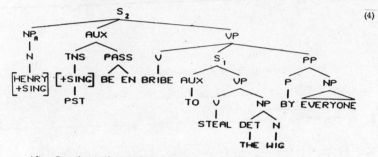

(4)

After <u>Complementizer Deletion</u> has applied on S₂.

Q. What do we have?
A. After <u>Affix Hopping</u> we have <u>Henry was bribed to steal the wig by everyone</u>. Note we could not generate the unacceptable S (4) (p. 231).

The last derivation (pp. 231-235) has illustrated another major difference between verbs undergoing <u>END</u> and those undergoing <u>It-Replacement</u>: Verbs undergoing <u>It-Replacement</u> can passivize full object NP clauses; verbs undergoing <u>END</u> cannot <u>passivize</u> full object NP clauses (as shown by the ungrammaticality of S (4) on p. 231) or NP's containing relative clauses, since object NP clauses can never be present in that position in the deep structure of these verbs (see S (4) on p. 231).

It-Replacement vs. END
(Sentential Subject)

We have already discussed some of the structural differences between the intransitive adjective, <u>be likely</u> (pp. 220-221), which may undergo <u>It-Replacement</u>, and the transitive adjective, <u>be eager</u>, which may undergo <u>END</u> (pp. 221-227). Another difference between these two adjectives and the class of adjectives each represents (with <u>likely</u> we have <u>sure</u>, <u>certain</u>, etc., and with <u>eager</u> there is <u>happy</u>, <u>sad</u>, etc.) is parallel to the difference between <u>believe</u> and <u>bribe</u> shown on pp. 231-235. As <u>believe</u> may take sentential subjects, so may <u>likely</u>; and as <u>bribe</u> may not have sentential subjects, so <u>eager</u> may not have sentential subjects:

    That John will perish is believed.
    That John will perish is likely.
  *That John will perish is bribed.
  *That John will perish is eager.

It is also the case that <u>believe</u> may have <u>there</u> as its object NP, just as <u>likely</u> may have <u>there</u> as its subject:

    He believes there to have been an explosion.
    There is likely to be an explosion.

But <u>bribe</u>, as <u>eager</u>, may not have <u>there</u> as its object (or subject) NP:

  *He bribed there to be an explosion.
  *There is eager to be an explosion.

To illustrate this difference between <u>likely</u> and <u>eager</u>, let us look at the derivation of <u>There is likely to be an explosion</u> and, finally, the deep structure of *<u>There is eager to be an explosion</u>.

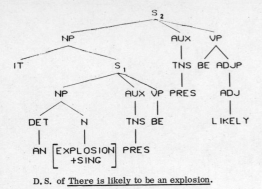

D. S. of <u>There is likely to be an explosion.</u>

Q. What rule may apply on S_1?
A. Both <u>Number Agreement</u> and <u>There-Insertion</u> must apply. <u>There-Insertion</u> is obligatory because <u>be</u> is intransitive. As we have seen (pp. 212-214), the order of <u>There-Insertion</u> and <u>Number Agreement</u> is not crucial within a simplex S. We will apply <u>Number Agreement</u> first.

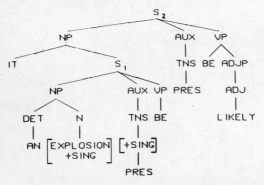

After <u>Number Agreement</u> has applied on S_1.

Q. What is the next rule?
A. We must now apply <u>There-Insertion</u>.

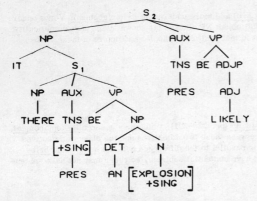

After <u>There-Insertion</u> has applied on S_1.

No other rules apply on S_1. We go to S_2.

Q. What rule must apply first on S_2?
A. <u>Complementizer Placement</u>. We'll choose <u>for-to</u>.

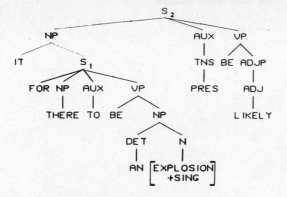

After <u>Complementizer Placement</u> has applied on the S_2 cycle.

Q. Can <u>END</u> apply?
A. No, because its S.D. is not met.
Q. Does <u>It-Replacement</u> apply?
A. Yes, because <u>likely</u> belongs to the class of adjectives which undergoes <u>It-Replacement</u>.

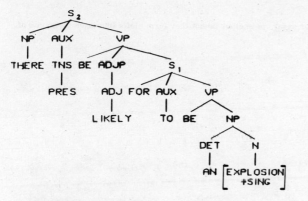

After <u>It-Replacement</u> has applied on the S_2 cycle.

The newly derived NP <u>there</u>[8] has moved up into subject position of S_2.

Q. What rules must now apply?
A. <u>Complementizer Deletion</u> and <u>Number Agreement</u>.

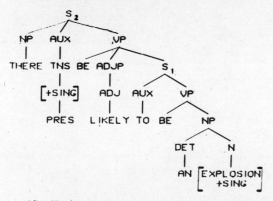

After <u>Number Agreement</u> and <u>Complementizer Deletion</u> have applied on the S_2 cycle.

Q. What S do we have?

[8]We have been assuming that <u>there</u> is an NP. This is not a groundless assumption, however. First of all, <u>there</u> takes part in <u>Subject-Verb Inversion</u>: <u>Was there an explosion</u>? Second, <u>there</u> forms tags: <u>There was an explosion, wasn't there</u>? Third, <u>there</u> is made the derived subject by <u>Passive</u>: <u>There was believed to have been an explosion</u>. Fourth, <u>there</u> has <u>Number Agreement</u>: <u>There were five men in town</u>. And finally, <u>there</u> undergoes <u>It-Replacement</u>: <u>There is likely to be an explosion</u> (as in our example).

A. After <u>Affix Hopping</u> we have <u>There is likely to be an explosion</u>. Because <u>likely</u> is an intransitive adjective which must take abstract subjects, the sentence is good. Now let's look at the deep structure of *<u>There is eager to be an explosion</u> (which exists only doubtfully).

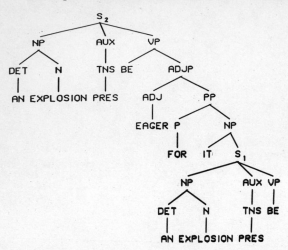

D. S. of *<u>There is eager to be an explosion</u>.

Finally, another difference between verbs like <u>expect</u>, or <u>likely</u>, as opposed to <u>bribe</u>, or <u>eager</u>, is whether or not they form clefts (the exact formation of which we will not go into):

> <u>What was expected was that there would be an explosion</u>.
> <u>What is likely is that John will win</u>.

as opposed to:

> *<u>What was bribed was that there would be an explosion</u>.
> *<u>What is eager is that John will win</u>.

Ordering of Rules Presented in Part IV

<u>Complementizer Placement</u>

<u>END</u>

<u>It-Replacement</u>

<u>Passive</u>

<u>Number Agreement</u>

<u>Reflexive</u>

<u>There-Insertion</u>

<u>Extraposition</u>

<u>It-Deletion</u>

<u>Preposition Deletion</u>

<u>Complementizer Deletion</u>

Appendixes

Sentences Illustrating the Necessity for Ordering the Rules

Part I

1. <u>Reflexive</u> precedes <u>Imperative</u>, otherwise we will have *<u>wash you</u>, and the grammatical <u>wash yourself</u> could not be generated (pp. 13–14).
2. <u>Neg-Emp Placement</u> precedes <u>Do-Support</u>, otherwise the grammatical S <u>John doesn't eat bananas</u> could not be generated (pp. 18–19).
3. <u>Tag Formation</u> must apply before <u>Do-Support</u>, otherwise the grammatical S <u>Churchill hated bagels, didn't he</u>? could not be generated (pp. 20–22).
4. <u>There-Insertion</u> precedes <u>Tag Formation</u>. If <u>Tag Formation</u> is first, we have *<u>There is a devil among us, isn't he</u>? If <u>There-Insertion</u> is first, then <u>Tag Formation</u> will correctly copy over the subject NP <u>there</u>, and we obtain the grammatical <u>There is a devil among us, isn't there</u>? (pp. 23–25)
5. <u>Question Formation</u> precedes <u>Subject-Verb Inversion</u>. Only after <u>Question Formation</u> is the environment for <u>Subject-Verb Inversion</u> met; i.e., the S.D. for the <u>Subject-Verb Inversion</u> is not met until <u>Question Formation</u> has applied (p. 26).
6. <u>Adverb Preposing</u> must precede <u>Subject-Verb Inversion</u>. If a negative Adverb is preposed, <u>Subject-Verb Inversion</u> must take place, as in <u>At no time did Willy put his finger in a crevice</u> (p. 29).
7. <u>Subject-Verb Inversion</u> precedes <u>Affix Hopping</u>. Otherwise, we could generate only *<u>At what time put Willy his finger in a crevice</u>? If <u>Subject-Verb Inversion</u> precedes <u>Affix Hopping</u>, we can obtain <u>At what time did Willy put his finger in a crevice</u>? (pp. 28–29)
8. <u>Question Formation</u> is unordered with respect to <u>Neg-Emp Placement</u> (pp. 30–31).
9. <u>Neg-Emp Placement</u> must precede <u>Subject-Verb Inversion</u>, otherwise we could not generate <u>What doesn't John like</u>? (p. 32).
10. <u>Dative</u> must precede <u>Passive</u>. If <u>Passive</u> applied first, we could generate only the S <u>Jane was sent some B.O. bomb yesterday by Lucifer</u>. We could not generate <u>Some B.O. bomb was sent to Jane yesterday by Lucifer</u>. To obtain both of these sentences, <u>Dative</u> must precede <u>Passive</u> (pp. 39–41).
11. <u>Passive</u> precedes <u>There-Insertion</u>. Only with that order can we generate the S <u>There was a stone being thrown by Jupiter</u> (pp. 41–42).
12. <u>Passive</u> precedes <u>Tag Formation</u>. Otherwise, we can generate only the unacceptable *<u>An arrow was shot by Paris, wasn't he</u>? If <u>Passive</u> is first, we can obtain the S <u>An arrow was shot by Paris, wasn't it</u>? (pp. 42–44)
13. <u>Passive</u> precedes <u>Question Formation</u>. If Q-Formation is first, we can generate only *<u>This show is being run by who</u>? (which is acceptable only as an echo question). If <u>Passive</u> is first, we can obtain <u>(By) whom is this show being run (by)</u>? (pp. 44–46).
14. <u>Tag Formation</u> precedes <u>Neg-Emp Placement</u>. Otherwise, we will generate the unacceptable <u>Mary wasn't cooked by the Chief, wasn't she</u>? If <u>Tag Formation</u> is first, the Tag will have no <u>Neg</u> in it (since there is still a <u>Neg</u> in the PreS), and we have the desired <u>Mary wasn't cooked by the Chief, was she</u>? (pp. 46–47)
15. <u>Tag Formation</u> precedes <u>Imperative</u>, otherwise the sentence <u>Come, won't you</u>? could not be generated (pp. 48–49)
16. <u>There-Insertion</u> precedes <u>Question Formation</u> and <u>Subject-Verb Inversion</u>. If <u>Question Formation</u> is first, we generate the odd S *<u>There is what in the drink</u>? (an acceptable echo question, but not good as a normal question). Only if <u>There-Insertion</u> is first can we generate the S <u>What is there in the drink</u>? (pp. 49–51). These two rules are said to be <u>extrinsically</u> ordered; i.e., the rules can structurally apply in either order, but only one order produces a good S (pp. 55–57).
17. <u>There-Insertion</u> and <u>Reflexive</u> are unordered with respect to each other (pp. 51–53). Either way, we can have the S <u>There is a boy washing himself</u>.
18. <u>Passive</u> must precede <u>Agent Deletion</u>. This ordering is said to be <u>intrinsic</u>; i.e., there is no agent to be deleted until <u>Passive</u> has created it (pp. 53–54).
19. <u>Affix Hopping</u> and <u>Agent Deletion</u> are unordered with respect to each other (p. 55).
20. <u>There-Insertion</u> must precede <u>Adverb Preposing</u>. Otherwise, we can generate only <u>Tonight a man will be leaving</u>. (After <u>Adverb Preposing</u>, the S.D. for <u>There-Insertion</u> is no longer met.) To obtain <u>Tonight there will be a man leaving</u>, we must apply <u>There-Insertion</u> first (pp. 57–59).

21. <u>Relative Clause Formation</u> precedes <u>Extraposition from NP</u>. If <u>Extraposition from NP</u> applied first, <u>Relative Clause Formation</u> could not apply, for the clause to be relativized would no longer be within an NP. The only S we could get is *<u>A performer is dressing now a performer will appear shortly</u>. If <u>Relative Clause Formation</u> is first, we can derive <u>A performer will appear shortly who is dressing now</u> (pp. 74-75).

22. <u>Relative Clause Formation</u> must apply before <u>Relative Clause Reduction</u>, since one cannot reduce a relative clause until it has been formed (p. 78).

23. <u>Relative Clause Reduction</u> applies before <u>Modifier Shift</u>, because <u>Relative Clause Reduction</u> sets up the environment in which <u>Modifier Shift</u> can apply (pp. 86-88).

24. <u>Agent Deletion</u> must apply before <u>Modifier Shift</u>, or else we wouldn't be able to have NP's like <u>the murdered man</u>, at all (p. 83)

25. <u>Extraposition from NP</u> must apply before <u>Relative Clause Reduction</u>. Otherwise, we will generate *<u>Someone must have done this crazy</u>. To prevent this S and to derive the desired <u>Someone crazy must have done this</u>, <u>Extraposition from NP</u> must apply before <u>Relative Clause Reduction</u> (pp. 84-86).

26. <u>Extraposition from NP</u> must follow <u>Question Formation</u>, because otherwise we could only have <u>Who, who is unfair, do we know</u>? We could not generate the sentence <u>Who do we know who is unfair</u>? To obtain both sentences, <u>Extraposition from NP</u> must follow <u>Question Formation</u> (pp. 88-91).

27. <u>Relative Clause Formation</u> must precede <u>Possessive Formation</u>, since the S. D. of <u>Possessive Formation</u> is not met until <u>Relative Clause Formation</u> has applied (p. 92).

28. <u>Possessive Formation</u> must precede <u>Possessive Shift</u>, because only after <u>Possessive Formation</u> has applied is the S. D. for <u>Possessive Shift</u> met (pp. 92-93).

Part III

29. <u>Passive</u> must precede <u>Extraposition</u>. Otherwise, we can obtain only the sentence <u>That Andy smoked pot was proven by someone</u>. If <u>Passive</u> is first, we can also have the sentence <u>It was proven that Andy smoked pot</u> (pp. 96-98).

30. <u>Extraposition</u> (optional) must precede <u>It-Deletion</u> (obligatory), because otherwise we must postulate two separate rules of <u>It-Deletion</u> (pp. 98-100).

31. <u>Extraposition</u> must precede <u>Relative Clause Formation</u>. Otherwise, we will generate the unacceptable *<u>The hat which that Tom bought is obvious is made of gold</u>. To derive the desirable <u>The hat which it is obvious that Tom bought is made of gold</u>, we must apply <u>Extraposition</u> before <u>Relative Clause Formation</u> (pp. 102-106).

32. <u>Extraposition</u> must precede <u>Question Formation</u>. Otherwise, we will generate the unacceptable *<u>What hat is that Tom bought obvious</u>? To obtain the S <u>What hat is it obvious that Tom bought</u>? <u>Extraposition</u> must precede <u>Question Formation</u> (pp. 106-108).

33. <u>Complementizer Placement</u> must precede <u>Extraposition</u>, otherwise we will generate *<u>It worries me our being criminals</u>. To prevent this, <u>Extraposition</u> follows <u>Complementizer Placement</u> (pp. 112-115).

34. <u>It-Deletion</u> must precede <u>Preposition Deletion</u>, because otherwise the S. D. for <u>Preposition Deletion</u> would not be met, and the rule could not apply (pp. 116-117).

35. <u>Complementizer Placement</u> must precede <u>END</u>, otherwise we will generate *<u>This little Indian expects that will be chief next year</u>. To prevent this S, <u>Complementizer Placement</u> must be first (p. 123).

Part IV

36. <u>END</u> must precede <u>Passive</u> within a simplex S (pp. 138-140).

37. <u>Complementizer Placement</u> must precede <u>It-Replacement</u>, otherwise we will generate *<u>John is certain that will find out</u>. To prevent this S, <u>Complementizer Placement</u> must precede <u>It-Replacement</u> (p. 170).

38. <u>It-Replacement</u> precedes <u>Reflexive</u> within a simplex S, since only after <u>It-Replacement</u> are there two identical NP's within a simplex S in sentences of the form <u>John believes himself to be cool</u> (pp. 186-187).

39. <u>Passive</u> precedes <u>There-Insertion</u>. Otherwise, we will generate *<u>A bike was a cow being ridden by there</u>. To prevent this and instead obtain the acceptable <u>There was a bike being ridden by a cow</u>, <u>Passive</u> must apply first (pp. 188-189, see also pp. 41-42).

40. Although <u>There-Insertion</u> and <u>It-Replacement</u> are not ordered with respect to each other within one simplex S, to obtain sentences of the form <u>John believed there to have been a bean in his bed</u>, <u>There-Insertion</u> must apply on the lower S_1, so that it can be <u>It-Replaced</u> into the next higher S (S_2) on the S_2 cycle (pp. 189-191).

41. <u>It-Replacement</u> must apply before <u>Passive</u>, otherwise we could not generate sentences of the form <u>Some ants were believed by Mary to have been eaten by John</u> (pp. 191-200).

42. <u>Passive</u> must apply before <u>Number Agreement</u> so that the <u>Tns</u> will agree in number with the derived subject after <u>Passive</u> has applied. This order will prevent sentences like *<u>The buffaloes is put into the air by a snowstorm</u> and generate instead <u>The buffaloes were put into the air by a snowstorm</u> (pp. 209-211).

Phrase Structure Rules

$$S \rightarrow \begin{Bmatrix} \underline{and} \\ \underline{or} \end{Bmatrix} \quad S^n, \ n \geq 2$$

$$S \rightarrow (PreS) + NP + Aux + VP + (Adv_{Time}) + (Adv_{Place}) + (Adv_{Manner})^+ (Adv_{Purpose})$$

$$PreS \rightarrow (\begin{Bmatrix} Q \\ Imp \end{Bmatrix}) \ (NEG) \ (EMP)$$

$$VP \rightarrow \begin{Bmatrix} V \ (\begin{Bmatrix} NP \\ PP \end{Bmatrix}) \ (\begin{Bmatrix} NP \\ PP \\ S \end{Bmatrix}) \\ be \ (\begin{Bmatrix} Adj\ P \\ NP \\ PP \end{Bmatrix}) \end{Bmatrix}$$

$$Adv \rightarrow \begin{Bmatrix} Adv_{Time} \\ Adv_{Place} \\ Adv_{Manner} \\ Adv_{Purpose} \end{Bmatrix} \begin{Bmatrix} PP, \ \underline{yesterday}, \ \underline{tonight}, \ etc. \\ PP, \ \underline{somewhere}, \ \underline{here}, \ etc. \\ PP, \ \underline{carefully}, \ \underline{thus}, \ etc. \\ PP, \ \underline{on\ purpose}, \ etc. \end{Bmatrix}$$
$$\quad\quad i \quad\quad\quad i \quad\ i \quad\quad\quad\quad\quad\quad i$$

$$Adj\ P \rightarrow Adj \ (\begin{Bmatrix} PP \\ S \end{Bmatrix})$$

$$PP \rightarrow P + NP$$

$$NP \rightarrow Det + N$$

$$Aux \rightarrow Tense + (M) + (Perf) + (Prog) + (Pass)$$

$$Tense \rightarrow \begin{Bmatrix} Past \\ Pres \end{Bmatrix}$$

$$M \rightarrow \underline{will}, \ \underline{shall}, \ \underline{must}, \ \underline{can}, \ \underline{may}$$

$$Perf \rightarrow \underline{have} + en$$

Prog $\rightarrow$ <u>be</u> + ing

Pass $\rightarrow$ <u>be</u> + en

Det $\rightarrow$ $\left\{ \begin{array}{l} \underline{a}, \text{ (WH)}, \underline{some}, \ldots \\ \underline{the}, \underline{this}, \underline{that}, \ldots \end{array} \right\}$

N $\rightarrow$ <u>jungle</u>, <u>Mary</u>, <u>one</u>, <u>thing</u>, <u>place</u>, <u>time</u>, <u>fungus</u>, <u>acrobat</u>

V $\rightarrow$ <u>osculate</u>, <u>jump</u>, <u>buy</u>, <u>yawn</u>, <u>speculate</u>, <u>smell</u>

Abbreviations and Notations

* = unacceptable sentence
∅ = null
= word boundary
= sentence boundary
S = sentence
PreS = PreSentence
NP = noun phrase
VP = verb phrase
PP = prepositional phrase
P = preposition
Adj P = adjective phrase
Adv = adverb
Imp = imperative
NEG = negative
EMP = emphatic
Prog = progressive
Perf = perfect
Pass = passive
Q = question
Det = determiner
M = modal
PS = phrase structure
$\Longrightarrow$ = "is transformed into"

$\overset{X}{\triangle}$ = abbreviation for a string dominated by a constituent, X, where the detailed constituent structure below X is not relevant.

$\left\{ \right\}_i$ = braces with a numerical subscript designate parallel choice. If the top line within the pair of such braces is chosen, the top line of all other like braces with the same subscript must also be chosen. The same holds true for the second line. For example, $\left\{ \begin{matrix} X \\ Y \end{matrix} \right\}$ L T $\left\{ \begin{matrix} E \\ A \end{matrix} \right\}$ abbreviates XLTE or YLTA, but not: *XLTA or *YLTE.

(X) = parentheses designate an optional item, which may or may not be there. So a term like $[(P) NP]_{pp}$ stands for $[P NP]_{pp}$ or NP_{pp}.

245

X - YL - ZKG - = the dashes between X, Y, and Z, indicate the boundaries of that term.
1   2   3   Thus, term 1 = X, term 2 = YL, and term 3 = ZKG.

Transformations[1]

Complementizer Placement

S.D.
$$
\begin{array}{c}
X - [\ NP\ - [\ Tns\ (M)\ -\ X\ ]\ VP\ Y\ ]\ -\ Z \\
\ \ \ \ \ S\ \ \ \ \ \ \ \ \ Aux\ \ \ \ \ \ \ \ \ \ \ Aux\ \ \ S \\
1\ \ \ \ \ \ 2\ \ \ \ \ \ 3\ \ \ \ \ \ \ \ \ \ \ \ \ \ \ 4\ \ \ \ \ \ 5
\end{array}
$$

$$\Rightarrow \text{oblig}$$

S.C.
$$
1\quad
\underbrace{\begin{Bmatrix} that \\ \underline{for} \\ poss \end{Bmatrix}}_{1}
+\underbrace{\varnothing}_{1}
\ \underbrace{\begin{Bmatrix} \underline{3} \\ \underline{to} \\ \underline{ing} \end{Bmatrix}}_{1}
\ \underbrace{\ }_{1}\ 4\quad 5
$$

Equi NP Deletion

S.D.
$$
X\ -\ (NP)\ -\ Y\ -\ [\ \underset{S}{\ }\begin{Bmatrix} for \\ poss \end{Bmatrix}\ -\ NP\ -\ \underset{S}{Z}\ ]\ -\ W\ -\ (NP)\ -\ R
$$

$$
1\qquad 2\qquad 3\qquad 4\qquad 5\qquad 6\qquad 7\qquad 8\qquad 9
$$

$$\Rightarrow \text{oblig}$$

S.C.
$$
1\qquad 2\qquad 3\qquad 4\qquad \varnothing\qquad 6\qquad 7\qquad 8\qquad 9
$$

$$
2 = 5 \\
\text{or } 5 = 8
$$

Condition: 2 and 8 may not both be null.

Dative

S.D.
$$
\begin{array}{c}
XV\ -\ NP\ -\ NP\ -\ Y \\
1\ \ \ \ \ \ 2\ \ \ \ \ \ 3\ \ \ \ \ 4
\end{array}
$$

$$\Rightarrow \text{opt}$$

S.C.
$$
1\qquad 0\qquad 3\ \text{to}\ 2\quad 4
$$

[1]These are given in the order in which they can be applied. Note that S.D. is the abbreviation for "structural description" and S.C., "structural change."

247

Passive

S. D.
$$\text{## (PreS)} - \text{NP} - \underset{\text{Aux}}{[} \text{X Pass} \underset{\text{Aux}}{]} \text{V (Prep)} - \text{NP} - \text{Y}$$

1	2	3		4	5

$$\Longrightarrow \text{oblig}$$

S. C.
1	4	3	5 by 2

Agent Deletion

S. D.
$$\text{X Passive V} - \text{by NP} - \text{Y}$$

1	2	3

$$\Longrightarrow \text{opt}$$

S. C.
1	0	3

Condition: $2 = \underline{\text{by}} + \underline{\text{some}} \quad \left\{ \begin{matrix} \underline{\text{one}} \\ \underline{\text{thing}} \end{matrix} \right\}$

Number Agreement

S. D.
$$\text{(PreS)} - \text{NP} \quad \text{Tns} - \text{X}$$

$$\underset{1}{\left\{ \begin{matrix} \text{+Sing} \\ \text{-Sing} \end{matrix} \right\}_{1}}$$

1	2	3	4

$$\Longrightarrow \text{oblig}$$

1	2	3	4

S. C.
$$\underset{1}{\left\{ \begin{matrix} \text{+Sing} \\ \text{-Sing} \end{matrix} \right\}_{1}}$$

Reflexive

S. D.
$$\text{X} - \text{NP} - \text{Y} - \text{NP} - \text{Z}$$

1	2	3	4	5

$$\Longrightarrow \text{oblig}$$

S. C.
| 1 | 2 | 3 $[\overset{4}{_{+\text{reflexive}}}]$ 5 |

There-Insertion

S. D.
$$\text{# (Pres)} - \text{NP} - \left\{ \begin{matrix} \text{Aux} - \underline{\text{be}} - \text{W} \\ [\text{X} - \underline{\text{be}} - \text{Y}] - \text{Z} \\ \text{Aux} \qquad \text{Aux} \end{matrix} \right\}$$

1	2	3	4	5	6

$$\Longrightarrow \text{opt}$$

S. C.
1	<u>there</u>	3	4 + 2	5	6

Conditions: a) 2 has an indefinite determiner
  b) <u>be</u> directly follows <u>Tns</u>.

Extraposition

S.D.
$$X - [\underset{NP}{\underset{it}{\text{it}}} - \underset{NP}{S}] - Y$$

1   2 3   4

$\Longrightarrow$ opt

S.C.   1   2   0   4 + 3

Condition: Applies only with <u>that</u> and <u>for-to</u> complementizers.

It-Deletion

S.D.
$$X - [\underset{NP}{\underset{it}{\text{it}}} - \underset{NP}{S}] - Y$$

1   2   3   4

$\Longrightarrow$ oblig

S.C.   1   0   3   4

Preposition Deletion

S.D.
$$X - [\underset{PP}{P} - \underset{PP}{S}] - Y$$

1   2   3   4

$\Longrightarrow$ oblig

S.C.   1   0   3   4

Condition: Applies only with <u>that</u> and <u>for-to</u> complementizers.

Relative Clause Formation

S.D.
$$X - [\underset{NP}{NP} - [\underset{S}{Y} - (P) - NP - W]] - Z$$

1   2   3   4   5   6   7

$\Longrightarrow$ oblig

S.C.   1   2   4 $\begin{bmatrix} 5 \\ +pro \\ +WH \end{bmatrix}$ 3   6   7

Condition: 2 = 5.

Question Formation

S.D.
$$Q - X - [\text{ (Prep)} \underset{NP \ Det}{[[\text{ WH } \underline{\text{some}}] \underset{Det \ NP \ PP}{N}]}] - Y$$

1   2   3   4

$\Longrightarrow$ oblig

S.C.   3   2   4

Condition: N = $\begin{Bmatrix} \underline{\text{one}} \\ \underline{\text{thing}} \\ \underline{\text{place}} \end{Bmatrix}$

Extraposition from NP

S.D.
$$X - [\ NP - S\ ] - Y$$
$$_{NP}_{NP}$$
$$1 \quad\quad 2 \quad\quad 3 \quad\quad 4$$

$$\Longrightarrow opt$$

S.C. $\quad 1 \quad\quad 2 \quad\quad 0 \quad\quad 4 + 3$

Tag Formation

S.D.
$$\#\ \begin{Bmatrix} Q \\ Imp \end{Bmatrix} - \begin{Bmatrix} Neg \\ \emptyset \end{Bmatrix}_{1\ 1} - (Emp) - NP - \begin{Bmatrix} Tns \\ Tns \begin{Bmatrix} M \\ \underline{have} \\ \underline{be} \end{Bmatrix} \end{Bmatrix} \begin{matrix} -\ V\ X \\ -\ X \end{matrix}$$

$$1 \quad\quad 2 \quad\quad 3 \quad\quad 4 \quad\quad 5 \quad\quad 6$$

$$\Longrightarrow oblig$$

S.C.
$$1 \quad\quad 2 \quad\quad 3 \quad 4 \quad 5 \quad 6 \quad 5 \begin{Bmatrix} \emptyset \\ Neg \end{Bmatrix}_{1\ 1} [\ _{+PRO}^{4}$$

Condition: OPT if 1 = Imp.

Neg-Emp Placement

S.D.
$$\#\#\ \ \underset{PreS}{[\ (\begin{Bmatrix} Q \\ Imp \end{Bmatrix}\ ) - (Neg)\ (Emp)\ ]} - \underset{PreS}{NP} - \begin{Bmatrix} tense \\ tense \begin{Bmatrix} M \\ \underline{be} \\ \underline{have} \end{Bmatrix} \end{Bmatrix} \begin{matrix} -\ VX \\ -\ X \end{matrix}$$

$$1 \quad\quad 2 \quad\quad 3 \quad\quad 4 \quad\quad 5$$

$$\Longrightarrow oblig$$

S.C. $\quad 1 \quad\quad 0 \quad\quad 3 \quad\quad 4 \quad\quad 2 \quad\quad 5$

Imperative

S.D.
$$\#\#\ \ Imp - \underline{you} - Pres - \underline{will} - X$$
$$1 \quad\ 2 \quad\ \ 3 \quad\ \ 4 \quad\ 5$$

$$\Longrightarrow oblig$$

S.C. $\quad 1 \quad\ 0 \quad\ 3 \quad\ 0 \quad\ 5$

Adverb Preposing

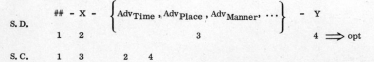

S.D.
$$\#\# - X - \begin{Bmatrix} Adv_{Time}, Adv_{Place}, Adv_{Manner}, \cdots \end{Bmatrix} - Y$$
$$1 \quad 2 \quad\quad\quad\quad\quad\quad 3 \quad\quad\quad\quad\quad\quad 4 \Longrightarrow opt$$

S.C. $\quad 1 \quad 3 \quad\quad 2 \quad 4$

Subject-Verb Inversion

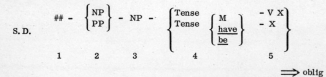

S.D.
$$\#\# - \begin{Bmatrix} NP \\ PP \end{Bmatrix} - NP - \begin{Bmatrix} Tense \\ Tense \begin{Bmatrix} M \\ \underline{have} \\ \underline{be} \end{Bmatrix} \end{Bmatrix} \begin{matrix} -\ V\ X \\ -\ X \end{matrix}$$

$$1 \quad\quad 2 \quad\quad 3 \quad\quad 4 \quad\quad 5$$

$$\Longrightarrow oblig$$

S.C.   1   2 4 3 5 ,

Condition: a) If 2 = NP, it must dominate WH or Neg.
            b) The transformation applies in main clauses only.

Affix Hopping

S.D.   X - [Affix] - [Verb] - Y

          1   2   3   4

$\Longrightarrow$ oblig

S.C.   1 # 3   2   #   4

Do-Support

S.D.   X - [Affix] - Y

          1   2   3

$\Longrightarrow$ oblig

S.C.   1 $\underline{do}$ + 2   3

Condition: $1 \neq$ W + [Verb]
Note: This condition means that the variable string which precedes the affix cannot end with a [Verb].

Complementizer Deletion

S.D.   X - $\begin{bmatrix} \begin{Bmatrix} for \\ poss \end{Bmatrix} \end{bmatrix}_S$ - $\begin{Bmatrix} to \\ ing \end{Bmatrix}$ Y $]_S$ - Z

          1   2   3   4

$\Longrightarrow$ oblig

S.C.   1   0   3   4

Relative Clause Reduction

S.D.   X - $[$ NP - $[\begin{bmatrix} NP \\ +PRO \\ +WH \end{bmatrix}$ Tns be - VP $]_S$ $]_{NP}$ - X
            $_{NP}$ $_S$

          1   2   3   4   5

$\Longrightarrow$ opt

S.C.   1   2   0   4   5

Modifier Shift

S.D.   X - $[$ Det - N - $[$ X $\begin{Bmatrix} V \\ Adj \end{Bmatrix}$ $]_{VP}$ $]_{NP}$ - Y
            $_{NP}$ $_{VP}$

          1   2   3   4   5

$\Longrightarrow$ oblig

S.C.   1   2 4 3   0 5

Condition: 2 - 3 $\neq$ $\underline{some}$ $\begin{Bmatrix} \underline{thing} \\ \underline{one} \end{Bmatrix}$

251

Possessive Formation

S. D.

$$X - [\underset{NP}{NP} [\underset{S}{-} \begin{bmatrix} NP \\ +PRO \\ +WH \end{bmatrix} - NP - Aux \underline{have}]_{S}]_{NP} - Y$$

1	2	3	4	5	6

$$\Longrightarrow opt$$

S. C.

1	2	0	of + 4 + poss 0	6

Possessive Shift

$$X - [\underset{Det}{[Def]} - N - \underline{of} - NP \; Poss]_{NP} - Y$$

S. D.

1	2	3	4	5	6

$$\Longrightarrow oblig$$

S. C.

1	5	3	0	0	6

Ordering of All Rules Given

Complementizer Placement	Oblig
Equi NP Deletion	Oblig
It-Replacement	Oblig
Dative	Opt
Passive	Oblig
Agent Deletion	Opt
Number Agreement	Oblig
Reflexive	Oblig
There-Insertion	Opt
Extraposition	Opt
It-Deletion	Oblig
Preposition Deletion	Oblig
Relative Clause Formation	Oblig
Question Formation	Oblig
Extraposition from NP	Opt
Tag Formation	Oblig
Neg-Emp Placement	Oblig
Imperative	Oblig
Adverb Preposing	Opt
Subject-Verb Inversion	Oblig
Affix Hopping	Oblig
Do-Support	Oblig
Complementizer Deletion	Oblig
Relative Clause Reduction	Opt
Modifier Shift	Oblig
Possessive Formation	Opt
Possessive Shift	Oblig

Index

71 72 73 7 6 5 4 3 2 1